A Short History of Malaysia

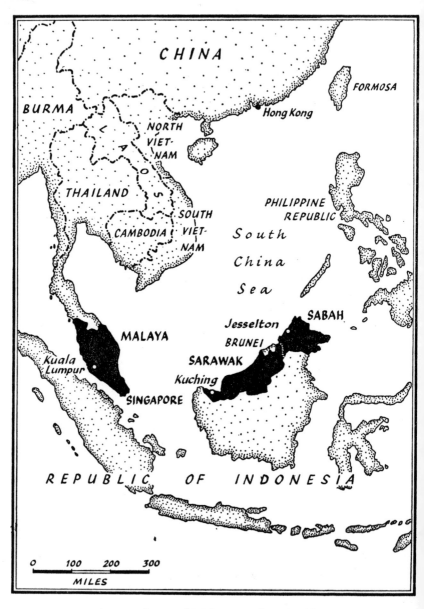

A general map of Malaysia and its neighbors

A SHORT
HISTORY OF
MALAYSIA

by

HARRY MILLER

FREDERICK A. PRAEGER, *Publishers*

New York · Washington

BOOKS THAT MATTER

Published in the United States of America in 1966
by Frederick A. Praeger, Inc., Publishers
111 Fourth Avenue, New York 3, N.Y.

Library of Congress Catalog Card Number: 66–10946

Printed in Great Britain

Contents

Illustrations

PLATES

9

MAPS

Preface

This book is really a history of the Federation of Malaya which includes the creation of Malaysia.

It is hoped that one of these days a Malaysian will write a history of that beautiful and invigorating group of countries. Many will agree with the view expressed by Mr. Lim Say Hup, of the University of Malaya, that there is a need for a reinterpretation and a reassessment of Malayan history from the Malayan point of view and based not only on Western but also on Malay, Chinese, Indian and Siamese sources. Professor K. G. Tregonning, Raffles Professor of History, University of Singapore, has also emphasized the same need and said that the correct way to study the history of any country is 'from within, looking outwards'.

This book is also an attempt to view Malayan history 'from within, looking outwards'—particularly the events of the last 25 exceptional years—by one who was born in Singapore, educated there, and worked there and in Malaya for over 25 years as a journalist. This book, I suppose, could be said to complete a trilogy dealing with Malayan history.

I owe a considerable debt to all those scholars, past and present, who have written so authoritatively on the history of Malaya before 1939. I relied very heavily on them for my account of Malaya up to the mid-1930s which was when I first became acquainted with court, *kampong*, and the makers of history in that country. I express special thanks to that eminent Malayan scholar, Sir Richard Winstedt, to Professor C. D. Cowan, Professor of the History of South-East Asia in the University of London, Mr. J. Kennedy, formerly Senior Lecturer in History, Malayan Teachers' Training College, in Kirkby, England, Mr. T. E. Smith, of the Institute of Commonwealth Studies, University of London, Mr. H. P. Bryson, of the British

11

Association of Malaysia, in London, and Mr. Roland Challis, a former colleague of mine in Malaya, for their advice and guidance.

I cannot unfortunately, and for obvious reasons, acknowledge others who have assisted me—those Britons and Malaysians who served, or are still serving, in high positions in Malaysia and who willingly guided my story of the modern Malaya and the events that established Malaysia, along the correct lines. I am grateful to them. I thank also the Straits Times Press (Malaya) Ltd., for help with the illustrations in this book.

To the Royal Asiatic Society, the British Association of Malaysia (which is building up a most useful collection of Malaysian historical papers), the Royal Commonwealth Society and the Colonial Office I express appreciation for the facility of research in their excellent libraries.

It is also necessary for me to add that any opinions I express in this book are my own.

HARRY MILLER

London
October 1964

NOTE: I have used the modern spelling of Malaysian states and towns; local values of exports, imports, et cetera, are expressed in Malayan dollars.

CHAPTER 1

Malaysia and its Peoples

Malaysia comprises fourteen states in South-East Asia which became a political entity and a monarchy on 16th September 1963. Its units were former British protectorates and colonies—the sovereign Federation of Malaya of nine Malay States and two British settlements which had achieved independence on 31st August 1957, the self-governing island State of Singapore immediately to its south, and the colonies of British North Borneo, now Sabah, and Sarawak, along the north-west coast of Borneo. Certainly no other federation in modern history was born after such a dramatic series of internal and external misunderstandings, tensions and crises, and finally threats of war from a once-friendly neighbour, Indonesia.

Malaya and Singapore are linked by a threequarter-mile-long granite and concrete causeway carrying a road and the railway line which eventually reaches the Malayan frontier with Thailand. They are separated from Sarawak and Sabah by about 400 miles of the South China Sea. Malaysia's land frontiers of jungle and rugged hill country run with friendly Thailand in the north of the Malay peninsula and with, at the time of writing, an aggressive Indonesia in the island of Borneo. The British-protected sultanate of Brunei is almost surrounded by Sarawak. To the north of Malaya are Burma, Cambodia and Vietnam. Indonesia glowers to the south and beyond Sarawak and Sabah lies the Philippines Republic which was another opponent of Malaysia but which at the time of writing was seeking a formula by which it could re-establish diplomatic relations without losing too much prestige. Thus Malaysia lies at the crossroads of South-East Asia, is a focal point in communications between the West and the Far East, and is also of considerable strategic importance to the West.

13

Malaysia covers a land area of 130,000 square miles. Malaya itself is 51,000 square miles or slightly larger than England without Wales. The two largest states are Sarawak, which with its 48,250 square miles is nearly seven times the combined area of Lancashire and Yorkshire in Britain, and Sabah (29,388 square miles). Singapore is the smallest of the fourteen states (225 square miles) but its port, which is among the first five largest in the world, makes it the trading heart of the federation.

A flight over Malaysia shows as nothing else can that just over three-quarters of it is still dense jungle. Part of its interior is still unexplored because of inaccessibility. Down the centre and for three-quarters of the Malay peninsula runs a spine of jungle-covered mountains with peaks which rise to over 7,000 feet. The highest mountain here is Tahan (7,186 feet) standing on the northern fringe of a vast national park and big-game reserve where tiger (the 'national animal'), panther, leopard, elephant, *seladang*, the largest member of the wild ox family in the world, the quaint tapir, and declining numbers of two-horned rhinoceros, roam in freedom. Malaya's coastline runs for about 1,000 miles but the west and east coasts are strikingly different. The west is disfigured by mangrove swamps while the east is beautiful with sandy beaches stretching for miles and fringed with coconut palms and casuarina trees and dotted with picturesque Malay fishing villages. The atmosphere and pace of life are different also: the west bustles with the prosperity and vigour that comes with proximity to trade while the east, suffering for decades from the isolation caused by the lack of communications, is a different world in which the true Malay atmosphere prevails.

In Sarawak and Sabah, the alluvial coastal plains move into undulating country which then rise into a very mountainous interior. The mountains—Sarawak's highest is Murud (7,950 feet)—run into Sabah and culminate in the Crocker Range in the north. Here, Kinabalu (13,455 feet) stands not only as the highest mountain in Malaysia and the Indonesian archipelago but also as one of the most impressive in South-East Asia. The people living in its immediate vicinity venerate its summit as the home of the spirits of the dead. Almost the whole of the country between the Crocker Range and the Indonesian border is inaccessible.

Seen from that aircraft the rivers of Malaysia are brown threads twisting haphazardly in shadowy green depths. They rise in the mountains, slip sometimes through precipitous gorges, roar over rapids and then broaden out in the plains where their crystal-clear waters change into the colour of mud with the silts of commercial development. The longest rivers in Malaysia are Sarawak's Rejang and Sabah's Kinabatangan, each 350 miles long, and Malaya's Pahang (297 miles) which courses into the South China Sea. The rivers are still the only highways for the peoples living deep in the hinterlands of Malaysia; but the heavy day-time silence of jungle and plains is broken by the rapid putt-putting of outboard motor-boats owned by aborigines in the peninsula and tribesmen in the Borneo states—signs of the affluence that has been reaching into the interior.

Malaysia's temperature is uniform—never above 90° F. or below 70° F.—but humidity is generally high. Lying in the tropics between latitude 1° and 7° north and longitude 100° and 119° east, it also has no clearly defined seasons, not even a clear-cut 'wet' and 'dry', for the rains vary with the monsoons and rainfall is high. From the Indian Ocean between May and September (the summer of the northern hemisphere), south-west winds bring rain to the west coast of Malaya and to Singapore while south-easters produce afternoon thunderstorms in the Bornean states. Then between October and March (winter), the north-east monsoon builds up in the South China Sea and lashes the east coast of Malaya and the coasts of Sarawak and Sabah with ferocious storms. The lofty coconut palms and casuarina trees arch themselves before the fury of the gales and the sandy beaches are churned up by great grey breakers; then almost suddenly, perhaps after a few hours or a few days, the skies clear and the lush green country is bathed again in brilliant sunshine and freshness.

A diversity of peoples compose Malaysia's population of 10 millions. They represent every stratum from the primitive Negritos, roaming the jungles of north Malaya and hunting with blowpipes, to Malay Royalty. Two races, the Malays, the indigenous people of Malaya, and the Chinese, descendants of immigrants, dominate, both largely in the peninsula and the latter in Singapore. On Malaysia Day, the Malays totalled about 40 per cent of the Malaysian population, the Chinese 43 per cent, Indians and Pakistanis 9 per cent, and the indigenous tribes of Borneo and other races 8 per cent. The racial proportions varied from territory to territory. In the Malay peninsula itself, the Malays were in the majority with nearly 50 per cent of the population of 7·2 millions, the Chinese 37 per cent, the Indians and Pakistanis just over 11 per cent, and people of other origins, including Europeans, the balance. Of Singapore's 1·7 millions, the Chinese formed the absolute majority with 75 per cent, against 13·6 per cent Malays and 8·6 per cent Indians. In the two Borneo territories, the combined indigenous tribes were in the majority but Chinese came next (31 per cent in Sarawak, 23 per cent in Sabah). This very multi-racial make-up of Malaysia provides it with one of its serious political problems.

While their ancestors are believed to have originated from the Mongolian race, the modern Malays are descendants more of mixtures with immigrants from eastern and central Sumatra, Java, the Celebes, India and Arabia, and of some inter-marriage with Chinese and Siamese. Attractive, decorous, gracious and graceful people, and among the most courteous in the world, they have a great pride in race. Almost 90 per cent of them live in rural areas, in *kampong* (tiny villages) which are clustered prettily on the edges of ricefields or along rivers or the coasts. Until very recently a Malay saying, 'Better a handful of quietness than both hands full with travail and vexation of spirit', reflected the simple measure of life and aspirations among the peasants, the rice-growers and the fishermen. Affluence however has pervaded many *kampong*, and battery radios and oil-fired refrigerators are as important possessions—if not status symbols—as the buffaloes used to plough the ricefields or the outboard motors which alleviate the fishermen's existence. A gigantic rural development programme launched in 1960 promises to broaden the basis of the economy in the rural areas and bring the people a much higher standard of living.

The customs and beliefs of the Malays are the product of successive cultural forces—from the animism of the aborigines of the very early centuries to the influence of Hinduism which lasted until the sixteenth century, followed by the embrace of Islam, and finally the association with westerners. Islam is the State religion—and there is not one Malay who is not a Muslim. Nevertheless ancient beliefs in the spirits of the elements still persist particularly among the peasants and fisherfolk. Malay *pawang* (medicine-men), although a dying fraternity, are still figures of consequence in some areas and are called on to intercede with the spirits for better harvests in the ricefields and fishing grounds. The belief in the divinity of a Malay ruler is still so strong in the Pahang hinterland that during a visit he may he asked to lay his 'fruitful' hands on baskets of padi or fish. How is this latent belief in animism equated with the strict precepts of

16

Islam's belief in only One God? An authority explains it this way: the *pawang* 'compromises himself today in practising a pagan faith but his lapse from Islam is sanctioned by the devout but not very orthodox Malay as consistent with conflict between the ancient (common) law of custom which Islam recognizes everywhere (*Hukum Adat*) and the strict (statute) law of the Prophet (*Hukum Shara*)'.

Roaming the northern jungles of Malaya are some of the world's few remaining primitives, the small dark-skinned woolly-haired Negritos, generally accepted as the descendants of migrants who arrived in the peninsula probably about 3,000 B.C. Only in the past three decades have they come into more frequent contact with 'civilization', and not very long before that they had exchanged the bow and arrow for the *sumpitan*, the blowpipe, and poisoned darts used by more 'advanced' aborigines further to the south, for hunting and defence. Nomadic, the Negritos move around northern Kelantan, northern Perak and South Siam, living on roots, fruits, snakes, birds and small animals, and sleeping at night in shelters made of tree branches and leaves. Ethnic relatives of theirs are to be found in the Andaman Islands, the Philippines and New Guinea.

Spread through the rest of the peninsula are other aboriginal groups. The two major tribes are the handsome Temiar of northern Perak and Kelantan, and the Semai, fairer-skinned people of the mountains and foothills of Perak and Kelantan. The Temiar have a highly developed system of tribal ethics. Grouped in units related by ties of kinship, they have a love of traditional dancing. In the south of the peninsula are proto-Malay aborigines who have almost given up jungle life to settle in west coast villages. Very few aborigines have embraced Islam; they remain animists, their lives and customs controlled by their beliefs in good and bad spirits of the sky, the earth, trees, plants, fruit, crops and animals. Strangely enough, a Hell does not appear among their fears.

The Chinese in Malaysia are a microcosm of China in their tribal composition, their bewildering number of dialects, and the variety of their religious beliefs and superstitions. Most of them originate from the southern provinces of China, and the records of Chinese association with the peninsula and with the Borneo states go back to the very early centuries. Chinese settlement in the peninsula itself really began after the foundation of Penang by the British in 1786, increased with the birth of Singapore in 1819, and became a steady flow towards the end of the nineteenth century when Chinese labourers streamed in in their thousands to dig for tin to satisfy a world demand for the ore. In the years between the two world wars (1919–39) they flooded into the peninsula in such alarming numbers that a quota system had to be introduced; since 1942, Chinese immigration into Malaya has been almost entirely prohibited.

Through the centuries the Chinese played a leading role in the commercial and industrial life of the territories that make up Malaysia. They dug for gold and tin; they levelled jungle and planted, first pepper and gambier, then pineapples, rubber and vegetables; they were the tradesmen and shopkeepers, the carpenters, masons and smiths, artisans, teachers, boatbuilders, fortune tellers, clerks, house servants, and undertakers. They still form the major communities of miners, bankers, merchants, and the professions and are represented in almost every aspect of industrial and business life. But it was the partnership between the British and the Chinese—the one providing most of the money, the initiative, and the 'know-how', and the other some of the money, the enterprise and the industry—that shaped the Malay peninsula and Singapore into the thriving and prosperous territories they are today.

Politically the Japanese war (1942–45), and then the engulfment of China by Mao Tse-Tung and the Chinese Communist Party, wrought a vital change in the outlook of the modern generations of Chinese who had been born in the Malaysian territories. They began turning their faces inwards to the country of their birth instead of outwards towards China, the home of their fathers and forefathers, and strove to establish their birthright through rights of citizenships and equal opportunities. In Malaya particularly, this produced a serious political problem yet to be solved to the complete satisfaction of the locally-born Chinese, who however appear to be showing patience, tolerance and understanding.

Most of the Indians in Malaysia come from Southern India. Although Indian association with the peninsula reaches back nearly 2,000 years, the vast majority of those living in Malaya today descend from migrants of the nineteenth and early twentieth centuries who left their homes for political or economic reasons. They arrived principally as agricultural labourers and domestic servants soon after the foundation of Penang in 1786, but the great influx came towards the end of the nineteenth century when the birth of the motor-car and the invention of the pneumatic rubber tyre produced a world demand for rubber and workers were consequently wanted for the proliferating rubber estates in the western half of the peninsula. As the country's prosperity grew, the government launched an ambitious programme of road and railway construction so as to facilitate economic development. Indians provided the vast labour forces which laid Malaya's excellent roads and its railway. Their sons, with education behind them, became clerks in the government service, or schoolmasters, lawyers and doctors.

Apart from the labourers, there was a steady arrival of Indian traders, businessmen, merchants, moneylenders, lawyers and doctors and other professional men to cater principally to the special needs of their countrymen. There was a call, too, for the services of north Indians, particularly the tall, bearded and turbaned Punjabis, chiefly Sikhs, who made stalwart soldiers and policemen in the Malaya of the days before the Japanese war.

So it was too with the Ceylonese, a much smaller community. Many of them are to be found in the railway service (indeed the first section of the first railway track of eight miles between Taiping, a tin town in Perak, and Port Weld, was completed in 1885 by Ceylon Pioneers lent by the Ceylon Railways). There are Ceylonese in many other government departments and in the professions.

To glance finally at the other non-indigenous races to be found in Malaysia: there are Pakistanis, Arabs, Siamese (with settled communities in Kedah and Kelantan near their frontiers with Thailand), Bengalis, Sikhs, Filipinos, and of course, Europeans, particularly the British who find themselves still received with great warmth.

Sarawak and Sabah have as great a diversity in their indigenous tribes as in their Chinese population. Sarawak has the Sea and the Land Dyaks, the Kayans and Kenyans, the Kelabits, Muruts, Punans, Pennans and Melanaus. The Dyaks were the original headhunters who were subdued by the great Brooke family who ruled over Sarawak for more than a hundred years; the Punans and Pennans are the nomads in the interior. Sabah has the Kadazans (the modern name for the Dusuns), the Muruts, the Bajaus, the Suluks and the Binadans. The Kadazans are the most progressive community, living mostly on the western plains, the Bajaus are fishermen and breeders of horses, and the Muruts are in the interior. And each tribe in Sarawak and Sabah has its own language, customs and beliefs. From this great diversity of peoples, Malaysia aims to produce unity.

Malaya and its 11 States

We turn now to the main subject of this book, that emerald pendant in a sapphire sea, the peninsula that is generally known as 'Malaya', which the Malays call *Tanah Melayu*, 'The Land of the Malays', and the capital of which, Kuala Lumpur, is also the heart of the wider federation of Malaysia. Malaya, with its nine Malay States and two former British Settlements, is an amalgam of centuries of influence by foreigners, beginning with the Indians who arrived about the first century A.D. and introduced rule by rajas, continuing with the first westerners, the Portuguese, who arrived in the sixteenth century, and the Dutch, and concluding with the British whose influence began in 1786 and who in August 1957 gave up their sovereign rights over the settlements of Penang and Malacca and their obligations as a protecting power. The Siamese too held sway over the northern states of Kedah, Perlis and Kelantan in the eighteenth and nineteenth centuries; in 1909 they transferred their rights to the British. But one must not forget that before the Portuguese came, to conquer, trade and crusade, much of the settled part of the peninsula had for a century been vassals of the first truly Malay empire which had its heart in Malacca.

The nine Malay States have names that ripple over the tongue easily and delightedly—Johore, Kedah, Kelantan, Negri Sembilan, Pahang, Perak, Perlis, Selangor and Trengganu. The two former British Settlements are of course Penang and Malacca. The origins of some of the states are obscure, for instance Kelantan and Trengganu. Johore, Pahang and Trengganu can claim that their ruling houses descend from either the Royal house of Malacca or the *Bendahara*, the very powerful Prime Ministers of the Malacca empire which was succeeded by the Johore-Riau kingdom. Of all the states, however, Kedah has the longest-recorded history for the first Indian traders from the Coromandel coast arrived at its port in the first century A.D. to barter their fabrics, beads and iron implements, for gums, camphor, wood and gold.

Mula-mula (In the beginning . . .) is the traditional Malay introduction to stories of the origin of the country and to tales of long ago. The aborigines, sitting around their flickering fires in the depths of the jungle, say it too as they recall the belief, passed down to them from the mouths of their fathers and grandfathers, that their tribal hunting grounds—their world—were created by Karei, their supreme deity, who expresses his displeasure with thunder and lightning—an anger which their women try to assuage by standing in the rage of the

21

storm and drawing blood from their body with a bamboo sliver.

The earliest written records of the peninsula come from Indian and Chinese sources for there is nothing written in Malay before the sixteenth century. The earliest Malay history, the *Sejarah Melayu*, loosely called the Malay Annals, written about 1541, is purely a collection of the 'tales told by men of bygone days' about the birth and growth to greatness of the Malacca empire and about its decline. Its greatest value lies in its detail of the life and customs of the period, the wars and court intrigues, and the exploits of Malay heroes, but the episodes described are unconnected and the historian cannot separate fact from romanticism. The unknown author had been writing, not for posterity but, as he put it, 'for the greater pleasure of my lord and king' who was striving to regain the kingdom of Malacca.

It is assumed that the human story of Malaya goes back to the remote Ice Age, that great change in the world's weather which lowered the levels of oceans so that what is now the Malay peninsula became part of a great land mass which encompassed the islands of Sumatra, Java and Borneo. Down from what is Yunnan, in China, where all the great river systems of mainland South-East Asia have their source, moved the first migrants seeking warmer climes. Groups of them remained in parts of the peninsula while others forged on somehow to as far east as the Polynesian islands of Samoa and Tahiti, as far south as Australia and New Zealand, and as far west as Madagascar. It is also believed that about 3,000 B.C. another migration occurred from Yunnan. Tribes—the 'proto-Malays'—arrived in the peninsula and drove the original inhabitants into the interior. They brought with them the culture of the Stone Age. Examples of their simple tools have been found in north Malaya but the most important—and exciting—archaeological evidence of Stone Age settlement in Malaysia has been emerging from diggings in the bat-guano-covered floors of massive caves in limestone hills one mile away from Niah, in northern Sarawak. The discoveries since work started in 1954 have, according to the archaeologists, begun to alter the whole concept of Bornean (and so Malaysian) prehistory. Among the finds were the almost-perfect skeletons of small people with beautifully made and polished stone axes and adzes lying among them, wall paintings in red haematite (iron ore) among the limestone walls of another cave, and fragile relics believed to date back to 50,000 B.C. In 1963 diggings began in deeper strata possibly relating to an even earlier period.

Finally, probably about 300 B.C. fresh migrants brought the Iron Age to the peninsula. Relics of this era have been found in Pahang, Selangor and Perak and include curious objects which look like tools that could have been used in mining or boat-building or as elephant goads. The remarkable point is that similar articles have not been found outside Malaya. By the beginning of the Christian era, small settlements stood at river mouths, up rivers and on islands; the people led circumscribed lives, cultivated rice, probably used the ox or buffalo for ploughing and as transport, fished, built shallow boats and perhaps traded with one another. Then into their lives came the Indians, the first of a series of foreigners who sought an overseas route to China and found the peninsula lying athwart the bows of their ships. Ever since then, the peninsula's destiny has been profoundly influenced by its geographical position on the major sea-route from west to east; the narrow Straits of Malacca has been an international highway for centuries.

The Indians reached the peninsula early in the Christian era, arriving in sailing ships each of which was reportedly 200 feet long and carried a considerable crew as well as about 1,000 tons of cargo and a year's supply of food, including live chickens and goats; a corner of each vessel was devoted to vegetable gardens. The Indians found that the peninsula had gold—mined in what are now Kedah, Perak, Malacca, Johore, Pahang and Kelantan (where traces of the ancient sites of the mines may be seen today although there is little gold left in Malaya)—and so trade began. Indians began to settle in the neighbourhood of Kedah Peak, married local women, and introduced the Hindu influence which lasted about fourteen centuries. (In the past 30 years, more than 30 sites of ancient Hindu temples, halls of audience in palaces, and forts have been excavated in Malaya, particularly in Kedah which had perhaps more Indian settlements than any other part of the peninsula simply because it gave Indian sailing ships their first landfalls. Recently on the lower slopes of Kedah Peak—which rises nearly 4,000 feet and has been a landmark for travellers from the west for centuries—a stone Hindu tomb-temple of impressive dimensions, built either in the tenth or eleventh centuries, has been uncovered and reconstructed.)

Rule by rajas replaced the simple patriarchal organizations of the peninsula tribes. Individual 'river-states' developed around the mouths of the larger rivers. Each had its own Hindu Malay ruler and tiny court in which the ceremonies were Hindu in form. Today old

Hindu rituals persist in certain Royal courts of Malaya. For instance, the ruler of Perak, at his formal installation, is anointed, taken in procession round his palace, and shows himself to his people wearing regalia which have associations with ancient Hinduism. In Negri Sembilan, the chief herald adopts an ancient Brahminic attitude when he proclaims the installation of the *Yang di-Pertuan Besar* (Head of State): he stands on his left leg with the sole of his right foot touching his left knee, his right hand shades his eyes and the fingers of his left hand press into his left cheek.

The Hindu Malay rulers lived in walled-in 'palaces' and worshipped Hindu gods in elaborately decorated temples. Slowly they were isolated from the peasants who were encouraged to believe in the divinity of their king, which was the basic Indian idea of kingship: 'Kings', said the Laws of Manu, 'are vastly superior to other created beings, because they are made of the essences of the gods.' Absolute despotism was introduced into the peninsula. Around the rulers grew an aristocracy from among whom were appointed the administrators in a ministerial form of government over which the king sat supreme.

The next to find the Malay peninsula were the Romans who had sailed across the seas from Egypt looking for China. The western world learned in A.D. 150 through Claudius Ptolemy, a celebrated Greek geographer, astronomer and mathematician, about the 'Golden Chersonese', the 'Golden Peninsula', which was identified later as the Malay peninsula. Ptolemy said that Roman sailors spoke of visiting two ports in the peninsula, one in the north and the other in the south, but these have proved impossible to identify. As a commentary, glass beads found near Kota Tinggi, in eastern Johore, have been identified as of Roman origin, though this does not necessarily mean that Romans called at any point in Johore. The Romans however did not continue to use the eastern sea route for long, principally because of the collapse of their empire. Fourteen centuries were to pass before the next Europeans, the Portuguese, arrived as traders— and conquerors.

With kings came empires, some to glory briefly, others to leave a mark in history. Chinese records of the sixth century A.D. speak of Langkasuka, an important kingdom situated somewhere in the northern part of the peninsula, a vassal of the Indianized empire of Funan—the earliest known empire of its kind in South-East Asia— which had its heart in the delta of the Mekong river in Cambodia and which apparently existed from the first century A.D. until 627. It was believed that Langkasuka had been situated in north Kedah because Kedah records mentioned it. (Malay mythology gave it the name of a fairyland, *Negri Alangkah-suka*, 'The Land of the Delights'.) However the cold analyses of available facts by modern historians have produced the more likely theory that Langkasuka stood where Patani, in South Siam (itself once an old Malay kingdom), is today and that the great emporium mentioned by the Chinese was not in Kedah but had possibly been the town of Patani itself. Langkasuka disappeared completely when Funan disintegrated.

About A.D. 682, Sri Vijaya, a powerful Buddhist kingdom, began flourishing in South Sumatra, with its capital at Palembang. It established a close relationship with the river-state (and port) of Kedah. By the early tenth century Kedah had risen to great importance in the kingdom and flourished with trade from India, China and Arabia. During the eleventh century, Sri Vijaya was invaded by the Chola kings of India's Coromandel coast. Kedah itself was sacked. Sri Vijaya recovered from the Chola onslaught but its power began to decline and it sank into oblivion towards the close of the thirteenth century. However, in the last half-century it had established Tumasek, a thriving settlement and port on an island in the south of the Malay peninsula. Tumasek was the 'Singhapura' of Indian records, the Singapore of today. Another Chola expedition also sacked Tumasek which, however, rose phoenix-like and flourished again. In 1366 it survived an attack by the powerful Javanese Hindu empire of Majapahit, centred in east Java, but in 1380 a Siamese force razed it and its inhabitants fled. The jungle closed over Tumasek until 1819 when an Englishman selected it as a pre-eminently suitable site for a trading settlement.

However it was the Siamese invasion of Tumasek which led to the birth of the Malay empire of Malacca, which was to become renowned from Europe to China.

CHAPTER 2

Foundation of the Malacca Empire

A short row of wood and *atap*-thatched sheds standing on sturdy *bakau* (mangrove) piles and ranged along a stretch of beach near the mouth of a river, laid the foundations of the Malay kingdom of Malacca which eventually embraced an empire receiving tribute from rulers and chiefs on the peninsula and in neighbouring islands. Those sheds formed the original bazaar from which developed an international emporium in which goods from the east and the west were exchanged. From Malacca the trade routes eventually extended eastwards to China and westwards through Ceylon and India to the Persian Gulf and Red Sea and thence into Europe via Venice and Genoa. The Portuguese who conquered Malacca confirmed its importance and affluence; one of their chroniclers, Tomé Pires who worked in Malacca after its capture wrote, 'Men cannot estimate the worth of Malacca on account of its greatness and profit.'

The true circumstances behind the foundation of the original village of Malacca are lost in the inextricable mixture of fact and legend that runs through old Malay writings and the Chinese and Western chronicles of the fifteenth century; but it would appear that its founder was a fugitive prince from Palembang, in South Sumatra. A Hindu by religion, he first came into Malayan history after his marriage to the daughter of the ruler of a state in Java. His wife was of higher rank, he adopted the honorific title of 'Parameswera', meaning 'Prince Consort', and it is as the Parameswera that he is initially known in Malayan history. His real name, his age, his height, his features—none of these personal details exist, but he must have worn his black hair shoulder-length like the Indians, possibly had a flowing moustache, again like the Hindus, was of average height, with a strong face and penetrating eyes.

After his marriage, he was forced to flee his country. Two different stories explain his flight. One says that he was forced out by his father-in-law because he failed to pay just tribute to him. The other, a Portuguese account, relates that 'when he realized how nobly he was married and how great was his power in the neighbouring islands' the Parameswera forswore allegiance to his father-in-law who sent an expedition against him. Accept whichever account we may, the Parameswera's flight was the inglorious opening to events which culminated in the foundation of Malacca.

With his wife, loyal followers and slaves, he sailed northwards and came ashore at Tumasek, a vassal of Siam and governed by a Siamese named Tamagi who welcomed the Parameswera. It proved a fatal gesture; for the Parameswera, having lost one kingdom, had an opportunist eye open for another and considered that as Tumasek had once been subject to his ancestors it should now become his. He murdered Tamagi within eight days of his arrival. The Parameswera ruled Tumasek for the next five years and reports paint an ugly picture of tyranny and wretched piracies on ships that went round the island. However, retribution overtook the Parameswera when Tamagi's brother, who was overlord of the Siamese state of Patani in the north, sent an avenging force which sacked Tumasek.

The Parameswera fled again, this time overland to the north with about 1,000 followers, moving from one place to another and finally settling somewhere along the Muar River where he remained for six years, living principally off the proceeds of piracies along the coast. Then he received reports about a fertile plain further north. A reconnaissance party returned with enthusiastic descriptions of the region: a river ran through it and it was inhabited only by aborigines. The Parameswera went to see for himself. A delightful Malay story purports to explain what swayed him to decide that the plain should be his new seat and that its name should be Malacca. Apparently he was leaning against a tree by the river watching his hunting dogs holding at bay a *pelandok*, a tiny mousedeer—the Brer Rabbit of Malay folk-tales—when it suddenly kicked one of its aggressors into the water, an incredible feat for such a small animal. The Parameswera exclaimed, 'This is a fine place for a city. It breeds bravery; even its mousedeer are full of fight. Let us make a settlement here.' He asked his followers the name of the tree against which he was resting. One answered that it was a *malaka* tree. 'We will call our town after it,' declared the Parameswera.

Malays generally accept the fact that Malacca was named after the tree which bears a nut that is used medicinally and which has a bark that forms a dye-stuff and a trunk that makes good charcoal. However, the name could have been derived from the Arabic word *malakat*, meaning a mart or emporium, applied by Arab traders long before the Parameswera's arrival to a tiny market that existed on Water Island, one of five islets lying off Malacca. About the year 1360 patrolling Siamese warboats demanded tribute. The traders hastily transferred their bazaar to the mouth of the Bertam River, and it became known as Malakat. The river itself was known as Malacca River, or the river of the market.

The Parameswera's river-state of Malacca is believed to have been born in 1403. Its settlers planted sugar-cane, bananas and other crops, and discovered small tinfields in the hinterland. Trade began with the exchange of tin for rice and other essential products. Native craft spread the news about the settlement and down from Kedah and across from Sumatra came other traders. So the Malacca bazaar began to flourish. The Parameswera seemed to change character with age. He settled down to the duty of promoting his village by peaceful means. He gave up piracy and literally turned merchant and businessman. Within two years, Malacca's population was 2,000. To ensure protection, the Parameswera accepted Siam as his overlord (probably much against his inclination for reasons connected with his usurpation of Tumasek) and for some years sent it an annual tribute of gold—until he found a new and more powerful protector in China.

The earliest recorded details about the Parameswera's Malacca come from Chinese historical records. As the fifteenth century opened, the new Emperor of China, Chu Ti (1403–24), looked outside his realm for sea routes to the west and south which would help expand China's trade. The admirals who took the fleets out on long voyages also had orders however to 'show that China was rich and strong' by offering protection to neighbouring countries in exchange for tribute. Thus in 1405 when Admiral Yin Ch'ing sailed into Malacca with a great fleet, he presented the Parameswera with gifts of silk brocades—and invited him to send envoys to the Imperial Court. The Parameswera accepted, and in Peking, according to the Chinese Dynastic Histories, the Emperor spoke to the envoys 'in praise of their master, appointed him king of the country and sent him a commission, a seal, a suit of silk clothes and a yellow umbrella', the authority and vestments of a Chinese-appointed ruler.

28

Yin Ch'ing personally delivered them to the Parameswera in 1406. From a Chinese chronicle comes a brief picture of the Malacca of those days. The Parameswera had his palace on the beach near the river mouth. Along the seashore and on the other side of the river ran a row of sheds supported by 20 pillars. Here trading took place. The people sold fish, tin, ebony and resin. They lived in huts built on wooden stilts. The men wore a kerchief about their heads and the women did 'their hair in a knot behind'. Their boats were 'dug out of logs of wood'. Another Chinese writer added almost disparagingly that the country had no donkeys or horses.

The more historic event for Malacca was the arrival in 1409 of the famous Admiral Cheng-Ho, a remarkable man who had risen through the ranks of the army until he became powerful in the Emperor's court. Cheng-Ho had shown China's flag overseas in several extensive expeditions, the first taking place in 1405 when he commanded an armada of 62 vessels. His mission to Malacca was momentous for the tiny river-state; on behalf of the Emperor, he formally proclaimed Malacca a city and a kingdom and the Parameswera its king. (The Chinese official record gratifyingly added that from that moment Malacca 'ceased to be a dependency of Siam'—but Malacca cautiously continued to pay tribute to Siam for some time.) As a gift, Cheng-Ho presented the Parameswera with fine Chinese tiles for the roof of his palace. Cheng-Ho returned to Malacca several times and local legends credited him with performing 'miracles' there although their nature was never detailed. His name is still fresh in Malacca where some Chinese venerate him. In the oldest Chinese temple in the town, inscriptions cut in stone commemorate his visit to the cemetery on a hill behind the town known as 'Bukit China' (Chinese Hill) but called by Chinese 'Bukit Sam-Po', after Cheng-Ho's local name.

In 1411 the Parameswera accompanied Cheng-Ho back to China to present his tribute in person and to receive the Emperor's confirmation of his status as 'king' of Malacca. He was accompanied by his wife and son, ministers and chiefs, and a retinue of nearly 500. In Peking, the Emperor entertained him and presented him with 'two suits of clothes embroidered with golden dragons and one suit with unicorns', gold and silver, and, among other gifts, curtains and mattresses. The Parameswera received more presents on his departure including 'a girdle studded with gems, horses and saddles, 100 ounces of gold and 500 of silver', and lengths of plain and embroidered silk.

In modern diplomatic parlance, the Parameswera's visit was a tremendous success.

Subsequently Malacca received favoured-nation treatment from China. Chinese trading ships—high, ungainly-looking junks with eyes painted in their bows to help the vessels 'see' their way—sailed in heavily laden with goods. The first Chinese also began to settle in Malacca. When word of China's interest in Malacca spread, traders gravitated to the port from Sumatra, Java and both coasts of India. Arabs made Malacca a chief port of call. The former fishing village was on its way to riches and consequence.

It was ideally situated for a port. The monsoons blew in the right directions twice a year. In January, Chinese, Siamese, Javanese and Bugis vessels came in with the north-east winds and returned with the south-easters in July having had enough time to barter their goods. From May, the south-west winds brought the Arabs and the Indians and they returned home with loaded vessels when the winds changed and blew from the east. Those very fastidious sailors and explorers, the Portuguese, later described Malacca as an ideal port. One of them wrote, 'There are no storms to injure it and never was a ship lost here. It forms a point where some monsoons commence and others end . . . and Malacca is the middle of all this. . . . Every year there used to come to Malacca ships of Calicut, Aden, Mecca, Coromandel and Bengal, of the Chinese and Javanese, of Pegu and all those ports . . . and I believe that if there was another world, and another navigable route, yet all would resort to the city, for in her they would find every different sort of drugs and spices which can be mentioned in the world, by reason of the port of Malacca being more commodious for all the monsoons than any other parts. . . .'

The Chinese sold cotton, silk, brocades, porcelain and other wares, the Indians and Burmese perfumed woods, carvings, gold, silver and precious stones. The islands to the east sent prodigious cargoes of fragrant spices. From the hinterland of the Malay peninsula itself came camphor, ebony, tin, gold and jungle produce. From Sumatra there were rice, gold and pepper. So the Parameswera's friendship with China paid dividends in trade and in the lustre that it brought.

In his old age, the Parameswera entered into a political alliance with the northern Sumatra state of Pasai when he married a daughter of its ruler. This marriage had its religious consequences for the peninsula. The ruler of Pasai was a convert from Hinduism to Islam which had spread slowly from Arabia to India and indeed to China.

In the thirteenth century it had begun to establish itself in states in northern Sumatra and there is evidence that towards the end of the fourteenth century it was the religion of a Malay settlement in Trengganu on the east coast of the peninsula; this evidence is in a block of stone found in Trengganu in 1902 which bears an inscription in Arabic characters and dated the Muslim year 788 A.H. (A.D.1386) recording the introduction of Islam somewhere in Trengganu.

As the bride was a Muslim, the Parameswera himself had to shake off Hinduism and adopt her religion. His conversion had two almost immediate sequels. The royal example was followed by some courtiers and resident traders, and subsequently Arab traders gave preference to a state ruled by a Muslim. But the significant historic point was that the Parameswera was the first Malay ruler to become a Muslim, a step which later led to Islam becoming the religion of all the Malays in the peninsula.

In keeping with his new-found religion, the Parameswera adopted a Muslim name—Iskandar Shah, which perhaps was some compensation to a ruler who, by becoming Muslim, had been deprived of some of his 'divine' Hindu attributes. (Iskandar Shah was the Islamic rendering of the name of that illustrious Greek warrior, Alexander the Great, whose exploits figure so largely in Muslim legends.) His was no conversion of convenience for Iskandar Shah encouraged Islam in Malacca. He welcomed missionaries and, to quote a record, 'did them honour, gave them places to live in and a place for their mosque'.

Iskandar Shah died in 1424 after reigning over Malacca for an eventful 21 years during which he had seen it grow from a fishing village to a trading port of repute. His burial place is not known but he left his monument in the city-state he had founded and nurtured. Malacca was to become the centre of an empire and the heart of Islamic learning in the archipelago and for 200 years eastern and western nations would war over it.

What was the town like in Iskandar Shah's last days? In the harbour bustled an incredible variety of craft from the *perahu* of the local traders to the long boats of the Javanese, the high-prowed vessels of the Indians and the great junks of the Chinese. Around the mouth of the river stood the great bazaar of raised booths and stalls, protected by a fence and the gates into it locked at night. Import and export duties were paid at a shed at the mouth of the river. Goods were unloaded at a pier and taken to the bustling bazaar where their owners added their voices to the babble of shouting and bargaining for cloves from the Moluccas, sandalwood from Timor, mace and nutmeg from other parts of the archipelago, camphor from Borneo, gold from Sumatra, tin from the peninsula, and a variety of spices, drugs, dyes and perfumes from Java, Siam, China and the Philippines, silks and rich cloths and cottons from China and India, to say nothing of sugar, livestock, weapons—and slaves. Malacca was cosmopolitan; there was little doubt about that. Only white faces were missing from the crowds that incessantly shuffled across a wooden bridge over the river. Malay was the *lingua franca* of the traders.

On a hill near by stood the new palace of the ruler, a long, rambling building with a many-tiered pagoda roof, the influence of China. Its pillars were gilded and its walls painted in several colours. It looked down on the narrow crowded streets which were lined with wood and *atap* homes and on the shops which stretched along the beach. The palace was the centre of life. It was open to peasants, traders, nobles, and princes who clustered into the *balai* (audience hall) a wide, doorless barn of a room decorated with the silks of China and Gujerat. Towards the back of the *balai* stood a dais, carpeted and cushioned, where the ruler, sitting cross-legged, gave audience. On formal occasions, he was dressed in rich embroidered costume. Pages, the sons of nobles, and attendants and guards flanked him. They bore the Royal regalia which included a fan, a betel-nut set, and the ruler's personal silver cuspidor.

In the fields beyond the town waved the leaves of quick-growing crops like sugar-cane and bananas. Stretches of vegetable gardens were interspersed with climbing pepper and other spice plants. There were some ricefields but most of the rice for Malacca came from Java, bearing out the assertion of a Chinese writer that agriculture was not favoured in Malacca. In the sea and in the river, the fishermen of Malacca caught fish with primitive bamboo spears.

CHAPTER 3

A Muslim State

Iskandar Shah was succeeded by his grandson, Raja Tengah, who adopted the Sri Vijaya kingly title of 'Sri Maharajah and remained Hindu. He reigned for 20 years but little is known about him except that he introduced into his court the first elaborate Hinduized rituals for ceremonies and royal occasions which were to be added to and perpetuated through several centuries. They tended to shroud the ruler in an aura of sanctity and some divinity. The royal person became sacred and was treated accordingly. He never walked, not outside the palace anyway. He was either borne on an elephant with the *Temenggong*, Minister of War, in front of him and another minister behind bearing the Sword of State while swords-and spearmen walked along the flanks and to the rear, or he was carried in a royal hammock by major chiefs. On short distances, a slave bore the ruler on his back. A court language, the *bahasa dalam*, language inside the palace, was evolved especially for the ruler's personal activities. For instance, he was never 'carried' but 'borne about on high'; he never ate but 'regaled' himself; he did not 'sleep' but 'reposed'.

The rituals for the installations of the ruler and major chiefs and for the ceremonials at banquets and levees came eventually to be laid down to the smallest detail. At formal ceremonies, the ruler, sitting high on a raised and decorated dais, was flanked by the highest officers of the state. Behind them stood the umbrella and regalia bearers. No man could come into the presence of the ruler unless he was formally dressed. His *kris* had to be tucked inside the front of his waistbelt as a sign that he came in peace. The colours, white and yellow, were exclusive to Royalty as was the wearing of gold ornaments unless they were gifts of the ruler. The privilege of using yellow colour in clothes and receiving gold and jewellery and rich garments became 'honours' which a ruler bestowed for services rendered.

Foreign envoys were received with appropriately graded ceremonials. The envoy from a ruler considered to be the equal of the ruler of Malacca was greeted with the beating of royal drums and was borne in procession through the town on a royal elephant while two yellow royal umbrellas were held over him. The elephant halted at the entrance to the Audience Hall and the envoy was taken in solemn procession into the presence of the ruler. Representatives of lesser princes were accorded the beating of only one drum—and they descended from the elephant at the outer gate to the palace.

The ruler was supreme in the state. The administration was carried out by ministers, heads of departments and chamberlains who were selected from the aristocracy—or were close royal kinsmen. The most powerful man after the ruler was the *Bendahara* (Chief Minister). Next came the *Temenggong*, who commanded the armed forces and the police and was concerned with defence and justice. The *Penghula Bendahari*, the Chief Treasury Officer or Finance Minister, 'accounted for' the 'Sultan's slaves and his financial clerks and all collectors of inland revenue or port dues'. Inevitably, the community was divided into two classes, the ruling and the ruled; it continued to be so for almost four centuries. A commoner was rarely permitted to enter the rarefied atmosphere of the ruling class.

The Sri Maharajah's death in 1444 set off the kind of struggle for the throne which was already a familiar feature in the region. The choice of his successor rested with the most senior chiefs for there was no automatic right of succession by a son or a brother. A ruler could designate his successor who however had later to gain the support of the chiefs. Their agreement depended not only on the personal qualities of the Heir Apparent but also on the status of his mother. In the days of Malacca, they preferred her to be a lady of the Bendahara's family but eventually she had to be of royal blood.

Towards the end of his life, the Sri Maharajah had married a young princess from Rokan, a State on the east coast of Sumatra. Upon bearing him a son, Raja Ibrahim, she insisted that as he was royal and also of pure Malay blood, he should be given precedence in the succession over the eldest son, Raja Kasim, whose mother was the daughter of a part-Indian noble. Apparently the Sri Maharajah capitulated against his better judgment for he had wished Raja Kasim to succeed him. On his death the court inevitably split into two factions. The situation was exacerbated by the presence of the Raja of Rokan, father of the royal widow, who reputedly was a tyrant in his own state. He forced the chiefs to proclaim the infant, Raja Ibrahim, ruler with the half-Hindu, half-Muslim title of 'Sri Parameswera Dewa Shah'. The Raja of Rokan appointed himself regent. His first act was to expel Raja Kasim from the palace. Raja Kasim became a fisherman and hawked fish aboard vessels arriving in Malacca until 17 months later, when he suddenly sprang a coup with the assistance of his ambitious uncle, Tun Ali, a Tamil nobleman. Raja Kasim was astride the leading elephant when he and his supporters stormed the palace one night in 1445. The Raja of Rokan and the boy ruler were both killed in the attack. Raja Kasim's first act as ruler was to invest his dead half-brother with the posthumous title of 'Sultan Abu Shahid' (The Martyred Sultan). He himself adopted the name 'Muzaffar Shah' and the Muslim title of 'Sultan'.

He was a fervent Muslim and he set his place in Malacca—and Malayan—history by declaring Malacca a Muslim sultanate and Islam the State religion. However, the process of the conversion of the Malays from Hinduism and Buddhism to Islam was gradual and was not completed in the peninsula until about the middle or end of the seventeenth century; but the results were startling and had an intense effect on the people themselves. They renounced Hinduism in all its aspects. They destroyed Hindu temples in which they had worshipped and religious symbols which had had such an influence in their life. They loosened, then irrevocably broke off, all their Indian ties and embraced Islam completely. They replaced the Indian script with the Arabic, indeed ceased adopting Sanskrit words in their language. Local rulers substituted their grandiose Indian title of 'Maharajah' for the Muslim 'Sultan'. One authority said, 'Indian aestheticism gave way to Muslim rigidity, and the convivial habits of the Malays were replaced by the strict teetotalism prescribed by Islam.' As the power of Malacca extended so did its religious influence and it became the centre for the teaching and study of Muslim theology for the entire Indies. From Malacca, the history, precepts, mysticism, and the romances of Islam spread to South Sumatra, Java, Borneo, the Celebes and the Moluccas.

As Malacca continued to prosper, a new element—imperialism—began to engross the thoughts of Muzaffar Shah's court in which his uncle, Tun Ali, had become *Bendahara*. The extensive Sri Vijaya kingdom was not yet forgotten history, and the wars that had brought the

Hinduized Javanese their Majapahit kingdom were still recent enough to stimulate and inspire ambitions. Why should not Malacca become the heart of a truly Malay kingdom? Muzaffar Shah took a calculated risk in the first year of his reign. He ceased paying tribute to Siam—so breaking off relations with it—but continued to acknowledge the overlordship of China in the hope that in time of military stress it would come to Malacca's aid. His defiance of Siam immediately projected Malacca into its first war. Overland from the north came a Siamese army. Muzaffar Shah appealed to neighbouring districts for help. From Klang, north of Malacca, arrived a large contingent of warriors led by Tun Perak, son of Muzaffar Shah's former *Bendahara* who had committed suicide after a misunderstanding with the ruler. (After his father's death Tun Perak had been given an appointment in Klang as a district chief.)

The Malacca army forced the Siamese to retreat. Tun Perak featured largely in this victory and Muzaffar Shah invited him to remain in Malacca. In 1456, Tun Perak was appointed *Bendahara*, and thus this powerful office was restored to his family. He guided Malacca's fortunes for 42 years until his death in 1498. He was all-powerful and, as Winstedt put it, he was 'the brain of Malacca's imperialist policy in Malaya and Sumatra for more than three reigns'.

In 1456 Siam attempted another invasion of Malacca by sending an armada into the straits. Tun Perak gathered a fleet which defeated the Siamese off Batu Pahat. In 1459 Muzaffar Shah died before he could launch his first campaign for territorial expansion. He had however shown that Malacca had sinews. He had underscored its promise as head of a Malay empire. During the reign of his son, Mansur Shah, who succeeded him, Malacca—with the brilliant and vigorous inspiration of Tun Perak behind the throne—began to move quickly towards fulfilling its vaulting ambition. Tun Perak urged Mansur Shah to spike Siamese influence by attacking its vassal state of Pahang, on the east coast. This was the first phase in Malacca's aspirations. Pahang then embraced almost the whole of the southern part of the peninsula. An important trade route connected it with Muar, in Johore, and with Malacca. Rather than use this arduous approach to Pahang, Tun Perak led an expedition by sea. 'Two hundred sail, big and small' moved round the tip of the peninsula, sailed up the Pahang River and captured Pekan, the capital. The Malay Annals dismiss the victory with a laconic, 'The men of Malacca fought with the men of Pahang. By the will of the Almighty and All-Powerful God, the country was easily conquered.' The Siamese governor of Pahang fled into the jungle but was captured. He and his daughter, Puteri Onang Seri, were brought to Malacca. There, to use modern parlance, the former was detained but treated with courtesy. Malay records say that he was eventually appointed head of the royal mahouts—because he was an authority on elephants. Mansur Shah placed a viceroy over Pahang.

He also married Puteri Onang Sari who bore him two sons, Raja Ahmad and Raja Muhammad. Both were destined to become rulers in the peninsula, though not of Malacca. Mansur Shah's favourite was Raja Muhammad, the younger, whom he designated as his successor. For the sake of continuity, although grossly out of chronology, the futures of these two princes might well be dealt with here. Raja Muhammad grew into a hot-tempered and spoilt youth. When he was 15, he killed a boy who was playing *sepak raga* (a game in which a ball made of rotan is kept aloft by kicks) and whose only offence was accidentally to knock off Raja Muhammad's head-dress with the ball as he was passing. The murdered youth, however, was a son of Tun Perak who, bowing to tradition that Royalty was sacred, asked Mansur Shah for no reprisal but pointedly hinted that Raja Muhammad could never become sultan—an illustration of his considerable power. Mansur Shah made Raja Muhammad the first ruler of Pahang, so creating a new dynasty there. Muhammad died in September 1475 after reigning for five years. He was succeeded by his elder brother, Raja Ahmad—who had for a second time been passed over for the succession to the Sultanate of Malacca.

Women and war filled the reign of Mansur Shah. He married often, and with women of various races. Purity of blood did not appear as important to Malays then as it was to become later. A Portuguese record says, 'He took all the beautiful daughters of the Parsee merchants and Klings (Indians) who pleased him to be his concubines, made them turn Moors (Muslims) when he had to give them in marriage and he married them to mandarins' sons and gave them dowries, and this custom of marrying people of different sects caused no surprise in Malacca.' One wife was a sister of Tun Perak, and great was the joy of the *Bendahara* when a son, Raja Husain, was born. The way lay open at last for the *Bendahara's* family to provide a ruler in Malacca (and in time Raja Husain did ascend the throne). A man of 'little force of character, colourless and unwarlike',

Mansur Shah was content to leave policy to Tun Perak who fanned the heat of a new Malay spirit that pulsated in Malacca. He built a formidable fighting force whose *sorak*, battle-cry, as it went into action, presaged victory. Warriors were the pride of the court. Around him Mansur Shah gathered brave and skilled fighters whom he honoured with a titular prefix of 'Hang', an abbreviation of *Hulubalang*, 'Captain'. Best known of them was Hang Tuah, a swashbuckler who was appointed *Laksamana*, the equivalent of an Admiral. His exploits became legendary; he was the epitome of courage and loyalty to the ruler and his name became immortal. A kris of Hang Tuah's is preserved in the royal regalia of Perak today.

Malay expeditions conquered the eastern Sumatra states of Kampar, Siak, Indragiri, and Rokan. Others in the region voluntarily began to pay homage. On the mainland, Kedah was subjugated, a conquest which gave Malacca suzerainty over the river-states of Perak, Selangor and Bernam. Other small river-states along the coast down to a settlement on Tumasek became willing tributaries to Malacca. This was the peak of Malacca's 'golden age'.

Mansur Shah lived in a splendid palace on that commanding hill behind the town. It had a 300-foot frontage with a roof of many tiers tiled with red glass which flashed in the sunlight. Its outside walls were covered with small Chinese mirrors which also dazzlingly reflected the sun. The author of the Malay Annals swelled with pride as he wrote, 'So fine was the workmanship of this palace that not another royal palace in the world at that time could compare with it.' But one day lightning struck and fire gutted the palace. Mansur Shah replaced it with a more impressive and ornate building.

He died in October 1477. During his reign the trading port had become an empire. Strangely enough the headstone to his grave is the only one of all the Malacca rulers still in existence. After conquering Malacca the Portuguese destroyed the royal tombs and used the stones for building fortifications. How Mansur Shah's headstone survived has never been explained, but it was found by Sir Richard Winstedt in 1918 'reclining against the wall under the front verandah of the Malacca Residency (home of the Resident) where it had been placed as a curio'. It had been unearthed not very far away and was still in a remarkable state of preservation. On it is inscribed a verse which appears on many ancient Muslim gravestones in North Sumatra, 'The world is but transitory; the world has no permanence; the world is but as a web by a spider.'

Although Mansur Shah had designated his eldest son, Raja Ahmad, as his successor Tun Perak easily persuaded the major chiefs to place his nephew, Raja Husain, on the throne. Raja Ahmad, furious over being passed over a second time, left for Pahang where in due course he succeeded his younger brother as ruler of the State. Raja Husain became Sultan Alaedin Riayat Shah and left his mark on Malacca by enforcing law and order—to the extent of taking a personal interest in the way the police carried out their duties—and waging war only when it was forced upon him. Malay sources describe him as perhaps the ablest of all Malacca's rulers but there is little in the records about his reign of 11 years. He died suddenly in 1488 when still a young man, and there is a theory that he was poisoned, for the Malay Annals hint at unusual circumstances surrounding his death; this would not have been surprising because a king who really ruled made many enemies.

Alaedin's eldest son had become Sultan of Kampar but was not summoned back to Malacca to succeed his father. Again Tun Perak swayed the chiefs to elect the younger son, Raja Mamat, who became Sultan Mahmud Shah. Ten years afterwards, in 1498, Tun Perak died of old age. He was indubitably one the greatest Malays in the history of the peninsula. 'With single-minded devotion', as one chronicler puts it, he had created a Malay empire. At the time of his death, Malacca was a strong centralized state as well as a great port filled with the ships of the countries of the Near and the Far East. Tun Perak had also expanded the fortunes of his own house but then that was the practice of the day. 'King-maker' he had undoubtedly been too—but he had deliberately manœuvred his own young relatives on to the Malacca throne. For almost his entire career as *Bendahara* he had been the real ruler of Malacca.

Tun Perak was succeeded as *Bendahara* by his brother, Tun Puteh, also an aged man, who died in 1500. The great office then went to the *Temenggong*, Tun Mutahir, a Tamil-Muslim, and an uncle of the ruler. Ambitious, vain, proud and arrogant, he created enemies among the major chiefs, was disliked by the Malays and hated by most of the traders upon whom he made blatant 'demands'. He mismanaged his high post and, although he did not quite dominate the young sultan completely, he was the power in Malacca. Sultan Mahmud Shah left politics and further territorial expansion to Tun Mutahir while he devoted himself to the study of the mysticism of Islam. During Mahmud Shah's reign, the frontiers of the empire

The Malay Empire of Malacca at its peak in the early 16th century

were extended for the last time and embraced, among other states, Kelantan in the north-east of the peninsula and its northern neighbour, Patani.

In 1509 came the event that led to the downfall of the empire. On 1st August that year the sails of five strange ships appeared on the Malacca horizon. The people packed the water-front in great curiosity and excitement as the vessels approached and finally dropped anchors. They were flying the flag of Portugal, and were the first

40

European vessels to arrive at Malacca. The commander of the small fleet was Dom Diogo Lopez de Sequeira who had come from Goa, then the easternmost point of the Portuguese empire, in search of trade. When he came ashore with his men, he realized that they were the first white men ever seen by the citizens who crowded round them with excited cries of 'These men must be white Bengalis', a reference to the bearded northern Indians. Portuguese faces were touched, their beards twisted and pulled, their armour felt, and their helmets examined. The reception was perhaps a little alarming at first but it was friendly. De Sequeira was taken with due ceremony to the Sultan who treated him with courtesy, tinged with curiosity. De Sequeira delivered a message of friendship from his king, Manoel, and asked for opportunities to trade.

As the days passed Mahmud Shah seemed amenable to the trading proposals. However, the Gujerati and Javanese merchants—with knowledge of Portuguese practice in India—saw the Portuguese as threats to their monopoly of the Malacca trade. They used their financial influence with the nobles of the court, especially the *Bendahara* who agreed to a plot to seize the Portuguese ships and to throw de Sequeira and his crew and troops into prison. De Sequeira however received a warning from a friendly source and he quickly hoisted sail for Goa, but his sudden departure forced him to leave behind 20 men who had been ashore collecting cargo. These the *Bendahara* flung into gaol. In Goa de Sequeira reported the unfriendliness and 'treachery' of the ruler of Malacca and asked for an expedition to rescue his crew. Malacca had a little less than two years left as an independent Malay kingdom. Tun Mutahir was executed a year later (1510) for high treason after he had made an unsuccessful attempt to seize the throne.

CHAPTER 4

Under Western Rule

The Portuguese appearance in Malay waters came 12 years after Vasco da Gama had sailed round Africa and landed at Calicut on the Malabar coast of India to become the European pioneer of the sea route to the Far East. Inspired by Prince Henry 'the Navigator', third son of the king, the Portuguese were the greatest explorers of the era, though exploration was not the compelling motive. They wanted trade (they hoped to find the spice islands of the east); they were also ardent missionaries of the Christian faith—and Muslims were their mortal enemies.

In India, the Portuguese established trading posts at Calicut and at Cochin further south on the west coast. A 'Viceroy of India' was based in Calicut. As maritime supremacy in the Indian Ocean was essential to keep their trade routes open, they garrisoned posts along the east coast of Africa, and Portuguese warships patrolled the sea lane to India. The next phase of Portuguese expansion in India came in 1510 when the second Viceroy of India, Alphonso d'Albuquerque, conquered Goa which he made his headquarters. It was from here that he and his successors extended the Portuguese empire eastwards until eventually a series of fortified Portuguese trading posts ranged from Ormuz in East Africa to Macao in South China and to the Moluccas. The Portuguese dominated this extensive eastern empire for more than a century. De Sequeira had been sent to Malacca to investigate the possibilities of trade with this fabulous market. However, even if he had reported favourably it is doubtful whether Malacca would have remained independent for long, because its position was of considerable strategic value to the Portuguese expansionist policy. De Sequeira's treatment merely hastened the conquest of Malacca.

Early in 1510 four ships left Portugal for Malacca to gain the release—by force if necessary—of the Portuguese prisoners and to extract a trading agreement from the ruler. However, when they reached Goa, d'Albuquerque refused to let them sail on to Malacca. Sarcastically he said that the town could not be won by 'four rotten ships and two rusty swords'. On 2nd May 1511, d'Albuquerque himself sailed for Malacca with the largest fleet he could gather—18 ships carrying 800 Portuguese soldiers and 300 Malabari Indian auxiliaries. At the beginning of July the fleet anchored in Malacca harbour. D'Albuquerque added to the impressive—and ominous—spectacle by firing salutes from every ship and sounding all trumpets.

Sultan Mahmud Shah was among thousands of people who, with some anxiety, watched the Portuguese fleet come to anchor in formation. After de Sequera's escape, he had expected the 'Franks' to return —and here they were. He sent a messenger to d'Albuquerque to ask, 'Have you come in peace or in war?' The answer said 'Peace', provided the Portuguese prisoners were released, the ruler was paid compensation for the losses sustained by de Sequeira, and the Portuguese were given the right to build a fortress to protect their trade. The Sultan prevaricated and d'Albuquerque threatened to attack the city. In the Malay court opinion was divided: the army commanders, confident of their overwhelming superiority in numbers, wanted battle while the Sultan's new *Bendahara* and advisers urged caution. The merchants, concerned only about their trade, vociferously urged war. They—like the army commanders—were confident that the 20,000 soldiers, comprising the Malay forces and a large number of Javanese and Turkish mercenaries, all well-armed and possessing abundant artillery in the shape of large bombards and cannon, could easily defeat the small Portuguese force.

Portuguese and Malay accounts of what followed naturally draw different pictures. The Portuguese chronicles show a patient d'Albuquerque holding back from assault for days even though the Malacca ruler 'never wanted peace . . . and would hear nothing of peace'. The Malay Annals describe the Portuguese threats of war and relate how the Sultan began to assemble his forces and to erect stockades on the hill on which his palace stood as well as on the vital bridge over the river and along the sea front.

D'Albuquerque's principal objective in his war plans was the bridge; its importance had been underlined by one of the Portuguese prisoners who, in a note smuggled out of the prison, declared, 'The occupation of the bridge which divides the city in two parts might decide victory or at least deal a heavy blow to the enemy.' The Malays themselves concentrated their troops and artillery around and on it.

D'Albuquerque waited until 25th July, the feast day of one of his favourite saints, St. James the Greater, before storming Malacca. His troops moved up the river in boats in a pincers movement towards the bridge. They were met, says a Portuguese writer, by an 'infinite number of Moors' armed with bows and arrows, long lances and shields and matchlocks who 'for a good space of time fought very bravely and defended the stockades' on the bridge. All Portuguese accounts say that the Malacca defenders put up a stout resistance. Down the centuries has come the picture drawn in the Malay Annals of Sultan Mahmud Shah and his son in the thick of battle mounted on caparisoned elephants. 'The Franks', said the Annals, 'fired their cannon from their ships so that the cannon balls came like rain, and the noise of the cannon was as the noise of thunder in the heavens and the flashes of fire of their guns were like flashes of lightning in the sky; and the noise of their matchlocks was like that of groundnuts popping in the frying pan. . . . The King went forth on the bridge and stood there amid a hail of bullets.'

The Portuguese captured the bridge and then the mosque along the seashore to the east of the bridge. Street fighting occurred in the town on the other side of the river. The pace as well as the heat began to affect the Portuguese soldiers who wore armour. Just after midday the commanders told d'Albuquerque that their men were 'tired and suffering from the great heat' and were 'quite out of heart with their work'. They recommended withdrawal of the troops for rest. D'Albuquerque unwillingly agreed and the bridge returned into the hands of the Malays who also regained possession of their mosque; during the lull that followed, they reconstructed and strengthened all their defences in anticipation of a fresh attack. It is clear from Portuguese records that, after the first day's fighting, a number of d'Albuquerque's commanders were convinced that Malacca could not be taken or that if it was captured it could be usefully maintained as a fortress. D'Albuquerque summoned them to his flagship for a council and swayed them back to a fighting mood by reminding them of the Imperial policy of Portugal, the economic advantages of possessing this 'ancient market', and the religious implications of casting the Muslims out of Malacca. He was convinced, he said, that if Malacca's trade was taken from the Muslims 'Cairo and Mecca are entirely ruined and to Venice will no spiceries be conveyed except that which her merchants go and buy in Portugal'.

On the morning of 10th August, the Portuguese ships opened up a continuous bombardment of the city, and under its cover d'Albuquerque sent his entire force directly against the strongly defended bridge. The Malays resisted grimly but were forced back and retired to the mosque where the Portuguese found, according to one of their writers, that they had 'a heavy and troublesome task before them for there was the King with a large body of men and elephants, and the defence was maintained so vigorously that a considerable space of time elapsed without our men being able to get in'. The Portuguese captured the mosque after several hours' desperate fighting but as they followed the retreating Malays they found themselves attacked by reinforcements under the command of Sultan Mahmud Shah and his son, Ahmad. The Malay forces were behind a vanguard of 25 elephants which charged the Portuguese, a counter-attack which might have proved successful had not one of the leading animals been speared in an eye, become berserk, turned wildly in its tracks, and transmitted its agony and terror to the other animals which panicked.

D'Albuquerque spent the night on the bridge with his men who waited behind strong barricades for an expected assault by the Malays. Fires were raging in the city; a Portuguese wrote of the night scene, 'It was a terrible thing to look at the city for it seemed as if it were all on fire.' Morning brought no counter-attack. On 24th August, d'Albuquerque launched his third attack, sending his troops six abreast through the streets. There was little resistance. 'And Malacca fell,' said the Malay Annals. 'The Franks advanced on the King's Audience Hall and the men of Malacca fled.'

In the sacking of the city that followed a considerable number of Malays were killed. D'Albuquerque's son recorded, 'Of the Moors, women and children there died by the sword an infinite number for no quarter was given to any of them.' The loot included 3,000 large and small cannon, matchlocks, bows and arrows, armour-plated coats, lances, 'much merchandise of every kind', and treasure such as 'bars of gold, jars of gold dust, jewels, priceless silks, rare perfumes and scented woods'. D'Albuquerque selected his own booty, a gold bracelet embedded with precious stones, and six large bronze lions, for his own tomb. He also reserved royal jewellery and the royal brocaded howdahs and gold-clothed palanquins for King Manoel and Queen Maria of Portugal. (All these treasures however were lost the next year when the vessel taking d'Albuquerque back to Goa was wrecked off the Sumatran coast.)

D'Albuquerque stayed for three months to set up an administration. As he had done in Goa and elsewhere, he also supervised the construction of a fort—made first of wood, then of stone—siting it near where the mosque had stood along the seashore south of the river. Sultan Mahmud Shah hid a short distance from the town in the hope that the Portuguese would leave with their plunder, but when he received news of the fort he realized that they meant to stay. Malacca could therefore only be his again by reconquest. He went south to Pagoh, on the Muar River, but the Portuguese chased him and he turned eastwards and journeyed by elephant and boat to Pahang, a home from home for there he was still 'Sultan of Malacca'. He sent vain appeals to vassal states for armed assistance to regain Malacca. An uncle even sailed to the Emperor of China with a *cri de cœur*, but this proved an unavailing journey.

A sidelight on the atmosphere under which the Portuguese troops existed in the days that followed their conquest of Malacca comes from a contemporary letter written by a Portuguese soldier to his father: 'We remained on shore twenty days, always carrying our weapons, on guard day and night, as we were attacked by sea and land every hour, and they troubled us much.' Of the fort, he said, 'As soon as it was made strong we set about making one of stone. . . . We made it with great difficulty, carrying the stones ourselves, as everyone was mason's labourer and stone-cutter. As we were building it there came many noises from the enemy; almost every day they attacked us, now from one side, now from the other; and now from the sea and now from the land.'

The fort was completed in January 1512 and d'Albuquerque named it *A Famosa* (The Famous). An impressive stone and mortar citadel, its foundations sank to a depth 'of a war lance'; its outer stone wall was 8 feet thick and 20 feet high. A five-storied keep rose by the edge of the sea in a dark red mass. Reinforcements from ships in the harbour could pour into it safely for at high tide twice a day vessels up to 200 tons could come alongside it. Two towers at the rear wall looked towards the hill behind the town and their cannon commanded the entire position. *A Famosa* was the heart of fortifications which spread behind it in ramparts dominated by four bastions. When the fort and the fortifications were completed and guns peeped through embrasures and soldiers walked the ramparts, the people of Malacca were awed by their size and strength. Malacca was incessantly attacked during the next 130 years but no enemy succeeded in penetrating *A Famosa* and its walls; its commanders feared only famine by siege.

On the hill (now known as St. Paul's Hill) on which had stood the palaces of the eight Malacca rulers, rose a church dedicated to *Nossa Senhora da Annunciada* (Our Lady of the Annunciation). It became a landmark as inspiring to Portuguese sailing into Malacca, as was the target it presented for the guns of enemies. The church was often seriously damaged during bombardments but it was always repaired with deep devotion. Conversely the hill had its strategic uses in the defence of the city. A Dutch officer was to write, 'From there all the surrounding countryside can be shelled. . . . From the summit, the besieged could observe everything which happened in the trenches of the enemy unless their palisades were extremely high.'

A mediaeval Portuguese city developed within the walls of Malacca with a town hall, offices, hospital, and homes for the officers, civil servants and traders who arrived with every fresh south-west monsoon. No less than nine churches raised their spires in the town and the suburbs. Outside the walled town lived the Malays and other races in three different suburbs—Sabac (now Bunga Raya), Yler (Banda Hilir) and Upeh (Tranqueirah). The Malays and Javanese were in Upeh, north of the river, and during the frequent alarms of war and actual attacks which beset Malacca they sought refuge inside the fort.

Malacca was controlled by a Portuguese 'Captain of the Fortress' (an office changed in 1571 to 'Governor of the South' with responsibilities extending over other Portuguese territories in the Far East) who was responsible to the Viceroy in Goa. A Captain-General commanded the garrison. A Malay *Bendahara* looked after the interests of Malays, Chinese, Indians and people of other races who lived in the suburbs. A *Temenggong* had authority over inland Malays, and a *Shahbandar*, harbour master and comptroller of imports, watched over all shipping except that flying the Portuguese flag.

The early Portuguese arrivals in Malacca were astonished by its grandeur as a port. Duarte Barbosa, who served there, wrote of the 'great wholesale merchants of every kind, both Moors and Heathen, men of great estates and owning many great ships' who lived in

47

Malacca and traded 'everywhere in goods of all kinds'. Trade resumed for a time. Great four-masted carracks from Portugal sailed in with raw silk, porcelain, damask, brocades, pearls, fans 'and many other baubles', and returned to Lisbon with pepper, incense, saffron, cotton cloths, quicksilver, opium, dyes, garlic, cloves, tin and weapons such as the Malay kris and swords. Aboard also was 'much gold in ingots' which the Portuguese called *pandouro* (*pao de ouro*, or loaves of gold), gold leaf and dust and woodwork 'gilded with a thousand pretty designs'. Barbosa added with a little awe, 'This city of Malacca is the richest seaport with the greatest number of wholesale merchants and abundance of shipping and trade that can be found in the whole world'—perhaps an exaggeration, but it served to emphasize to the Portuguese at home the greatness of this new eastern possession. D'Albuquerque's son also wrote proudly of his father's prize: 'Men cannot estimate the worth of Malacca on account of its greatness and profit. Malacca is a city that was made for merchandise, fitter than any other in the world. . . . True it is that this part of the world is more valued and prized than the world of the Indies because the smallest merchandise here is gold which is least priced and in Malacca they consider it as merchandise. Whoever is head of Malacca has his hand on the throat of Venice.'

There were never many Portuguese civilians in Malacca; Portugal had too many overseas commitments for its size and small population (then 1½ millions only) and so 'rationed' out its civil service. The Portuguese in Malacca were therefore officially encouraged to marry local women in the hope that this would induce many of them to settle in the country and work in it for the rest of their lives. Relatively few Portuguese, however, became settlers. The climate was unhealthy for Europeans; the death-rate from malaria was high, and the local hospitals always lacked medicines and staff. In 1532, for instance, the Vicar of Malacca complained that in one hospital 'many sick perish through not having the necessary supplies'. Tomé Pires, proud of Portugal and its empire, nevertheless criticized the lack of good government in Malacca, and later Portuguese writers described Malacca as 'voluptuous' and a 'Babylon of the Orient' occupied by 'profligate inhabitants', meaning their own people.

As they traded, the Portuguese crusaded for the Faith, and Malacca became a centre for missionary work (in 1545, the great Francis Xavier, missionary son of a Spanish nobleman, arrived to spread the gospel, to teach children and to look after the sick), but Catholicism failed to appeal to the local people who also hated the Portuguese and their arrogance. The Portuguese found themselves ringed by Muslim enemies and their navy and army were continually engaged in fending off serious attacks or taking the fight into their enemies' strongholds. *A Famosa* was continually in a state of preparedness.

CHAPTER 5

Johore and Acheh Conflicts

From Pahang, Sultan Mahmud Shah, still acknowledged over-lord of a great part of the peninsula and certain states in Sumatra in spite of the defections of several vassals who had switched their allegiance to the conquering Portuguese, sailed south to the island of Bintang (also known as Riau). He set up a capital and a court at Kopak, deep up a river. From Bintang he sent expedition after expedition against the Portuguese in determined efforts to drive them from Malacca; he became their implacable foe and on occasions all but succeeded in defeating them.

In 1516 and 1519, for instance, his forces besieged Malacca and almost reduced it to starvation but were swept away by relieving troops. The Portuguese themselves tried several times to dislodge Mahmud from Bintang and only succeeded in 1526 when they sent a very strong force which captured his capital. Mahmud escaped from them again but this time there were no elephants to bear him away; he struggled through the jungle with his feet wrapped in cloth and eventually was rescued and taken to Kampar, in Sumatra, where he died in 1528. Mahmud Shah had been a strange mixture of despot and mystic. In history he became the ruler who lost a great empire but who until his death was a bitter foe of his conquerors.

When his successor had to be found history repeated itself. Mahmud Shah's young wife, daughter of Tun Mutahir, persuaded the chiefs to exile the Heir Apparent, Muzaffar, and proclaim her son, Raja Kechil Besar, ruler. Muzaffar, then in Johore, went north and was invited to become the first Sultan of Perak. His brother, Sultan Alaedin Riayat Shah II, founded the new kingdom of Johore, setting up his first capital somewhere on the Johore River, probably beyond the present-day Kota Tinggi. In the decades that followed, the site of the capital changed several times, principally for strategic reasons.

Alaedin continued the war against the Portuguese, harassing their ships in the straits and attacking Malacca in hopes of forcing the Portuguese to give up the fort. The Portuguese were also assailed by the war fleets of Acheh in Sumatra, which had become wealthy from trade that moved to it from India and the archipelago as a result of Portuguese trading restrictions. Acheh's capital was filled with traders and adventurers from many countries. It was a town as lawless as the Acheh court was cruel and ruthless, a place where people lived in ostentatious splendour. The Acheh ruler saw himself as the future head of the Malay world and with overlordship over Johore. There was little question, therefore, of the Malays and Achinese joining forces against the Portuguese. Their war fleets combined rarely against the common enemy and only when it suited them. Equally, whenever it was expedient they unblushingly allied themselves with the Portuguese. Until the Dutch took Malacca in 1641 the region was noted for the sea and land battles waged among the Malays, Achinese and Portuguese and for the series of sieges suffered by Malacca, some of which it barely survived.

For instance, in June 1551, Sultan Alaedin came close to starving out Malacca. While 200 boats blockaded the harbour, his army of 5,000 captured the suburbs and cut the walled town off from its land sources of food. The siege lasted three months and was only lifted when the Malays heard that Portuguese warships from Goa were attacking Johore, Perak, and Pahang and they hurried away to the rescue. As an illustration of the flexibility of alliances, in 1582 the Portuguese assisted Johore against an Achinese attack. The Johore ruler, Sultan Abdul-Jalil Riayat Shah II (1580–97), perhaps only out of gratitude rather than of friendship, visited Malacca afterwards to thank the Portuguese personally. What his feelings must have been as he entered the town, the first descendant of the Malacca dynasty to do so since 1511, can best be imagined. Had the years mellowed Malay feeling against the Portuguese? Certainly the Portuguese, harassed as they were by two enemies, must have hoped so. At any rate, the Johore Malays and the Portuguese established trade relations but these lasted a brief two years.

Johore hated the Portuguese but it possessed a deeper and bitter enmity against Acheh. In 1564 Acheh, still rankling over a severe naval defeat inflicted by Johore in 1539, suddenly attacked the Johore capital at Johore Lama, razed it, and took the ruler, Alauddin, into captivity. He died there under mysterious circumstances. During the

51

next 15 years, Johore breathed a little easier when the Achinese devoted their attention to the Portuguese and to efforts to capture
Malacca. Acheh still wanted to rule the Malay world and, as part of
its strategy, it built a fort in Perlis. Then in 1575 it conquered Perak,
an ally of Johore, and incidentally controlled it for the next 100
years. The capture of Perak gave the Achinese two advantages: first,
they had a foothold on the peninsula and thus they became a greater
menace to the Portuguese; second, they held a monopoly of the
state's valuable tin trade.

In January 1587, Johore made another determined effort to capture
Malacca by land and sea, and the siege was broken only by the
arrival of a Portuguese fleet from Goa where it had been raised by the
Viceroy from loans from merchants. After desperate council, the
Viceroy decided that Johore should be taught a lesson. He ordered
the destruction of its capital at Johore Lama. A special expeditionary
force under Dom Paulo de Lima Pereira set out from Goa. In July
1587, galleys and *fustas* towed Portuguese galleons up the Johore
River towards Johore Lama. The capital, which stretched along the
river bank, lay behind thick walls built either of stone or timber,
'backed', said da Couto, Keeper of the State Archives for India and
State Chronicler, 'so strongly by earth that no artillery shots could
pass through it'. Innumerable cannon of various calibre looked down
along the river. There appear however to have been no defences behind the town, either because the Malays had never expected an
enemy to attack from the jungle or because they wanted a withdrawal
route.

The Portuguese, who later claimed that Johore Lama was
defended by 12,000 men, launched initial attacks on the southern
'suburbs 'which lay about a mile away. The troops received little
opposition and set fire 'to everything both to the vessels which were
numerous and to the houses, which being of straw and wood, took
the fire most magnificently from one to another until they reached
some very large warehouses full of drugs and other goods, and it
took such possession of them and did so much damage that the world
seemed to be on fire'. On 10th August de Lima decided on a frontal
assault and 600 troops were rowed ashore under the umbrella of a
bombardment from the galleons. The Malays were pushed back from
their stockades and desperate hand-to-hand fighting occurred in the
narrow muddy streets of the town. On the stockades themselves,
tired but exhilarated Portuguese soldiers turned the cannon around

and fired into the retreating Malays who broke and fled. The Portuguese razed Johore Lama after gathering an immense quantity of booty which included 800 bronze cannon which the Malays had buried. They claimed to have suffered only 80 killed against the 'thousands' lost by the Malays.

The Sultan of Acheh hardly concealed his pleasure at the fate of Johore Lama; he sent his congratulations to the Portuguese and for a time gave up attacking their ships. Meanwhile, the Johore Sultan established himself at Batu Sawar, 12 miles north of Johore Lama.

The triangular war between the Portuguese, Johore and Acheh continued bitterly, and then in 1595 the formidable Dutch entered the scene, intent on seizing trade and power from the Portuguese who were their enemies in Europe. As the century turned, the English also appeared in the Indian Ocean and among the islands of the Malaysian archipelago. The Portuguese governor in Malacca could hardly have viewed the future with equanimity. The Portuguese position in the Indian Ocean and the Straits of Malacca had weakened considerably because of the continuous fighting around the peninsula; Portugal could not send adequate reinforcements in ships and men owing to commitments in Europe. The Portuguese were well aware of the fact that their hold on the Far East was doomed if their navy lost control of the trading routes; Francisco d'Almeida, first Viceroy of India, had warned King Manoel in an early despatch, 'Let it be known to your Majesty that if you are not strong in ships, little will avail you any force on land,' and later a Chinese had written, 'Drive the Portuguese from the sea and they will die like fish out of water.' Hence the persistent Malay and Achinese attacks on Portuguese warships and shipping. And it was this Portuguese Achilles' heel that the Dutch struck at also when they were ready to test their strength in the Far East.

The arrival of the Dutch and the English in Malayan waters had stemmed from events in Europe. In 1580, Spain, sworn enemy of Holland and England, had annexed Portugal; 14 years later it closed Lisbon to Dutch and English merchants as a trading port. So, impelled by economic as well as political motives, the Dutch and English turned eastwards and moved out to challenge the century-long supremacy there of the Portuguese.

In England in 1600, Queen Elizabeth I granted a Royal Charter to the 'East India Company' which had been formed by a group of English merchants. The first Company ships sailed to the east in

February 1601, reached Acheh in June 1602, and returned to England with full cargoes of spices. In 1602 Dutch trading companies also combined to form the 'United East India Company' which received the full support of the Dutch Government. Consequently it had far more funds and ships than the private English company; it also had power to found colonies, make war or peace, build fortresses, and draw up treaties. The ease with which English and Dutch ships picked up cargoes in the spice islands demonstrated weaknesses in the Portuguese naval strength along the trade routes.

Holland, however, was not ready to drive the Portuguese out of the east; so it played a waiting game, concentrating on establishing trading posts and obtaining trading agreements from local rulers. The Dutch also harried Portuguese ships and by 1618 they dominated the spice islands. The following year they occupied the Javanese capital, Jakarta, renamed it Batavia, were impressed by its position and made it their centre in the region. They developed it as their principal port and so struck a telling blow against the Portuguese in Malacca, for the native states welcomed them as rivals of the Portuguese and took their trade to Batavia.

The Dutch also formed alliances with Johore and Acheh. Indeed their treaty with Johore in 1606 called for a combined attack against Malacca on the promise that, if Malacca were captured, they would occupy the town only and pass control of the suburbs and the rest of the territory to the Malays in return for free trading rights up the Johore River. In the event, when the Dutch besieged Malacca that year, the Johore Malays failed to provide their promised support.

The Portuguese were certainly putting up an epic resistance to old and new enemies in spite of serious losses in men and ships and a consequent decline in their fighting strength. The situation for them became all the more desperate in 1612 when a new ruler of Acheh, the redoubtable Iskandar Muda, more familiarly known as Mahkota Alam, set out to conquer the Malay world and, if possible, Malacca before the Dutch got it. However, he selected Johore as his first victim, captured Batu Sawar in 1613 and took Alauddin, the ruler, prisoner although he later restored him to the throne. When Alauddin subsequently allied himself to the Portuguese, Mahkota Alam sent a fleet of 300 ships and 30,000 men and Batu Sawar was sacked. Alauddin was chased to Bintang where he was taken prisoner again; he died shortly afterwards.

Mahkota Alam placed his brother-in-law, Raja Abdullah, on the

Johore throne, perhaps in fond expectation of obedience from a close relative; he learned later that he had, on the contrary, installed a staunch friend of the Dutch who also made peace with the Portuguese. In 1623 Mahkota Alam took his revenge by descending on Batu Sawar for the third time. Abdullah became a fugitive and in May that year died 'of a broken heart' on the Great Tambelan Island. The kingdom of Johore appeared to have all but come to an end. The new ruler, Abdul Jalil Shah II, a youth, spent his initial years as an exile and a wanderer and did not gain his inheritance until 1636.

Between 1618 and 1620 Mahkota Alam conquered Pahang, Perak and Kedah, and so the Portuguese found themselves ringed on land by the Achinese whose fleets now began to blockade Malacca. The expected Achinese assault on Malacca came in 1629 when 236 vessels carrying 20,000 men sailed into the port. The great force landed in the suburb of Yler, took what is now St. John's Hill and began from there a heavy bombardment of *A Famosa*, captured another hill and was poised for an assault on the town when, once again, Portuguese reinforcements arrived to relieve the fort. They turned the tide of the battle and inflicted a most serious defeat on the Achinese.

Mahkota Alam died in 1636, still vowing to capture Malacca. With news of his death, Johore boldly and defiantly declared its independence from Acheh and began a new era. Mahkota Alam's successor died in five years' time before he could don his predecessor's conquering mantle. As the country was next ruled by four women in succession, the menace of Acheh quickly disappeared. By the middle of the seventeenth century the State stood without an empire. Perak finally regained its independence.

The Achinese assault on Malacca in 1629 had really weakened the fortress. Clearly the town's day as a Portuguese possession was numbered. The Dutch had all the time they wanted to decide when they should capture Malacca. They heralded their purpose by signing another agreement with Johore which again promised support in any other attempt to take Malacca. In 1640 Antonio van Diemen, the Dutch Governor-General at Batavia, ordered the investment of Malacca. Early in July, Dutch warships began to blockade the port and to bombard *A Famosa* almost every day. At the end of the month, Dutch troops, this time supported by 1,500 Johore Malays, landed in the north of the town, encircled it, and took up positions beyond the range of the heaviest Portuguese cannon. Over in India,

Dutch warships blockaded Goa to prevent rescue ships sailing out to help the besieged garrison.

As the Dutch cannon pounded away at the fort, the Malay allies scorched the ricefields and the fruit orchards; as the siege dragged on, hunger bit into the Portuguese garrison and the people inside the fort. Eventually they were forced to eat cats, dogs, rats and snakes; there is a record of a mother eating her dead child. The Dutch troops also suffered their own rigours as the weeks passed and the Portuguese resolutely refused to surrender. Monsoon rains turned the countryside into quagmires, and malaria, typhoid and cholera took a heavy toll among the Dutch and Malay soldiers. On 14th January 1641 after a siege lasting six months, the Dutch forces, shouting a beseeching, 'Help us God', stormed one of the bastions of *A Famosa* and surged on to eventual victory. It was estimated that 7,000 Portuguese troops and people were killed or died during the siege; the Dutch claimed the loss of 1,500 troops. The town and fort were in ruins and not a house stood whole in the suburbs.

So ended the Portuguese era in the peninsula and the straits. The Portuguese may have dominated the region for 130 years but their influence hardly went beyond Malacca. Today, the Santiago gate, one of *A Famosa's* bastions, is the sole relic of their occupation. But along the beach two miles from modern Malacca town is a settlement of descendants of the original Portuguese settlers. They speak an archaic patois, the 'Lingus de Christao' which modern philologists identify as sixteenth and seventeenth century Portuguese. Through 400 years of changing local history, this slowly-dwindling group has managed to preserve itself as a distinctive community.

With typical thoroughness the Dutch began to restore the fortifications and the town. They rebuilt the church on the hill and erected a town hall, the Stadthuys, which stands today as it did then. Hardheaded merchants arrived to trade but Malacca never returned to its former status as a commercial centre simply because the Dutch Government preferred Batavia as the chief trading port in the region. To the Dutch the capture of Malacca had been a strategic necessity, and in their plan of empire it was just an outpost.

The Dutch enforced a rigid monopolistic system in which all ships had to call at Batavia to pay duties on cargo and shipping tolls. Local traders had to have Dutch permits before they could sell their products—and they could sell only to the Dutch who 'bought cheap and sold dear', making enormous profits in the European markets. One inevitable result of this policy was a tremendous resuscitation of piracy in the region. Rulers and chiefs in the archipelago either openly financed pirate fleets or covertly encouraged them in exchange for a major share of the booty plundered from Western and local craft.

In 1641 the ruler of Johore, basking in the friendship of the Dutch, the new power in the East, still held some form of control over territory on the Malay peninsula between Klang and Singapore, over Pahang on the east coast, the islands of Karimon, Bintang, and Bangka around Singapore, and the kingdoms of Bengkalis, Kampar, Indragiri, Siak and Rokan on Sumatra. With the Portuguese out of the way and the Dutch anxious to trade, the reigning Sultan of Johore, Abdul Jalil Shah II (1623–77), envisaged the return of prosperity and splendour to his court and kingdom.

With peace, Batu Sawar, the capital, developed into a vigorous mart—and the Malays were not above contriving to evade the Dutch monopoly in trade. Indeed Batu Sawar attracted ships from China and India, to say nothing of those from Sumatra and the Moluccas, much to the annoyance of the Dutch one of whose chroniclers was to write in 1678, 'The Johorites are not well disposed towards Malacca, and must rather be regarded as false friends.' After 30 years of affluence and opulence (shades of Malacca), disaster befell Johore—over a breach of promise by Abdul Jalil Shah to marry his heir to the daughter of the ruler of Jambi, a rich pepper port in eastern Sumatra. This new war started Johore on the decline again. In 1673 Jambi sacked Batu Sawar and picked up loot which reportedly included four tons of gold, 100,000 Dutch guilders and guns and muskets. The Sultan, then aged about 86, fled to Pahang where he died, a broken man, at the age of 90.

For the next 15 years, the Johore River was deserted by the Johore Royal house. Abdul Jalil's successor, his cousin, Ibrahim, used the island of Riau for a capital. From there he continued the campaign against Jambi and, in the hope of ensuring victory, bought the help of forces outside his realm. They were the vigorous and fierce Bugis from the Celebes. His action had a boomerang effect for the Bugis were to impose themselves on the affairs of Johore and of other states in the peninsula. Good traders but better warriors, these swashbuckling chain-armoured mercenaries were to put their own

57

nominee on the throne of Johore; they also founded the State of Selangor which became the centre of their influence in the peninsula.

With Bugis help, Ibrahim kept the persistent Jambi forces at bay, and the war eventually ended in 1681. By then, several vassals of Johore, including Siak, had cut themselves off from Johore control. Ibrahim did not have much longer to live. His life was cut short in 1685 when, according to report, he was poisoned by three of his wives. . . . He was succeeded by his son, Mahmud, a minor, who was destined to be the last of the Malacca dynasty to occupy the throne. One of the first acts of the Regent of Johore was to move the capital back to the Johore River, to Kota Tinggi, in 1688. Seven years later, Mahmud began to rule Johore himself; his reign was marked by sadism and murder. Winstedt declares, 'Never a day passed when this mad prince did not kill some wretch with his own hands.'

Captain Alexander Hamilton, a British trader who called at Kota Tinggi, presented Mahmud with a pair of screw-barrelled pistols and demonstrated that a ball could penetrate wood from 50 yards. Hamilton related the cold-blooded sequel: Mahmud shot 'a poor Fellow in the Street' in order to see how far a pistol 'could carry a Ball into his Flesh'. One morning in August 1699, Mahmud was speared to death as he was being carried to a mosque on the shoulders of a slave; he had been assassinated with the full knowledge and approval of the major chiefs. He left no heir for he had never married. Indeed the Malays averred that he had had 'a fairy wife' because he had turned from all mortal women. The Johore chiefs elevated the *Bendahara* to the throne. So was founded the line from which the modern rulers of Johore have descended.

To complete the story of Johore up to the first quarter of the nineteenth century when it entered a new era: the empire continued to be afflicted with wars, internal and external, and gradually lost its grip on the remaining vassals in the peninsula while those in Sumatra showed defiance. In 1722 after a civil war in Johore, the Bugis exerted their influence and became masters of the state. They set up Raja Sulaiman, a younger son of the previous ruler, as sultan—and frankly described him as being in the position of a wife who had to do as she was told by her husband, to wit, themselves; in other words, he was a puppet, as were his successors until the Bugis no longer figured on the Johore scene. They also moved the capital to Riau because they considered it would be easier to defend. The Johore capital was destined never to return to the Johore River; nor did it return to the mainland until 1824 when the remnants of the kingdom were divided by the English and the Dutch with the approval of the Bugis and the Malays.

The Bugis used Johore as their base for extending their authority over much of the peninsula either through wars they themselves initiated or by offering their services to rulers in want of assistance against enemies. They became masters not only of Johore but also of a large part of the west coast of the peninsula. They established themselves in Selangor, declared it a State, and appointed a Bugis prince, Raja Lumu, as the first sultan. They intervened in internal struggles in Kedah and placed their own nominee on the throne there. By 1777 they were at the height of their power in the peninsula.

They showed the greatest contempt for the Dutch, attacking their ships, diverting trade to their own ports and smuggling tin out of the Malay States. They climaxed their scorn by laying siege to Malacca for six months in 1784. Strong Dutch reinforcements from Batavia drove them from the scene. Then the Dutch, with the bit strong in their teeth, decided to pursue hostilities into Bugis territory. They captured Selangor (which the Sultan regained in 1785 with help from Pahang), moved on to Riau, forced the Bugis out and terminated their régime in Johore. The Dutch recognized the existing ruler, Mahmud, who signed a treaty ceding the island to them, permitted them to install a garrison and agreed never to let Bugis back on Riau.

Mahmud found himself without many privileges and yearned for independence. He sought ways of ridding himself of the Dutch; and an opportunity came in May 1787, when a fleet of the notorious Illanun pirates of Mindanao arrived in Riau after having been blown off their course while sailing back to their base. He persuaded them to attack the Dutch garrison which evacuated the island. The Illanuns then turned on Mahmud and forced him to flee too. In 1795 the Dutch, who had reoccupied Riau soon after the Illanuns left it, permitted him to return as sultan.

But, before Mahmud could resume his throne, events in Europe again had repercussions in the peninsula. In that year of 1795, the French occupied Holland which then became an ally of England. The Dutch allowed the English to take over all their possessions in the Far East to prevent the French from doing so. The English occupied Malacca for a period and also restored Mahmud to Riau—as well as the Bugis. Mahmud died in 1812 and proved to be the last overlord of Johore, Pahang, the Riau and Karimon islands, and of the jungle-covered island that seven years later became Singapore.

Mahmud left two sons, Hussein, the elder, and Abdul Rahman, but had never indicated which should be his successor. Once again the court split into two factions and once again the Bugis stepped in. The Johore chiefs favoured Hussein not only because he was the elder but also because he was related by marriage to the *Bendahara* and the Temenggong. The Bugis however raised Abdul Rahman to the throne because he was younger and malleable.

In 1824, an Anglo-Dutch Treaty was signed. It brought into operation two distinct spheres of influence in the region. The Malay peninsula and the island of Singapore came within the orbit of the English, while Sumatra, Riau and the islands around, Java and the rest of the archipelago came under the Dutch. The division of the Johore empire had the agreement of the Bugis and the Johore Malays who themselves were anxious to be rid of the former. The division also took Abdul Rahman and the Bugis completely out of peninsular history.

CHAPTER 6

A British Foothold in the Peninsula

The English East India Company did not show the slightest interest in the Malay peninsula for more than 100 years after its ships first sailed the seas around it. Its merchantmen headed through the Straits of Malacca directly for Java and the Moluccas for a bite at the spice trade which was almost completely controlled by the Dutch. English trading stations sprang up at Sukadana in Borneo, the Sambas Islands, and Banjermasin and Indragiri, in Sumatra. Inevitably bitter rivalry developed on the spot between the English and the Dutch. The more powerful Dutch East India Company brought its local navy and army into action and asserted its monopoly. The English Company gradually forsook trading in the region, closed its factories, and turned its attention to India where it thought a better market existed for English woollen and other manufactures. Out of this enforced change in trading fields developed England's empire in India.

The only commodity from the Malay peninsula which could have interested the Company was tin, particularly from Kedah, but its ships brought back such small quantities, because of the Dutch monopoly, that by 1676 this trade lapsed. The Company thenceforth concentrated on expanding trade in India and with China. Nevertheless independent English traders operating from Indian ports became familiar faces in the Malay river-states, and it was one of them, Captain Francis Light, who in 1786 was responsible for bringing England its first foothold in the peninsula when naval strategy forced the English Company to change its policy about having a station beyond India.

Wars in Europe which had their repercussions in the Indian Ocean and further east made it imperative for a naval harbour to be found beyond India which could guard the eastern trade routes; Bombay, on the west coast of India, was the Company's sole naval base. When the French began to be interested in expanding their empire in the Far East, English factories along the east coast of India and English ships in the Bay of Bengal became vulnerable to French attacks, particularly at the time of the monsoonal changes. In those days of sailing ships, the monsoons over the Bay of Bengal played a vital role in naval strategy. In October and November the north-east monsoon lashed the Bay of Bengal and the Coromandel coast and an English fighting fleet was forced to move into a safe harbour—faraway Bombay. In the milder monsoon season, Bombay was also the only port available for repairing disabled ships or revictualling them.

English private captains and merchants were naturally anxious for protection and suggested possible sites for a naval base, but the Company found none of these suitable. In 1771, Francis Light, an ex-naval officer and now a trading master, informed the Company that his good friend, the Sultan of Kedah, was willing to cede his port at the mouth of the Merbok River in return for assistance against his enemies. English traders knew Kedah well and their stalwart Indiamen were familiar sights in the port as they arrived with cloth and other goods and took away tin, gold, pepper and elephants. (The records are replete with poignant tales of elephants either dying on the voyage west or falling overboard.) Alexander Hamilton, the Scots trader, has left a piquant picture of Kedah and its ruler. Writing about 1700, he described the country as 'small and poor'. 'The King shews no Marks of Grandeur, besides arbitrary governing', was 'poor, proud and beggarly' and never failed to visit 'stranger Merchants at their coming to his Port, and then, according to Custom, he must have a Present. When the Stranger returns the visit, or has any business with him, he must make him a Present, otherwise he thinks due Respect is not paid to him, and in Return of these Presents, his Majesty will honour the Stranger with a Seat near his sacred Person, and will chew a little Betel, and put it out of his Royal Mouth on a little gold Saucer, and sends it by his Page to the Stranger, who must take it with all the Signs of Humility and Satisfaction, and chew it after him, and it is very dangerous to refuse the Royal Morsel.'

Kedah was in constant fear of attack from Siam and Burma and from the Bugis in Selangor. Its ruler saw in the English an opportunity for arranging protection in exchange for free trading rights; hence his offer of 1771. Light emphasized to the Company the value of the concession which he said would exclude the Dutch and French from Kedah and would ensure that 'not a slab of tin, a grain of pepper, betel-nut or damar' would be sold to anyone but the English. Light also wrote to Warren Hastings, who had become Governor of Bengal, suggesting the island of Penang, opposite Kedah, as an ideal port between India and China.

Light's overtures at least resulted in the despatch of two missions by the Company. The first was to Acheh but the ruler refused to listen to the envoy's overtures. The second mission went to Kedah and was entrusted to a young and inexperienced officer who had the Sultan exclaiming, 'Have the Company no one to send me but this stuttering boy?' He rejected the Company's proposals because they excluded military assistance. The Sultan of Kedah's offer was shelved for more than 10 years. Then further anxieties were caused by the peregrinations of a French squadron after France became involved against England in the American War of Independence and when England itself was at war again with the Dutch (1780-4); Holland became an ally of France and permitted the French fleet in the Far East to use Dutch ports like Acheh and Mergui during the stormy monsoon months. The French ships sailed out of them immediately the monsoon turned and caused considerable damage to English shipping in the Bay of Bengal—while the English fleet waited in Bombay for weeks for a favourable turn of the wind which would sail them back into operations. In 1782 and 1783 the French proved a serious menace in the Indian Ocean and also nearly succeeded in blockading Calcutta. Peace in Europe thus set the English East India Company on a feverish search for an answer to the problem of a good naval station before another war broke out. It looked at Acheh, Riau, the Andaman and Nicobar Islands, and Trincomalee, in Ceylon, but dismissed them as unsuitable.

In 1786 Francis Light again pressed the possibilities of the largely uninhabited islang of Penang. He was then living in Junk Ceylon, an island off the coast of Mergui, in Burma, where he had set up a home and had become a successful trader in tin; he was also a close friend of the new Sultan of Kedah as well as a noble of the Court of Siam. Was the Sultan of Kedah willing to cede Penang? Light sailed to Kedah and obtained the promise of a grant of the island in exchange for military assistance and an annual payment of $30,000 for loss of trade. In his despatch to the Company Light emphasized that any clause relating to assistance against the ruler's enemies should be 'worded with caution, so as to distinguish between an enemy endeavouring or aiming at destruction of the kingdom and one who may simply fall into displeasure with either the King or the Minister'. Light well knew the ways and whims of eastern potentates. . . .

The Company agreed to accept the Kedah offer though it did not specify the compensation it was prepared to pay; on the point of Kedah's defence it merely agreed to maintain an armed vessel to guard Penang and that part of the mainland coast which belonged to the Sultan of Kedah. This reply appeared to induce the ruler to agree to cede Penang. The Company instructed Light to take possession of it and appointed him Superintendent of the new settlement.

Light presented the Sultan with gifts of blunderbusses, brass-barrelled guns and gold and silver brocades—and an extra hundred muskets 'which in their situation was of more consequence than all the rest'. He sailed across to Penang on 16th July 1786 and landed on the north coast; his troops began to clear an area of jungle pressing on to the beach for the settlement. On 11th August Light hoisted the Union Jack and took formal possession of the island which he named 'Prince of Wales Island' in honour of the Heir Apparent (the future George IV) 'it being the eve of his birthday'. This name however has rarely been used.

Light was no visionary when he suggested Penang as a settlement; he saw it only as a trading port and perhaps a naval harbour but not as an outpost of a growing British empire. He was however the forerunner of thousands of Britons who were to come to the peninsula to trade, to govern, and to become friends with the people and to receive deep friendship in return. He was the pioneer in the field of human relations and endeavour in this new country. History has unfortunately largely overlooked him. He was born in the market town of Woodbridge, in Suffolk, in December 1740, the illegitimate son of Colonel Negus, of the Foot Guards, Master of the Royal Buckhounds to the first King George, Member of Parliament, and a considerable landowner. The boy retained the surname of his mother.

Some historians take the line that had there been no Francis Light of Penang there would have been no Stamford Raffles of Singapore. In other words, if Penang had not been established, Singapore would not have been founded because the Dutch would have possessed both; the whole peninsula would probably have formed part of the later great Dutch East Indian empire. Indeed, but for Light's extremely good personal relations with the Sultan of Kedah, Penang might very easily have become Dutch, for, to use a racing collo-

1a. Top-spinning is a popular pastime in Kelantan. The tops are made of hardwood and are wound up with rope. A top can spin twenty minutes

1b. Horsemen of Malaysia are the Bajau who are found on the east and west coasts of Sabah. Apart from raising horses—used in horse racing in the country—they also rear cattle and plant rice

2a. The peace that belongs to Malay fishing villages is reflected in this scene taken
in Kuala Trengganu

2b. A Sea Dyak of Sarawak dressed in his old-time fineries as a warrior. The
Sea Dyaks are now generally known as Iban

quialism, he just pipped them at the post for possession. While he had been in Calcutta trying to persuade the Company to accept the Sultan's offer, the Dutch had been in Kedah asking the Sultan to make a treaty in which he would recognize their suzerainty, and give them a monopoly of tin, and also agree to keep other Europeans out of his territory. Of the Dutch reaction to the Company's use of Penang Light was to write: 'The Dutch are much grieved at our possessing this island and are sure we shall be cut off. It is very probable that they will secure some Banditti to attempt it and engage the Kings of Siak (on the east coast of Sumatra) and Selangor to attack Kedah in revenge for giving this place away.'

This is a useful point at which to remark on the strange historical coincidence that the beginnings of English influence in the peninsula should have been ushered in by a Sultan whose great-great-great-grandson, Tunku Abdul Rahman, was 171 years later to gain the independence of the whole country. . . .

Penang became a Residency subject to the Governor of Bengal. It almost immediately justified its promise as a settlement. The small clearing round the flagmast blossomed into a village which developed into a town as settlers and traders arrived. As Light put it, 'Before we could get up any defence we had visitors of all kinds, some for curiosity, some for gain and some for plunder.' Malays crossed from Kedah and Malacca to augment the original community of 50 Malay fishermen; Chinese, Indians, Arabs, and Sumatrans streamed in. Trade boomed. By 1789 Penang's imports and exports were worth $853,592, a figure that was to be doubled in the next five years. Light encouraged the growing of pepper and gambier; some years later great crops of pepper promised to make Penang the rival of the Moluccas as a producer but the price of the spice fell and eventually its cultivation ceased.

Light governed Penang tactfully but firmly. He had problems, particularly those relating to Kedah which were created solely by the Company's dilatoriness in signing a formal treaty with the Sultan. Light plagued the Company to confirm the amount of compensation the ruler would receive for having given over Penang, and also to accede to his now pressing demands for a flat promise of military help in case of invasion. Light suggested $10,000 annually 'as the value of the Sultan's friendship' and stressed the 'necessity for coming to some terms with the King of Kedah while the Siamese and Burmans are upon him; and I have reason to believe that nothing will be acceptable without the government promising the King protection'. The Siamese had considered Kedah a vassal, had been incensed over the cession of Penang and were making threats of war. Light feared that a Siamese conquest of Kedah would place next to Penang 'an insolent and troublesome neighbour' who would probably deprive the island of supplies from the mainland.

Light urged the Company to send Kedah two companies of Indian Sepoys with six-pounder fieldpieces, a force which he felt would be sufficient to keep the Siamese away for from personal knowledge he did not consider them formidable in battle. However he was merely given approval to fix compensation to a maximum of $10,000 a year for a period not exceeding ten years. Defence assistance was not mentioned. Angered by the Company's attitude, the Sultan of Kedah made two attempts to regain Penang by force. Both were unsuccessful, the first because of dissension among the Kedah commanders and the second, in 1791, because Light, in defence of Company property, took the initiative and flung 400 troops straight at 8,000 Malays assembled on the Prai River for an invasion; they broke in disorder. A few days later, the Sultan sued for peace. He accepted Light's offer of an annual payment of $6,000 for as long as the English continued in possession of Penang and he signed a treaty to this effect on 1st May 1791. The document, to the Sultan's chagrin and Light's personal shame, said nothing about protection against enemies. Nine years later the Sultan ceded to the Company a tract of the mainland opposite Penang—named Province Wellesley—for another $4,000 a year. The Company wanted the strip so that it could control passage through the strait between Penang and the mainland.

Light died on 21st October 1794 from malaria. During his eight years as Superintendent, Penang had grown lustily and prospered. On his tombstone in Penang was inscribed this eloquent tribute: 'In his capacity as Governor, the settlers and natives were greatly attached to him and by his death had to mourn the loss of one who had watched over their interests as a father.' It might be recorded here that the name of Light is also known in Australia. Light's happy and long association with a young Portuguese woman, Martina Rozells, had produced five children, one of whom, William, became aide-de-camp to the Duke of Wellington during the Peninsular War and later founded the city of Adelaide in Australia.

Nine months before his death Light had sent a despatch to the Governor-General in Council in Bengal drawing attention to the 'necessity of establishing a more regular form of government than that which exists at present under the sole administration of one person'. He estimated Penang's population at about 25,000 composed of over 3,000 Chinese (whom he described as 'the most valuable part of our inhabitants'), 1,000 Indians (shopkeepers and labourers), small communities of Siamese and Burmese (chiefly cultivators), Arabs (who were traders and 'good friends and dangerous enemies'), between 1,000 and 2,000 Bugis ('proud, warlike, independent people . . . the best merchants among the eastern islands'), a considerable number of Malays ('poor, knowing little of arts, manufactures or trade'), and the Company's officials and some European settlers. To the Company, however, Penang was still important only as a trading station, although its potentialities as a forward base had been tested in 1793 by events which followed another war between France and England, and by France's subsequent occupation of Holland, which then became an ally of the English who as a consequence took over almost every Dutch port in the Indies to prevent its capture by the French.

Among them was Malacca which they were to occupy for just over 25 years until France was defeated. Malacca had already become a backwater because of Batavia's headway as the Dutch centre of trade. The population was only about 15,000, very much less than that of Penang. *A Famosa* was still its pride. As the war with France dragged on, the local English authorities recommended the destruction of Malacca's fortifications—in case England should be forced to capture the town after it had been handed back to the Dutch. . . . The Directors in London agreed and also recommended that Malacca should be abandoned and its population encouraged to move to Penang.

A Famosa proved extremely difficult to destroy. Apart from its solid stone construction, local superstition held up demolition because the labourers believed that ghosts and devils inhabited the fort, and, said a Malay chronicle, 'many were afraid to go on because of the deaths and injuries'. Even doubling pay did not quell fears. After three months of delays explosives were finally brought into play and 'pieces of the fort as large as elephants and even some as large as houses' flew into the air. The Malay chronicler lamented this act of vandalism; 'the fort', he wrote, 'was the pride of Malacca and after its destruction the place lost its glory, like a woman bereaved of her husband, the lustre gone from her face'.

But Malacca was not abandoned. The Directors changed their minds after receiving a masterly report urging its retention. The author was a young Assistant Secretary in the Penang Government named Stamford Raffles, the future founder of Singapore, who argued that apart from the difficulties of 'doing justice' to the inhabitants, who declined to leave their homes anyway, the abandonment of Malacca could be of 'no real service to Penang but in all probability would be most injurious'. And as it turned out the fort need never have been destroyed. In 1818, at the end of the war with France, the Dutch reoccupied Malacca for only six more years. In 1824, under the Treaty of Holland, they ceded 'the Town and Fort of Malacca and its Dependencies' to England.

In 1805 the East India Company remodelled the government of Penang. They elevated it to a Presidency under a governor who was subject to the Governor-General of India. The Company had changed its opinion and had great hopes for Penang's future as a port, although the lack of suitable timber for building and repairing ships had negated its possibilities as a naval base (Trincomalee, in Ceylon, became the choice for this). However Singapore, after its foundation in 1819, took the lustre from Penang and much of its trade. But then for four years from 1826 Penang reached heady heights as the capital of the newly-established 'Straits Settlements' of Penang, Malacca and Singapore. Finally, in 1832, Singapore took over the role of capital of the Settlements and Penang played a secondary role from then on.

CHAPTER 7

The Rise of Singapore

T homas Stamford Raffles endures as one of the most singular and exceptional figures in British history. His monument is Singapore, that child of his own which he founded in 1819.

He was born on 6th July 1786 on a West Indiaman of which his father, Captain Benjamin Raffles, was master. When he was 14 years of age Raffles joined the East India Company in London as a 'temporary' clerk. He yearned for service in the Far East and he chafed in the office for the next ten years. In 1805 the Company, on making Penang an Indian Presidency, sent Raffles out as an assistant secretary to the first governor. Overnight, his salary of £70 a year as a clerk leaped to £1,500. On 19th September that year, Raffles arrived in Penang with a knowledge of Malay which he had learned on the voyage out. A thorough man, he devoted himself assiduously in Penang to further study of the language and its literature as well as the customs of the Malays and the history of the peninsula. This tireless quest for knowledge of the peninsula and the archipelago to the south held him enthralled for the rest of his life. He plunged into jungle, climbed mountains, sailed up rivers, met rajas and peasants and made friends among all.

A Malay scribe, Abdullah bin Abdul Kadir, familiarly known as 'Munshi Abdullah', who worked with Raffles from 1810 onwards has left this Malay picture and assessment of him. Abdullah saw Raffles as a man 'of medium height, neither tall nor short, neither stout nor thin', his head 'large, a sign of ability', his light hair 'a sign of courage', his ears 'broad to enable him to hear anything'. His nose 'was thin, the sign of a clever talker, and his tongue was persuasive. As to his manner, he always seemed lost in thought. He was very courteous, with a smiling face and word for everyone, great and small. He had a wide sympathy for all men alike and he was generous to the poor. He had a way of finding all about the past, and he never rested until he knew everything. He did his work with method, never mixing one thing with another.'

Raffles's letter about Malacca brought him to the attention of Lord Minto, the Governor-General of India. Raffles met Minto in Calcutta in 1810 when on holiday and impressed him with his detailed knowledge of the Malay world. Never one to miss an opportunity, Raffles, who disliked the Dutch intensely, went on to draw Minto's attention to Java as an island worth capturing and so reducing the power of the Dutch in the region. Minto reacted favourably and, in order to ensure a successful military expedition, appointed Raffles as his agent with the specific task of collecting the fullest possible information about Java and its rulers, the neighbouring islands, the size of the Dutch forces and the local political situation. When he was ready, Minto himself led a fleet to Java in August 1811. The Dutch capitulated on 18th September after an operation which had lasted 45 days, four days less than it had taken the expedition to sail from Malacca to Java. Raffles was appointed Lieutenant-Governor of Java with instructions 'to promote the prosperity and welfare' of the six or seven million people on the island. Minto said to him, 'While we are here, let us do all the good we can.' Raffles implemented his brief with eminent success during his seven years as Lieutenant-Governor.

England's possession of Java proved only temporary. In 1814 under the Convention of London signed in August, England undertook to return to Holland all her colonies in the Far East. In 1816 Java and the Moluccas were returned to the Dutch who were glad to resume possession of these valuable and beautiful islands. Raffles had returned to London in 1814 dismissed as Lieutenant-Governor by the hard-headed Directors of the East India Company, who respected his integrity and zeal but not the wisdom of some of his burning reforms because they had cost a lot of money. In Java, however, Raffles had forged what eventually became accepted as the correct role of a colonial administration—to serve the interests of the people of the country and not just that of the governing power.

In 1817 Raffles—'shunted out of the way' as his friends put it—became Lieutenant-Governor of Bencoolen, an unimportant trading post on the south of the west coast of Sumatra which since 1685 had been the Company's first sovereign possession outside India after its withdrawal from the spice islands. It had never been successful as a port because it was off the eastern trade route; it was a depressing, disease-ridden place, retained by the Company for reasons of 'face' than of necessity. From Bencoolen, however, Raffles continued to warn the Directors of the dangers to British interests in the Far East if the Dutch extended their trade monopoly, and again and again he stressed the importance of having an English station south of Penang and Bencoolen.

Raffles dreamed of a growing British empire in the east. In Java he had declared, 'The great island of Bali, the Sulu Island, Lingga and Rhio, the east coast of Sumatra, Cambodia, Cochin China, etcetera . . . want but the attention of an enlightened and liberal government to add extensively to the commerce of India and to the permanent ascendancy of British influence in these seas.' Now to his agony, the Dutch were back in the east in greater force and possessed 'the only passes through which ships must sail into this archipelago—the Straits of Sunda and Malacca—and the British have not now an inch of ground to stand on between the Cape of Good Hope and China; nor a single friendly port at which they can water or obtain refreshment'. He refused to be defeated by the London resistance to his project.

The turning-point came in October 1818 when Raffles visited Calcutta to discuss the future of Bencoolen with the Governor-General, now the Marquis of Hastings. Seizing his opportunity Raffles again put his arguments for a southern port, and so successfully that Hastings instructed him to establish a station 'beyond Malacca, such as may command the southern entrance of the Straits because the proceedings of the Dutch Authorities in the Eastern Seas leaves no room to doubt that it is their policy, by possessing themselves of all the commanding stations in that quarter, to extend their supremacy over the whole Archipelago' which 'would have the effect of completely excluding our shipping from the trade of the Eastern Islands, except on the terms which the Dutch Authorities might impose, and would give them the entire command of the only channels for the direct trade between China and Europe'. These words in Hastings's despatch reflected the thoughts of Raffles.

Hastings named Rhio as his choice for the port provided the Dutch had no rights over it—he warned Raffles to avoid any 'collision' with the Dutch—and if they had such rights Raffles could negotiate with the Sultan of Johore for a site in his territory, again provided the Dutch had not got in first. As it turned out, the Dutch had secured a treaty granting them the use of Rhio on the day Hastings had signed his instructions to Raffles.

Elated with his commission, Raffles sailed from Calcutta on 7th December bound eventually for Singapore which was his own choice for the new port; he felt that here history would repeat itself and the island would rise again as an important centre. When five days out of Calcutta Raffles wrote to a friend, 'We are now on our way to the eastward, in the hope of doing something, but I much fear the Dutch have hardly left us an inch of ground to stand on. My intention is principally turned to Johore, and you must not be surprised if my next letter to you is dated from the site of the ancient city of Singapura.' To him, as he once wrote, 'the island of Singapore, independently of the Straits and harbours of Johore which it both forms and commands, has on its southern shores and by means of the several smaller islands which lie off it, excellent anchorage and smaller harbours and seems in every respect most peculiarly adapted for our object. Its position in the Straits of Singapore is far more convenient and commanding than even Rhio, for our China trade passing down the Straits of Malacca, and every native vessel that sails through the Straits of Rhio must pass in sight of it.'

On the afternoon of 28th January 1819 Raffles anchored off Singapore. A Malay delegation which came aboard confirmed that the Dutch had neither been to the island nor concluded any treaty with the Temenggong who lived on it and who was the territorial chief of mainland Johore as well. Jubilant, Raffles called on the Temenggong the next day. On a clearing on the right bank about 400 yards up the river stood about 50 Malay huts raised on stilts and a larger home outside which waited the Temenggong. Raffles accepted refreshment in the shape of a local fruit called the *rambutan*, and then, as they sat on a grass mat in the front room of the Temenggong's house and talked, Raffles learned that the Temenggong had been in Singapore since 1811, and that the island was part of the Johore empire which was ruled by Tengku Abdul Rahman who had been placed on the throne by the Bugis and who lived in Lingga. Nevertheless the Temenggong asserted that the rightful ruler was the older brother, Tengku Hussein, who was living in exile in Riau.

As one of his biographers has put it, Raffles decided 'to exploit the peculiar political situation in regard to the sultanate'. It was necessary for him to have a title to the island so water-tight that it could not be assailed by the Dutch who could easily argue that, as they had a treaty with Tengku Abdul Rahman, Singapore came within their sphere of influence. Raffles decided to 'recognize' Tengku Hussein as the *de jure* ruler of Singapore. The following day he sent an emissary to Tengku Hussein with an offer, and also made a quick provisional treaty with the Temenggong who agreed to let the English establish a station on the island for an annual grant of $3,000 and protection; pending a final treaty with Tengku Hussein, the Temenggong also permitted Raffles to land his troops and equipment. That afternoon the Company flag flew from a masthead on the beach. That evening Raffles wrote a second letter to his friend: 'Here I am at Singapore, true to my word, and in the enjoyment of all the pleasure which a footing on such classic ground must inspire. . . .'

On 1st February Tengku Hussein arrived and from all accounts was welcomed by the 150 inhabitants on the island as their ruler. Raffles had little difficulty in persuading him to agree to be formally installed as ruler. The ceremony took place in the front room of the Temenggong's house—a unique setting for such a royal occasion—and in the presence of the people the Temenggong proclaimed Tengku Hussein ruler of Johore with the title of Sultan Hussein Muhammad Shah. It is worth recording that the first proposal of the freshly installed ruler was that he should personally lead Raffles and his troops to Riau to massacre the Dutch there. . . .

Sultan Hussein accepted the terms of a treaty which gave the English East India Company the right to settle in Singapore and trade. He also agreed not to allow any other European power to establish itself in any other of his territories. In return, Raffles agreed to pay him $5,000 annually and to protect Singapore for as long as the English remained on the island. On 6th February Sultan Hussein and Raffles signed the treaty with due pomp and ceremony. The ruler's 'audience hall' was a tent set up by English marines on the river bank. To bring the colour of majesty to the occasion, the sandy beach on which the tent stood was covered over with scarlet broadcloth. In the harbour were the English ships dressed in gay bunting. By the tent a guard of honour formed of Indian Sepoys presented arms as the Sultan, wearing silks, passed between their lines to take his seat on a special armchair brought from Raffles's cabin. After the ships' guns had fired a royal salute, Raffles ceremonially presented his commission from the Marquis of Hastings. The Sultan's secretary translated it, says an account of the day, 'in a loud voice to the inhabitants who had surrounded the tent and squatted, behaving throughout the ceremony with respectful decency and silence'. The treaty was inscribed on thick, white foolscap paper. Raffles sealed his signature with the great red wax seal of the East India Company. The Sultan and the Temenggong held their individual brass seals over the smoke of an oil lamp until they were covered with lamp black and then pressed them on the treaty. Afterwards Raffles presented them with gifts of opium, arms 'and woollens of a scarlet colour'. He sailed from Singapore the next day, leaving Major William Farquhar, R.E., behind as first Resident with detailed instructions on how Britain's new possession was to be developed.

What was Singapore like in February 1819? Munshi Abdullah has left a graphic picture of an island with an evil reputation. 'No man dared to pass through the Straits of Singapore; jinns and satans even were afraid for that was the place the pirates made use of to sleep and to divide their plunder. There also they put to death their captives and killed each other in their quarrels over the spoils. All along the beach there were hundreds of human skulls, some of them fresh with the hair still remaining, some with the teeth still sharp and some without teeth.' An exaggeration, perhaps; but certainly the creeks and mangrove swamps along the coast of Singapore provided the innumerable pirates in the region with more than adequate cover for their operations.

The Malays on the island fished for a living and were also part-time pirates. Along the coast to the east lived a colony of sea gypsies, the *Orang Laut* (people of the sea) whose only homes were the canoes on which they had been born and on which they lived until they died. Their principal occupation was piracy with fishing as a sideline.

Farquhar first set up a fort on a small hill behind the village. It was named, and is still called, Fort Canning. Raffles envisaged Singapore growing in an orderly manner with a free port which would become a focal point of trade in this quarter of the world. He planned for the future, or as he wrote, 'I have had to look for a century or two beforehand.' The new colony thrived almost from the moment Farquhar began clearing the jungle around the existing village. Within four months more than 5,000 people had settled on it. A year later the population, mostly Chinese, numbered between 10,000 and 12,000. In a year the imports and exports from native craft alone exceeded $4,000,000. Singapore continued to expand phenomenally and soon became what Raffles had envisaged, '. . . a great commercial emporium and a fulcrum whence we may extend our influence politically as circumstances may hereafter require'.

The Dutch soon protested vehemently against what they called Raffles's violation of the sanctity of treaties. As expected, they contended that their treaty with Sultan Abdul Rahman covered the whole empire of Johore and therefore Raffles had obtained Singapore under false pretences. In London, the Court of Directors became alarmed over the possibility that continued possession of Singapore against the claims of the Dutch would plunge England into an unwanted war with Holland. So they accused Raffles of 'intemperance of conduct'. Hastings, although worried, supported Raffles whose only concern was that the Directors in their apprehensions might order Singapore to be handed to the Dutch. Time, and the slow wheels of diplomacy, saved Singapore. As the Foreign Offices in London and The Hague pursued the regulated course for dealing with such disputes, Hastings exchanged temperate correspondence with the Dutch Governor-General in Batavia. And as Singapore continued to expand and trade multiplied, so the Court of Directors became impressed and slowly changed their minds until in March 1823 they wrote to Hastings, 'You will continue to occupy Singapore.' By then, as the British Government had guessed would happen, the Dutch were not anxious to go to war over Singapore.

In its early years Singapore was administered under the general supervision of Raffles as Lieutenant-Governor of Bencoolen. He left for England in June 1823 and died three years later on his forty-sixth birthday on his farm at Hendon after an epileptic stroke. A statue to this great man sits in Westminster Abbey while another stands in Singapore facing the point on the Singapore River where he is believed to have landed. But Singapore itself remains his most stirring monument.

In 1824, two years before Raffles died, some unfinished business was concluded between Sultan Hussein and the Company. The treaty of 1819, as John Crawford, who succeeded Farquhar as Resident, pointed out, 'amounted to little more than a permission for the formation of a British factory. . . . There was in reality no territorial cession giving a legal right of legislation. . . . The native chief was considered to be the proprietor of the land, even within the bounds of the British factory.' Crawford therefore concluded a second treaty in August 1824 which made British sovereignty indisputable. The

75

ruler ceded the island and 'the adjacent seas, straits and islets' lying within a radius of 10 miles in full sovereignty and property to the East India Company, its heirs and successors forever. Sultan Hussein undertook that as long as he continued to draw a British pension he would not form an alliance or correspond with any foreign power. The treaty also made it clear that no offensive and defensive alliance existed between the Company and the ruler and that neither party would interfere in the internal affairs of the other or in any political dissensions or wars that might arise or 'support each other by force of arms against any third party whatsoever'. In return the Company paid the ruler a sum of $33,000 and a pension of $1,300 a month for life, while the Temenggong received $26,800 and $700 a month for life.

The new era in Britain's history in the Far East was assured in 1824 when England and Holland signed the Anglo-Dutch Treaty under which the Dutch, *inter alia*, withdrew their objections to the British presence in Singapore and recognized it as a British possession. They ceded Malacca and all their factories in India to Britain and agreed 'never to form any establishment in any part of the Peninsula or to conclude any treaty with any native Prince, chief, or State therein'. England withdrew from Bencoolen and factories in Sumatra and also undertook not to form any new settlement in the new Dutch sphere of influence. In effect the treaty drew a clear line down the Straits of Malacca between English and Dutch possessions. To the right of the line lay the Dutch sphere of influence, to the left Britain was the paramount power. But it also divided what remained of the Johore empire. Sultan Abdul Rahman remained in Riau supported by the Dutch, and Sultan Hussein ruled mainland Johore, first from Singapore and then from Malacca where he died in 1825. The treaty notably suited Britain for it ensured that the trade route to China via the Straits of Malacca was secure.

The colonies of Penang, Malacca and Singapore were styled the 'Straits Settlements'. In 1826 they were formed into a Presidency with Penang as the centre of government. Four years later they were reduced in status to a 'Residency', and in 1832 the capital was moved from Penang to Singapore because of the latter's importance as a commercial centre. In 1851 the 'Straits Settlements' were placed directly under the jurisdiction of the Governor-General of India. In 1858, the East India Company was abolished, and the administration of India and the Straits Settlements was taken over by a special Government department in London known as the 'India Office'.

CHAPTER 8

Siamese Pretensions Frustrated

With possession of Penang, Malacca and Singapore, England stood as the predominant power in the peninsula. It would have been simple enough for the East India Company to have signed quick treaties with the rulers of the Malay States and so extended its patronage and protection in exchange for a trade monopoly, but it was not interested in moving further into the peninsula. The Company had no aspirations to further territorial expansion—India was providing it with enough vexing political and financial problems—and the China trade was far more important than the tin, gold and jungle produce which the Malay States could offer. To ensure therefore that its wishes were fully understood, the Company forbade its staff in the three settlements from interfering in the affairs of any Malay State. Although almost 50 years were to pass before this basic policy of non-intervention was radically altered, nevertheless, events in certain States forced British officers to intervene—indeed to sign a treaty in one instance—and then to present a *fait accompli* to the Company for approval.

While the Company was not anxious to become involved in the peninsula, it was at the same time quite prepared to prevent European or Eastern powers from gaining influence in the States. One such country of immediate concern was Siam, a growing power. Siam claimed sovereignty over Kedah, Kelantan and Trengganu although the last named vigorously disclaimed vassalship while admitting to sending occasionally the expensive and elaborate tokens of submission, the *bunga mas*, small flowered trees made of solid gold. (A *bunga mas* sent by the ruler of Kelantan to Siam in 1869 was described as having eight branches, four with snakes entwined round them, 980 leaves, 38 flowers, and four pairs of perching birds.) Siam showed a desire to dominate the whole peninsula, and had begun displaying its hand in 1818 when it instructed the Sultan of Kedah—whom it had never forgiven for ceding Penang to the English without first gaining Siamese permission—to invade his neighbour, Perak, subjugate it and force its ruler to render tribute to the Siamese. Kedah obeyed even though it had no quarrel with Perak.

This Siamese aggression against Perak was merely the prelude to their long expected act of vengence against Kedah itself which came in 1821 and which was undoubtedly planned and executed in the certainty that the English would not come to the help of the Sultan, for ever since 1786 the East India Company had appeared to be morally insensible about the original Kedah condition of providing 'protection against enemies' and had made it clear that it would not enter into a military alliance. A Siamese army laid waste to Kedah—a reliable account says they carried 'fire and sword wherever they went, killing the men, outraging the women, pillaging, torturing, destroying all over the land'—but the Sultan, Ahmad Tajuddin Halim Shah II, escaped. He went to Penang where the Governor gave him refuge but had to turn down his appeals for help. Only when Siamese troops, who were pursuing the ruler and thousands of fugitives, moved into Province Wellesley which was British territory, did the Governor find reason for intervention. A company of sepoys 'sent the whole army scurrying back to Kedah'. Shortly afterwards the Governor flatly refused a peremptory demand from the Raja of Ligor, under whom the Siamese had placed Kedah, to surrender the Sultan.

The East India Company's unfortunate approach to the subject of the defence of Kedah was resurrected by the Siamese conquest of the State. The Sultan demanded that the Company should, under the terms of the stipulation to Francis Light, help him to drive the Siamese out of his State and restore him to his throne, but the Company refused. It had no wish to become involved in war with Siam. Instead it offered to negotiate a settlement with the Siamese. The inflexible—some chroniclers of the day described it as 'immoral' and 'shameful'—attitude of the Company provoked bitter controversy in Penang and in London, where the supporters of Kedah contended that the Company must have been aware of its obligations because Light had several times underscored the fact that the Sultan's principal reason for offering Penang was to receive military assistance against his enemies. Some authorities bluntly declared that the East India Company had been guilty of 'cowardice'. If Ahmad Tajuddin's faith in the English was not completely shattered, it was because of the strength of the support he found in Penang and London.

The next Governor of Penang, Mr. Robert Fullerton, who had taken over in August 1824, tried to convince the Indian Government to help the Sultan to regain his throne as a measure 'not less supported by strict justice than by sound policy' and further to protect the Malay States from Siamese aggression by making representations to Bangkok. Fullerton considered it was 'indispensable to the future peace and tranquillity of the Malay Peninsula' that Siam should be called on to renounce all claims to sovereignty over every Malay State south of Patani. He advocated representations to Siam and 'stronger measures' if these should fail. For once the views of the man on the spot were accepted, although it was not just the Kedah question which swayed the Company to accept his recommendations for a mission to Siam but rather strategic and trade considerations. An Anglo-Burmese war had begun in 1824 and there was need to gain Siam as an ally. Economically English merchants had complained bitterly of 'unfair conditions' and wanted trading conditions in Bangkok to be relaxed.

Major Henry Burney, Military Secretary to Fullerton, who spoke Siamese fluently, was sent as envoy to Bangkok at the end of 1825 and after protracted and very difficult negotiations he concluded an ambiguously worded treaty in June 1826. He had been partially successful in his objectives. Although the Siamese refused to withdraw from Kedah, they recognized the independence of Perak and also agreed never to attack Selangor. Another clause was interpreted as giving the English the right to prevent Siam from interfering in Kelantan and Trengganu. (Like Kedah they had failed to persuade the East India Company to give them military assistance.) In the commercial sphere, Burney gained slightly more favourable terms for English trade.

The treaty had a mixed reception in Penang principally because of its failure to get the Siamese out of Kedah. The forceful Fullerton, who was leader of a violently anti-Siamese group, turned on Burney and expressed regret that the mission had been entrusted to a man so unfitted for the charge. . . . However the India Government was pleased with the treaty and ratified it, in spite of Fullerton's warnings that although the trading concessions appeared advantageous 'so little faith do I repose in their fulfilment that I scarcely think it worthwhile to enter into any serious discussion regarding them'. Too true; the Siamese violated the terms of the treaty time and again and the aggressive Raja of Ligor failed to withdraw his troops from Perak. Incensed over this, Fullerton sent Lieutenant James Low to Perak to explain to the Sultan that under the terms of the Burney Treaty he need not pay tribute to Siam unless he desired to do so and that he might 'rely on the assistance of the British in expelling any Siamese who may proceed to Perak'. The Sultan took the cue and said that he dared not exploit his rights under the treaty unless the English guaranteed him protection, at which Low, another anti-Siamese, without reference to Fullerton, signed a treaty with Perak—the kind the ruler had been seeking for ten years—promising British assistance in 'expelling from his country any Siamese or Malays' who might interfere in its internal affairs and declaring that he could 'in all future times rely on the friendly aid and protection' of the Company—provided he did not send tribute to Siam or hold any communication with it or any other State in the peninsula on political affairs or on the administration of Perak.

As he put his signature to the treaty, Low must have realized he was breaking the Company's strict instructions on intervention and possibly committing it to a war with Siam. . . . Inevitably the wrath of Calcutta descended on Low for having involved the Company 'to an extent which was never contemplated or desired'. The treaty was never ratified, although later events gave the impression that the Company regarded it as binding. The treaty however had its effect; the Siamese withdrew from Perak which thus regained its independence, and as it turned out the treaty also halted them from any thoughts of domination over the western States in the peninsula which were not already their vassals.

In Kedah the Siamese were rarely free from serious internal rebellions and external attacks by Malays, who at times were supported by professional pirates from the Borneo seas. Some of these failed simply because they originated from British soil (Province Wellesley) and the Penang Government felt bound under the Burney Treaty, however much it went against the grain, to assist the Siamese. Thus in April 1831, when 3,000 Kedah Malays living in Province Wellesley surged into Kedah with the help of several hundred Malays from Penang and Province Wellesley and drove the Siamese garrison out of the capital, the Penang Government blockaded the Kedah coast and stopped reinforcements and supplies from Penang reaching the rebels who had the mortification of being pushed out by the

3a. His Majesty the Yang di-Pertuan Agong (Supreme Head of State) of Malaysia, Tuanku Syed Putra ibni Al-marhum Syed Hassan Jamalullail. He was installed as the third Yang di-Pertuan Agong on 4th January 1961. He was born on 25th November 1920, and before his election as Supreme Head of State was the Ruler of Perlis

3b. The first Federation in Malaya was formed in 1895. Two years later, the rulers of the four constituent states met in Durbar in Kuala Kangsar, Perak. Seated from left: Mr. Hugh Clifford, Resident of Pahang (later to become Governor and High Commissioner), Mr. J. P. Rodger, Resident of Selangor, Sir Frank Swettenham, Resident-General of the Federation (soon afterwards to be appointed Governor and High Commissioner), Sultan Ahmad of Pahang, Sultan Abdul Samad of Selangor, Sir Charles Mitchell, Governor of the Straits Settlements and High Commissioner for the Federated Malay States, Sultan Idris of Perak, and Tuanku Mohammed, the Yang di-Pertuan Besar of Negri Sembilan. Seated on the ground are the regalia bearers of the four rulers

4a. An aborigine family of the primitive Negrito tribe in their overnight shelter made from bamboo, branches of trees and leaves

4b. Harvesting rice in a field in north Malaya

Siamese in October. Rebels again forced the Siamese out in 1838 but were unable to hold their positions again because British blockading ships prevented reinforcements reaching them. The repeated failures to oust the Siamese finally convinced Ahmad Tajuddin that he would never regain his State without adequate outside assistance—which he could not expect from the English. In 1841 he decided to submit to the Siamese and sent his eldest son to Bangkok to beg for pardon and for reinstatement. His appeal was backed by the Governor of the Straits Settlements, who took the opportunity of informing Siam that if the Kedah appeal was rejected he did not propose to use British forces to crush future revolts. This possibly helped to persuade the Siamese king that there was no future in holding a country whose people were prepared to go on fighting for their independence. The following year a compromise was reached. The Sultan of Kedah returned to the throne as a vassal paying the customary annual tribute —but shorn of the northern part of his State, for Siam retained the provinces of Perlis, Setul and Kubang Pasu.[1]

On the east coast Siam, in spite of the Burney treaty, continued to have designs on Trengganu and examined the possibilities of dominating Pahang. The Government in Penang kept a careful watch on these manœuvrings. In 1862 the Siamese supported plans for a take-over in Pahang. Here the major chief, the *Bendahara*, had assumed the throne and when he died in 1857 his two turbulent sons, Wan Mutahir and Wan Ahmad, fought over the succession. After a civil war lasting three years, the younger brother, Wan Ahmad, was driven out of the State. He went to Bangkok where he received a promise of support to capture the Pahang throne. In Bangkok also lived another exile, Sultan Mahmud Muzzaffar Shah of Lingga, who had been banished by the Dutch for intrigue. In search of a throne, he was claiming to be the rightful ruler of Pahang and Johore through his descent from Abdul Rahman whom Raffles had not recognized as ruler of Johore and Singapore. Here for the Siamese were two ready-made tools. They planned to help Mahmud to revive the Johore-Pahang Sultanate and at the same time assist Ahmad in Pahang.

From Bangkok in July 1862, sailed a Siamese warship taking the two pretenders and a great fleet of *perahu* (small boats) to be used for an invasion of Pahang. Mahmud and Ahmad landed in Trengganu. Very soon afterwards the latter invaded Pahang with the assistance of

---

[1] Later Kubang Pasu was returned to Kedah, Setul was absorbed into Siam and Perlis became an independent Malay State.

the Sultan of Trengganu (who incidentally was Mahmud's uncle). The civil war in Pahang resumed with fresh intensity. Again economic rather than political reasons influenced the Singapore Government to take notice of affairs in a Malay State, once it had read into the arrival of Mahmud and Ahmad in Trengganu fresh designs by the Siamese to dominate Pahang and Trengganu. Singapore's trade with the east coast States was slowly expanding—and had to be protected. Or as it was put by the Governor, Colonel Sir Orfeur Cavenagh, in a despatch to India, 'It is not to be imagined that the Sultan (of Trengganu) would yield his post without a struggle, and the whole country would in all probability be soon involved in a civil war to the utter frustration of our trade which is now of considerable value, and provided peace and quietness can be maintained is likely to increase. For general reasons of policy it is also apparently advisable that we should as far as practicable prevent any interference (by Siam) in the affairs of countries so intimately connected with the British possessions . . . as Trengganu and Kelantan.' Cavenagh emphasized that under the Burney Treaty neither Trengganu nor for that matter Kelantan had ever been considered as Siamese provinces even though the Sultan of Trengganu had admitted that once every thirty months or so he had sent the *bunga mas* and gifts of camphor, cloth and other articles to the Siamese court which had returned gifts of equal value.

Calcutta agreed that Cavenagh should ask Siam to withdraw Mahmud from Trengganu as a sign of good faith and to give no further help to Ahmad. Cavenagh's letter to the Siamese, in which he stressed he would take whatever measures seemed necessary to protect British interests and maintain peace in the peninsula, appeared to have some effect for they agreed to remove Mahmud—but then they delayed action and it became apparent that they were waiting for the north-east monsoon to break. This would isolate the east coast from shipping and would give them several more months in which to push ahead with their scheme.

Cavenagh decided on drastic action. He despatched H.M.S. *Scout* and H.M.S. *Coquette* to Kuala Trengganu, the capital, with instructions to 'request the Sultan to dismiss his intriguing guest' (Mahmud). Refusal would be met with force. The Sultan of Trengganu made no move so the commander of the expedition carried out his orders, fired a few shells into the town's fort, and then landed his troops who dismantled the guns and sank all the *perahu* which had come from Bangkok. This show of force induced the Siamese themselves to sail Mahmud back to Bangkok in March 1863 when the change in the monsoon permitted. In Bangkok he was discarded as a useless tool. As for Ahmad, he won all the honours of the game. He finally defeated his brother early in 1867 and was installed ruler by the chiefs—with the blessings of his erstwhile antagonists, the British. The Siamese made no further attempts to insinuate themselves in either Pahang or Trengganu.

In 1867 the Straits Settlements were transferred to the administration of the Colonial Office in London following many years of incessant local agitation by English and Chinese merchants, backed by powerful connections in Britain. Several factors had motivated this demand for separation from Indian control. In the 1830s, the Government in India had attempted to impose tariffs on imports into Singapore which would have interfered with its free trade policy. The merchants successfully contended that these proposals would seriously injure the island's flourishing trade. This effort by India—as well as a later attempt to interfere with the local currency—served to increase the dissatisfaction over the way that it was running the affairs of the Straits Settlements.

One Singapore newspaper bitterly commented: 'This is not the first time by any means, that it has been sought by the Government of India to introduce duties at Singapore, in one form or another. . . . Statesmen of all parties in England have ever recognized the importance of maintaining in all its integrity the system on which Singapore is conducted, and which has been productive of such beneficial results to the trade of England as well as to that of India. Our immediate rulers in India, however, have never been able to regard the Settlement of Singapore through any other medium than a revenual one; and whenever, therefore, there has been an excess of expenditure over receipts, whether arising from ordinary sources of disbursement or from measures required for the protection of trade, they have frowned upon the unfortunate place, and the one sole remedy propounded—the only suggestion they have had to make on the subject—is the imposition of duties on the trade.'

The merchants themselves criticized the Indian Government for showing very little interest in the affairs of South-East Asia. Third-rate residency and an isolated outpost of the Indian Empire the Straits Settlements or Singapore itself may have been in the eyes of the lofty Indian Government, but the spirit of Raffles and his dream of a commercial empire in the Far East ran strong among the merchants who already saw Singapore not only as a great free port between Britain and China but also as a strategic centre and citadel of British power in the East.

The Indian Government's decision in 1855 to impose Indian currency (the rupee and the anna) on the Straits Settlements (which used dollars and cents) set the mercantile blood really on the boil, and the agitation for separation from India was raised to fever heat. The merchants called a public meeting in Singapore on 11th August that year, to protest against the new Currency Act on the grounds that the two quite dissimilar systems of coinage could not exist side by side and that forcing a rupee currency upon the Straits would injure trade very seriously. However, the meeting passed a strongly-worded resolution which really marked the beginning of an intensive agitation for separation from India. This resolution declared that the meeting was 'forced into the painful conviction that the Legislative Council of India, in treating with utter disregard the remonstrances of the inhabitants (against the Currency Act), have shewn that they are neither to be moved by any prospect of doing good nor restrained by the certainty of doing evil, to the Straits Settlements, and that it is therefore the bounden duty of this community to use every exertion and to resort to every means within its reach to obtain relief from the mischievous measures already enacted and to escape from the infliction of others of the same nature, more comprehensive and still more hurtful'. (The Act was repealed in 1857 when the Indian Government ordered that only dollars should be used in the Settlements.)

The Indian Mutiny in 1857 provided the occasion for the termination of the East India Company's reign over India and the Straits Settlements. After the mutiny, the merchants in Calcutta petitioned that the Crown should take over the government of India; in Singapore another public meeting decided that the Straits Settlements should take similar action regarding its own future, and a forceful petition was presented to the British Parliament. It argued that the Straits Settlements were so far away from India and their problems so different from those of the British possessions in India, that the Government of Calcutta had failed to understand their needs and had also taken very little interest in them; it had also entirely neglected to cultivate good relations with the neighbouring Malay States and consequently Britain's interests had suffered and her influence had declined. The petition appealed for Straits separation from India. In August 1858 the Crown created an 'India Office' under a Secretary of State to administer India and the Straits Settlements. The new department however showed itself more amenable than the Company had been, to the wishes of the Settlements for transfer to the Colonial Office. Indeed, the attitude of Lord Canning, the first Viceroy of India, swayed the home government to accept the policy in principle; he stressed several points: that the Indian Government was not competent to deal with the affairs of the Settlements the conditions of which differed so widely in every respect from those of India, that it found almost insuperable difficulty in providing competent officials for the Straits civil service and had no means of training them to deal with the peculiar problems of the Chinese and Malays, and that in case of war India would be powerless to defend the Settlements against a strong hostile fleet.

By early 1860 both the India and the Colonial Offices had agreed in principle to the transfer of the Straits Settlements to the latter, but interminable discussions between the Treasury, the War Office, the India Office and the Colonial Office on whether the finances of the Settlements were adequate to cover all contingencies, delayed the event for another nine years. Finally on 10th August 1866, the Parliament passed an Act transferring the Straits Settlements to the control of the Colonial Office. On 1st April 1867, the Straits Settlements became a Crown Colony with its own officially-nominated Executive and Legislative Councils headed by a Governor.

What was Singapore like by 'Transfer Day'? It had a population of about 100,000 people, of whom nearly 60,000 were Chinese. The town was divided into distinct racial areas. The Chinese lived on one side of the river, the Indians and Malays in their own settlements on the other. The Europeans, apart from those in the army, numbered less than 1,000 and lived in spacious cool bungalows set in extensive gardens about two miles from the town. From there they could hear the 68-pounder gun on Fort Canning, which overlooked the harbour, boom reveille at 5 a.m. for everybody.

The Europeans followed a pattern of gracious living. They went for a ride or a walk at sunrise, breakfasted at nine o'clock ('a little fish, some curry and rice, and perhaps a couple of eggs washed down with a tumbler or so of good claret' was apparently considered to provide a 'firm foundation' on which to 'begin the labours of the day', according to one chronicle). The men worked from 10 a.m. until 1 p.m., lunched lightly, and returned home before 5 p.m. In the evening, the families drove along the seafront in their carriages, and when they turned for home in darkness a runner lighted their way with a flaming resin torch held above his head. Dinner, when compared with modern tables, was a gargantuan feast. Soup and fish were followed by beef, mutton, turkey or chicken—and also rice and curry. Pudding, cheese and local fruit ended the meal which was washed down with beer cooled with ice manufactured locally by an American company. As we read, 'The good folks of Singapore are by no means inclined to place too narrow restrictions on their libations, and it has been found in the experience of older residents that a liberality in this respect conduces to good health and long life.' . . . As it was early to rise and there were no other amusements beyond billiards, reading or conversation after dinner, it was also early to bed at 10 p.m.

A day that was always looked forward to by the European community was the arrival of the ship carrying mail from England. The journey to Singapore from London took about two to three months now that the steamship with its tall, ungainly-looking funnel standing starkly upright from dead amidships, and its paddlewheels churning the waters, had superseded the graceful sailing schooner. Instead of going right round the Cape of Good Hope (a route still used for cargo bound for the Far East), the traveller from London was taken first to Alexandria where he crossed the Isthmus of Suez by rail and transferred to another vessel which brought him to Penang and Singapore. The Suez Canal was under construction; when it was opened in 1869, it brought a new era of prosperity to Singapore.

The trade of Singapore had risen fantastically—from £2,563,124 in 1823, four years after its foundation, to £13,252,175 in 1864. It had fast become a centre of commerce with the East Indies, China, Siam and Cochin-China, and with Western countries. Singapore's predominance as a market had almost spelt disaster for Penang which, however, recovered from the almost crippling blow caused by Singapore's early capture of trade; its figures rose from £1,106,924 in 1810 to £4,496,205 in 1864. Malacca had become a backwater; nevertheless its trade figures of £821,698 contributed towards the Straits Settlements' total in 1864 of £18,570,080. The prosperous merchants were satisfied that on these figures the new Crown Colony had every prospect of being able to pay its own way.

CHAPTER 9

Anxieties Over the Malay States

A very important stage in the history of the Straits Settlements and the rest of the Malay peninsula had been reached. As a Crown Colony, the Straits Settlements was to run itself through its own executive and legislative councils under its own governor, and to have its own civil service (which later became the 'Malayan Civil Service') of officers specially recruited and specially trained to understand the problems, languages and customs of the people of the territories. In 1867, therefore, the Straits Settlements stood poised to carry out the aims of Raffles and of the men who thought like him. One of these aims, which was to provide the next phase in the history of the peninsula, was the extension of British influence in the Malay States.

The first Governor of the Colony of the Straits Settlement was Colonel Harry St. George Ord, of the Corps of Royal Engineers. 'Transfer Day', on which Ord was installed as Governor, was a public holiday. Chinatown was decorated and the Chinese let off fire crackers as a sign of joy in the release from 'Indian' control. Singapore at least could now forge ahead on its own destiny. Ord himself never achieved success as a Governor from the moment of his installation. A chronicler wrote that he 'stalked' into the town hall for the ceremony 'without removing his hat, and sat down on the dais without taking any notice of anyone. The impression thus created was never removed and was justified in the years that he remained in the Straits'.

Gratified over owning a measure of freedom in running its affairs, Singapore was concerned only with the enlargement of trade. With this went the determination to try to force the British Government to recognize the necessity for altering its policy of non-intervention in the Malay States where strife and wars were affecting Straits trade.

87

Ord himself was in favour of a forward policy and of intervention in the Malay States; during his term of office he visited them as often as he could. He urged the British Government to recognize Siam's suzerainty over the northern States and to take a parallel control over the States to the south, but he was smartly brought to heel by the Colonial Office. Ord therefore stolidly performed the mission he was given—which was to ensure that the new colony paid its way and did not become a burden on the home government.

Little was known then about the Malay States and few European and Chinese cared to know more than that they existed and presented trading potentialities if only the official line were changed. Swettenham, that great Malayan administrator, scholar and historian, was appalled at the lack of interest in the peninsula and wrote that from 1867 to 1874 it was 'almost inconceivable how little was actually known of the independent Malay States in the Peninsula. . . . What was understood was that in many of the States there was going on some kind of domestic struggle between rival claimants to power who from time to time as they could raise funds or gain credit, sent to the Colony for arms and ammunition to carry on a warfare which claimed comparatively few victims, and in which the fortunes of the combatants varied with bewildering rapidity.' The Government had its answer for those people who had supported Malay rulers or chiefs or Chinese factions with money or material and then found themselves unable to recover the debts and appealed for official assistance. They were told, 'If persons knowing the risks they run, owing to the disturbed state of these countries, choose to hazard their lives and properties for the sake of the large profits which accompany successful trading, they must not expect the British Government to be answerable if their speculation proves unsuccessful.'

Johore and Trengganu were the only really peaceful States in the peninsula. Trengganu was ruled by a singularly strong monarch, Baginda Omar, who had sent envoys to England in 1869 with gifts to Queen Victoria and letters asking (unsuccessfully) for British protection. Baginda Omar, strangely enough for a feudalist, had centralized his authority and administration of his State; in the 1870s Trengganu was an oasis of quiet.

By 1867, Johore itself had entered a new and peaceful era in its turbulent history. It was moving slowly towards prosperity under the able guidance of its ruler, the Raja Temenggong Sri Maharajah Abu Bakar, grandson of the Temenggong who had helped Raffles over

Singapore. Abu Bakar's family had come to the throne under unusual circumstances. In 1855, Ali, the indolent son of Sultan Hussein who had ceded Singapore to Raffles, was persuaded by his Temenggong, Ibrahim, and by the Government in Singapore to abandon his sovereignty over Johore in favour of Ibrahim in return for a pension of $5,000 and a small area in Muar, on the west coast, where some of his ancestors were buried. Ali also signed away the claims to the throne of his heirs and successors.

Ibrahim was a very much stronger and steadier man than Ali. He also had considerable business abilities and he started Johore on the road that eventually made it the richest and most prosperous State in peninsula. He took full advantage of Johore's proximity to Singapore to develop its economy as well as to enhance his own fortunes. He opened the State to Chinese who planted gambier and pepper estates; by 1861 more than $1 million had been invested in such plantations in the State. Ibrahim died in 1862, and his son, Abu Bakar, who succeeded him was to overshadow him in his achievements.

In 1866, Abu Bakar became the first Malay ruler to visit England. There he had an audience with Queen Victoria and this cemented his deep attachment and personal feelings for the British Government and the British people. Paradoxically, although Malay State after State agreed to accept British Residents or Advisers to help them in administration, Abu Bakar declined to follow suit. He wished to remain quite independent—in the full knowledge that the government in Singapore, for obvious reasons, valued having a friendly State on their doorstep, particularly when its sultan was amenable to informal advice. It was not until 1885 that Abu Bakar signed a treaty which brought Johore under British protection, and it was not until 1914 that his successor, Sultan Ibrahim, signed another treaty which gave the British any right—through a 'General Adviser'—to advise in Johore's internal affairs. Even then the agreement laid down some very forthright conditions. For instance, the ruler stipulated that when he found himself at differences with the General Adviser he would take the opinion of the State Council and communicate it to the High Commissioner. He also reserved to himself the right to appoint Europeans to membership of the Executive and State Councils and to the Bench, and also insisted that he could recommend the dismissal of any European officer appointed or seconded to the State service.

In 1895, Johore became unique among the Malay States. Sultan Abu Bakar gave it a written constitution which not only provided for the Sovereign, his election to the throne, his State allowance, and the descent of the Crown, but also for the constitution and duties of a Council of Ministers, a Council of State, and for the basis of law to be administered in its courts of justice. According to Braddell, an authority on the constitutions of the Malay States, it was clear from this document 'that the status of the Sultan of Johore is entirely different from and juristically much higher than that of any Indian prince or any other Malay Sultan'.

In much of the rest of the peninsula, life existed under a dark pall of lawlessness and internecine warfare in which the chiefs with the best fighters remained in possession of a port, or a stretch of river, or a slice of country in the interior, and a ruler clung to his throne by armed might. Robbery and murder went unpunished unless Royalty or the nobility were victims. Taxation on the peasants was crushing, and the homes of rulers and chiefs were stocked with slaves who worked off their debts in years of subjection. To the immediate outside world, many of the Malay States were reaching a stage of complete disintegration; Winstedt, in one of his histories, described some of the States as 'committing hara-kiri'. Perak and Selangor were the worst. Internal war threatened to crush them out of existence. In Pahang, Wan Ahmad, the victor of the long fratricidal struggle over the throne, had become a despot but his country was still riven by civil strife because his predecessor's three sons continued the conflict in vain efforts to regain their throne.

To deal with Selangor first. Between intervals of comparative quiet, said Swettenham in his book *British Malaya*, 'the normal state of Selangor was robbery, battle and murder'. Over Selangor ruled a singular individual, Sultan Abdul Samad, himself a warrior who boasted that he had killed 99 men with his own hands. In him ran the turbulent fighting blood of the Bugis who had founded Selangor. The State's tribulations began during the weak reign of Sultan Muhammed (1826–57). As the chiefs fought over tin and the State turned into a battlefield, the inhabitants of villages fled southwards into Malacca in fear. In the south in Lukut (now a part of Negri Sembilan), Chinese murdered the heir to the throne and his family. It was in Lukut however that the man of the moment lived—

Raja Jumaat, a Bugis, one of the six territorial chiefs of Selangor, who had married Sultan Muhammed's eldest daughter. Jumaat, more businessman than warrior, had invested heavily in developing local tin fields. By 1850 his income from export dues was about $15,000 a year, a fortune in those days. He treated his Chinese miners well and administered Lukut wisely.

The year 1857 was important for Selangor for two events. First Raja Jumaat sent 87 Chinese miners up the Klang River to find tin. They got off their boats at the junction of the Klang with the Gombak River and began to dig at a place which was later called Ampang. They found a rich lode of tin but paid a terrible price for within a month malaria killed all but 18 of them. The mining force nevertheless grew. A village named Kuala Lumpur sprang up at the confluence of the Klang and Gombak Rivers as boats arrived daily with labour or supplies and returned to Klang with tin for export. Kuala Lumpur developed rapidly and in the passage of years became not only the capital of Selangor but also successively the capital of the Federated Malay States (from 1894 until 1946), of the unpopular 'Malayan Union' (1946–8), of the Federation of Malaya (1948–57), and finally the capital of Malaysia.

In 1857 too, Sultan Muhammed died and Raja Jumaat persuaded the other major chiefs to agree to place the ruler's nephew, Abdul Samad, on the throne instead of the eldest son who was still a minor. Abdul Samad changed character after he ascended the throne. He turned to gardening and smoking opium and left the chiefs to battle disputes out among themselves. When they came to him with long complaints, he waved them away with a *'Benar, benar'* ('Right, right') without explaining to them—as he confessed much later—that he meant, 'Right from their point of view, not mine.'

In 1867 civil war broke out in Selangor. It originated from an attempt by Raja Mahdi, the son of a territorial chief, to gain control of the Klang estuary into which the cargoes of tin from around Kuala Lumpur arrived for export. Sultan Muhammed had presented Raja Mahdi's father, Raja Suleiman, with Klang as a domain but had later cancelled the gift in favour of Raja Abdullah, younger brother of Raja Jumaat. Bitter about being ousted from what he considered was his inheritance, Raja Mahdi planned vengeance. He bided his time, which came after Raja Jumaat's death. He gained the support of Sumatran Malays in the hinterland of Selangor who felt no loyalty towards the Bugis chiefs; it was a hostility which had been maturing for generations. Raja Mahdi and his Sumatran Malays captured Klang; Raja Abdullah fled to Malacca where he died but one of his sons, Raja Ismail, took up his banner.

Into the Selangor scene in 1868 came a visiting Kedah prince, Tengku Kudin, brother of the ruler of Kedah. He married Sultan Abdul Samad's daughter, was appointed 'Viceroy' of the State and was handed the responsibility of administering it on behalf of the Sultan. Tengku Kudin found that his first major task was to try to settle the dispute over Klang, when Raja Mahdi refused to arbitrate. Tengku Kudin threw his influence behind Raja Ismail and added 500 Kedah warriors to the latter's mixed force of Bugis and Chinese who were led by European mercenaries. They besieged Klang and blockaded the river so effectively that neither food nor tin entered the town. Nine months later, in March 1870, Raja Mahdi was forced to flee, but he remained a vigorous opponent of Tengku Kudin.

Meanwhile strife had broken out between the Chinese miners in Ampang and those at a new but less abundant tinfield in Kanching, 10 miles to the north-west—and Kuala Lumpur became the prize. The field of battle extended as Malay chiefs allied themselves with one side or the other; Raja Mahdi emerged to lead the Kanching miners. Head of the Chinese in Kuala Lumpur was an ambitious young man named Yap Ah Loy, who had arrived in the peninsula in 1854 at the age of 17 and worked as a mine labourer. He rose to become a mine owner and in 1868 the Sultan appointed him 'Capitan China' (Chinese headman). Yap had supported Tengku Kudin in the siege of Klang and now Tengku Kudin sent his forces in to the defence of Kuala Lumpur, which changed hands several times before the resources of its enemies were exhausted and peace reigned in the region by the middle of 1873. But two years before this the Singapore Government had made its first intervention in Selangor affairs. . . .

In March 1871 Ord had left for England on holiday and Colonel Archibald E. H. Anson, Lieutenant-Governor of Penang, became Administrator of the Straits Settlements. Anson favoured closer association with those Malay States which were not subject to any power, but London continued to be adamant on the point even though the Selangor hostilities had seriously affected the British tin trade. A piracy in the Straits of Malacca plunged Anson into an unauthorized intervention which might be described as the first of a series of local moves that finally led to a change in British Government policy. A Penang Chinese merchant reported that his junk, which had left Penang on 14th June that year for Larut in Perak, had been overdue and that he suspected it had been pirated. The Government steamer *Pluto* found the junk in the estuary of the Selangor River with six Chinese aboard but its cargo sold. Police who tried to arrest other members of the pirate crew who were ashore were attacked by Malays identified as Raja Mahdi's men. The police managed to regain the *Pluto* with a total of nine prisoners whom they delivered to Penang.

Anson despatched the sloop H.M.S. *Rinaldo* and the *Pluto* to the Selangor River to arrest others concerned in the piracy and to try to recover the missing cargo. After a skirmish ashore, the commander of the *Rinaldo* decided on punitive measures. He sailed up the river and shelled Raja Mahdi's stockades for 12 hours—spending the day, as he reported, 'in utterly destroying this nest of pirates'. Anson next sent the Colonial Secretary, Mr. J. W. W. Birch—whom we shall hear more about in connection with the affairs of Perak—to the Sultan of Selangor at his home in Kuala Langat to ask him to co-operate in arresting and surrendering the remaining pirates and to guarantee that 'pirates shall not again be allowed at Selangor or to occupy the forts there'. Birch travelled in the *Pluto* with H.M.S. *Teazer* in support, and landed at Kuala Langat with a large force of marines. Behind him, the *Teazer's* guns bore upon the Sultan's home. The Sultan denied responsibility for the actions of Raja Mahdi and others—he described them as 'bad men and pirates who had long devastated my country'—and said he had already captured the remaining pirates concerned in the interception of the Penang junk and had sent them to Malacca. Birch, in accordance with Anson's instructions, then broached the question of the appointment of a chief acceptable to the Straits Government who would be in charge over the district around the Selangor River. The Sultan averred that Tengku Kudin was still 'Viceroy' and therefore in control. There had been reports however that Tengku Kudin, because of his strong character and forceful administration, had fallen out of favour with the Sultan, so Birch suggested that Tengku Kudin's authority should be renewed as this 'would be very acceptable to the English Government'. The Sultan said he could not do this without consulting his chiefs. Birch threatened to use force within 24 hours. The following day the Sultan sent Birch two letters, one of which declared Mahdi and the other chiefs supporting him to be outlaws and gave the British Government leave to arrest them. The second letter reappointed Tengku Kudin '*Wakil Yamtuan*' (the Sultan's agent or representative) with full powers. Birch delivered these two letters and two other 'trophies' to Anson; one was a pair of elephant tusks to be presented to Queen Victoria on behalf of Sultan Abdul Samad, and the other $1,000 worth of tin belonging to Raja Mahdi and handed to him by the ruler, probably as compensation for the piracy.

Birch's threats to the Sultan were clearly intervention in the internal affairs of a Malay State and therefore contrary to the policy of the British Government. Anson was undoubtedly pleased with the results of Birch's mission, but privately he was uneasy over Birch's show of force when asking for the appointment of a 'governor' whose duties he had also defined. When a public outcry broke out in London over what was described as an 'unprovoked attack' on a 'small and defenceless state', Anson hastened to assure the home government in a despatch that he had expressed to Birch his 'disapprobation' of his peremptory attitude to the Sultan. However, the Colonial Office finally decided that no important aspect of policy had been breached, and not only approved Anson's handling of the Selangor incident but also complimented Birch on 'conducting a difficult negotiation with ability'—an attitude which baffled the merchants in the Straits Settlements and the London firms with which they were associated, for it showed that on the one hand the Colonial Office was inflexible about extending influence over the Malay States while on the other it was apparently ready to condone action which could be legally described as intervention.

CHAPTER 10

The Borneo Territories

In the same era, other events were contributing to the development of the Malay peninsula and eventually to the creation of Malaysia. These were the suppression of what was described then as the 'great and blighting curse' of piracy in Malaysian waters, the cession of the province of Sarawak, in the island of Borneo, to a young British adventurer, James Brooke, and finally the foundation of the territory of North Borneo by British businessmen.

Pirates had ranged from the Indian Ocean to the China Sea for centuries. The seas around the Indies and Borneo were the happy hunting-grounds of thousands of pirates, the Illanuns from the island of Mindanao, and the Balanini from Sulu. Around the Malay peninsula itself were Malay, Bugis and Achinese pirates. In the China Sea swarmed hordes of Chinese pirates in their great junks, but they are not part of this history. The whole Malaysian region was peculiarly favourable for piracy because the innumerable estuaries, deep creeks, rivers and narrow channels were excellent hideaways either for an attack or for a quick escape. From all accounts, the Malay, Bornean, and Chinese pirates were the most villainous and vicious of their ilk in history. Callous and cold-blooded, they impassively tortured and killed their captives or sent them into slavery.

Thousands of men and women disappeared every year from villages after raids by pirates. They were sold as slaves to rulers, major chiefs and petty nobility in depots which existed in the extensive archipelago for the sale of pirate loot, both human and material. With the proceeds the pirates bought supplies to refurbish their boats or repair their guns in armouries they had set up in isolated parts of the region.

European sailing ships which ventured into the then unknown and uncharted seas of the Far East feared nothing more than being encircled by a fleet of long, low *perahu*, manned by hundreds of scarlet-coated and befeathered pirates who beat gongs and shrieked and danced on the narrow decks of their craft as a prelude to an attack. The pirates, though, were wary of the heavily-armed western merchantmen and attacked them only when they were becalmed or wrecked; then they overpowered the crew by sheer weight of numbers.

The rigid trading policies of the Dutch, which destroyed the local inter-island trade, turned rajas and chiefs to backing pirates either openly or covertly in order to replenish their depleted treasuries. The royal patrons provided arms and gunpowder in return for a share of the plunder and royal patronage made piracy an 'honourable' profession in the archipelago. In the Malay peninsula, Sultan Hussein of Johore and his Temenggong and rulers of other States were suspected of encouraging pirate groups. By the 1820s the situation was so bad that local trade around the peninsula almost came to a halt. The Straits Settlements Government frankly admitted that it was powerless to deal with the pirates and that its fleet was 'totally inefficient' for protecting trade. In 1830, sailing warcraft of the Royal Navy arrived in Singapore for anti-piracy operations, but the beginning of the end of piracy around the peninsula only came when the East India Company sent that new-fangled invention, a steamer, the *Diana*, to assist in operations. A coal-fired paddle-wheeler, spuming black smoke out of its single tall funnel, the steamer was excellent for anti-piracy operations simply because it did not have to depend on favourable winds to move or pick up speed—so the pirates found themselves overtaken by the churning monster. *Diana* worked closely with H.M.S. *Wolf*, a sailing man-o'-war, for two years in a most effective partnership. By 1839 the Royal Navy had reduced the menace of piracy around the peninsula; 10 years later, it had all but disappeared.

But along north-west Borneo the Sarebas and Sakarrang pirates kept a tight blockade and controlled life and trade along the coast and up the larger rivers. The Sarebas and Sakarrang—their names came from the rivers on which they had their headquarters—were Sea Dyaks, magnificent sailors but ferocious killers who between them could call on 20,000 men and hundreds of light *perahu*. Their days began to be numbered in 1841 when James Brooke, an Englishman, was formally installed ruler of the province of Sarawak in the island of Borneo.

James Brooke, son of Thomas Brooke, a judge of the High Court of Benares in the East India Company's Bengal Civil Service, was born on 29th April 1803 in Benares, the fifth of six children. In 1819, the year of Singapore's foundation, James became an ensign in the 6th Native Infantry in Bengal, fought in the first Anglo-Burmese War six years later and was severely wounded. In 1830 he resigned from the Company and took a long voyage home via the Malay peninsula, China and Borneo. In 1835 he bought a schooner, armed it with six-pounders, named it the *Royalist*, and three years later set off for Borneo with a hand-picked crew of 14 to 'scrape acquaintance with the natives and explore the rivers and the mountain of Kinabalu. After that to the Celebes. After that, Timor and Port Essington, etcetera, collecting knowledge all the way.' Brooke, a botanist and zoologist by inclination, planned to collect botanical specimens and to make notes on natural history. A personal 'empire' was never in his mind.

Early in August 1838 the *Royalist* dropped anchor in the bay outside the Sarawak River. Sarawak was then the southernmost province of the Malay sultanate of Brunei which was already in the last stages of disintegration. Brunei had risen to greatness in the sixteenth century when one of its rulers, Sultan Bulkiah, a renowned rover of the seas nicknamed '*Nakhoda Ragam*', the 'Singing Captain', conquered States in Borneo and the Sulu seas and some of the southern islands of the Philippines; he had even seized the city of Manila. Brunei's sovereignty extended over the whole island of Borneo and over sultanates in a large number of neighbouring islands. Magellan visited the capital of Brunei during his celebrated but ill-fated voyage round the world in the sixteenth century and Pigafetta, the historian with him, left a vivid description of the city. He said it was 'entirely built in the salt water, the king's house and those of some chieftains excepted'. This immensely rich sultanate welcomed the western visitors grandiosely. After receiving rich gifts borne to them on caparisoned elephants, wrote Pigafetta, 'we mounted the elephants . . . (and) proceeded to the house of the Governor who gave us a supper of many dishes. From the Governor's house to the palace the streets were full of people armed with swords, lances and shields. The King had so ordered it.

'Still mounted on the elephants we entered the court of the palace. . . . We entered a great hall full of courtiers. . . . As a guard to the King there were 300 men with naked rapiers in hand resting on their thighs. At the further end of this smaller hall there was a great window with a brocade curtain before it, on raising which we saw the King seated at a table masticating betel, and a little boy, his son, beside him. Behind him women only were to be seen. A chieftain then informed us that we must not address the King directly but that if we had anything to say, we must say it to him, and he would communicate it to a courtier of higher rank than himself. . . . This person, in his turn, would explain our wishes to the Governor's brother, and he, speaking through a tube in an aperture of the wall, would communicate our sentiments to a courtier near the King who would make them known to His Majesty.'

Brunei's power began to decline towards the end of the seventeenth century. When the Dutch established trading stations along the south and east coasts of Borneo and extended their influence over semi-independent sultanates which owed allegiance to Brunei, the sultanate slowly lost control. By the beginning of the nineteenth century all that remained of it was the whole of the west coast of Borneo (what is now Sarawak and Brunei) and that part of the north-western coast which later became British North Borneo.

On 11th August the *Royalist* sailed up the Sarawak River and two days later dropped anchor outside the village of Kuching. James Brooke landed and met Raja Muda Hassim, a relative of the Sultan of Brunei, who was in Sarawak trying to quell a rebellion of the Dyaks against the rule of the Pangeran Mahkota, another kinsman of the ruler. When Brooke returned to Sarawak two years later he agreed to help Raja Muda Hassim to bring the four-year-old civil war to an end. He did so and was rewarded with a kingdom. As he wrote to his mother in England, 'The war being over, the little man (Raja Muda Hassim) offered me the government of the country of Sarawak.' On 24th September 1841, with Kuching *en fete* and British and Malay guns firing salutes, James Brooke, aged 38, was installed as the ruler of Sarawak 'with the fullest powers'. He wrote in his journal, 'I have a country but oh, how beset with difficulties. . . .' His first act was to draw up a code of regulations enforcing law and order; he also promised 'the extirpation of piracy' so that trade could flourish untrammelled and without fear. In this he received the support of Raja Muda Hassim on the one hand and, on the other, the enmity of nobles and chiefs who were actively participating in piracy.

Brooke was visiting Singapore in 1843 when he met Captain (later

Admiral of the Fleet) the Honourable Harry Keppel, twelfth child of the fourth Earl of Albemarle. Keppel said of this meeting, 'I was initiated into the mysteries, depths and horrors of pirates.' Three weeks later he and Brooke agreed on a campaign against the Sarebas and Sakarrang pirates. Keppel led two expeditions against the latter, his vessels daringly sailing up 100 miles of unknown rivers, destroying pirate strongholds and the numerous craft that lay along the banks. It was not until 1849 however that the final blow against the Sea Dyak pirates was struck. The navy waited in ambush at Batang Mura for a very large fleet manned by about 4,000 men. Between 300 and 500 pirates were estimated killed in the engagement while another 3,000 abandoned boats, swam ashore and fled. Mopping-up operations along the Sarebas and Sakarrang Rivers finally forced the two piratical tribes to submit to Brooke; their leaders promised to abandon piracy—and kept their word. In 1854 the Sultan of Brunei ceded Brooke the country occupied by the tribes in return for an annual fixed payment.

(Britain itself had earlier gained a new colony, the island of Labuan, off the coast of Brunei, which the Sultan had ceded in 1844 as a gesture for British assistance in the suppression of piracy, but Britain did not take possession of it until 1846.)

Freed of pirates, Sarawak settled to trade and development under the patriarchal rule of James Brooke who continued to extend his State with further cessions of territory by the Sultan of Brunei. He laid the foundations of an administration and also began the pacification of the interior of his territory where the head-hunting Dyaks and other tribes were fighting each other. He died in 1868 and was succeeded by his nephew, Charles, who in a long reign of 50 years enlarged the State still further, reduced head-hunting, expanded trade, and brought a measure of prosperity to the country. In 1888, he placed Sarawak under British protection.

It was also at James Brooke's persistence that the Royal Navy cleansed the northern Borneo seas of the Illanun and Balinini pirates. By 1879 full-scale piracy around this region ended. In the meantime, British and Chinese businessmen from Hong Kong had been investigating the possibilities of trade in northern Borneo. Early British attempts to establish settlements in the region had failed for various reasons. Then in the 1870s came the men who laid the foundation of the future British North Borneo. An American named Torrey, who had received concessions in northern Borneo from the Sultan of Brunei, sold the rights to Baron von Overbeck, consul at Hong Kong of the Austro-Hungarian Empire and also local agent of the British firm of Dent Brothers in Shanghai. Overbeck then entered into partnership with Alfred Dent, a son of one of the Dent brothers, to exploit the concessions. On 29th December 1877 they were ceded further territory in northern Borneo by the Sultan of Brunei who also created Overbeck 'Maharajah of Sabah and Raja of Gaya and Sandakan', the provinces concerned, with powers of life and death over the local people. However, the northeastern part of this territory was claimed by the Sultan of Sulu who no longer recognized the ruler of Brunei as his overlord. Overbeck appreciated this delicate point and visited the Sultan of Sulu, who on 22nd Janaury 1878 ceded the area to him and, not to be outdone by the Sultan of Brunei, created the Austrian 'supreme and independent ruler' of the territory. Soon afterwards Overbeck withdrew from the partnership and Alfred Dent and his associates found themselves in control of about 30,000 square miles of country with a coastline stretching for 850 miles. In 1881 they formed the British North Borneo Chartered Company (it received a Royal Charter) which became the first of the vigorous merchant adventurers that developed trade in new regions in that era and so assisted in expanding the British Empire. The Company administered North Borneo benevolently until the Japanese war in 1942.

An end had to come to the territorial concessions which the Sultan of Brunei had been making either to the Brooke family or to the Chartered Company, each of which vied for land while accusing the other of 'piracy' and 'extortion'. A Colonial Office minute in May 1885 testily said, 'If something is not done soon to cool the exasperation of Messrs. Brooke and Treacher (Governor of North Borneo), there will not be a *pengeran* (major chief) left in Brunei.' Britain stepped into this 'scramble for Brunei' but only when the French and Germans began to show an interest in Borneo. It offered the Sultan of Brunei protection which he accepted early in 1888; he also agreed that the foreign relations of the State should be conducted by the British Government. It was thus that the territories of Brunei remained at its present narrow limits.

CHAPTER 11

A Treaty Signed

Ord returned to Singapore in March 1872 fresh with the memory of another rejection by the Colonial Office of a further appeal from him to change their policy towards the Malay States. As he wrote afterwards, 'The Secretary of State, whilst acknowledging to some extent the force of my statements, expressed in the most decided terms his objection to extend in any way the Governor's authority to deal with native affairs. . . .' It seems clear now however from the records that had the Colonial Office decided to change their minds at the time they would probably not have entrusted the task of diplomatic intervention to Ord, who was unpopular in the Straits Settlements as it was. Colonial Office papers of the day bear a pungent minute by Sir Robert Herbert, the Permanent Under-Secretary, who after receiving a bitterly-worded despatch from Ord in October 1873 about conditions in Selangor wrote, 'Most certainly the present Governor cannot be trusted to interfere wisely.'

Ord found conditions in the peninsula worse. The civil war in Selangor was bitter, but in Perak the Malays were embroiled in a serious dispute over the succession to the throne which threatened to burst into civil strife, and the situation was aggravated by the continuing war among Chinese miners in the tinfields of Larut. For good measure, a small war was also in progress between Sungei Ujong and Rembau, two small States south of Selangor and bordering on Malacca.

In March 1873 Ord received a petition from about 250 Chinese merchants and traders in the Straits Settlements asking the British Government to restore order in the Malay States 'not by expeditions' but by 'a moral intervention and a determined attitude in respect of the Territories'. They pointed out that the richest parts of the peninsula were in the hands of the lawless and the turbulent and they contrasted the peace of Johore under the *de facto* supervision of the British with the chaos in States which were not influenced by Britain or by Siam. They contended that a policy of non-intervention might be in accordance with the view which European governments took of their responsibility toward each other but it had no proper place in the peninsula. This petition was the culmination of a series of demands for intervention which had appeared in the local Press and which became more vehement in tone as time dragged on and the British Government refused to move.

The sequence of events during the next few months had significance. For some unaccountable reason Ord did not send the Chinese petition to London until July; it arrived in the Colonial Office in the third week of August. In May, because Ord's term of office was drawing towards its end, the Secretary of State had offered the Governorship to Colonel (later Sir) Andrew Clarke, aged 49, of the Royal Engineers, a man with considerable army and administrative experience in Australia and New Zealand. Clarke had accepted and was due to leave London for Singapore on 20th September. In the month between the receipt of the Chinese petition and Clarke's impending departure, the Colonial Office appeared to have decided to reverse its policy on intervention in the Malay States. On the petition appeared this minute, 'Lord Kimberley (Secretary for the Colonies) is about to consider how far it may be desirable for the Government . . . to interfere actively in an endeavour to stop the dissensions in the Malay States.' Three days later Kimberley ended passive policy with this directive, 'The interests of the British Settlements require that we shall exert our influence to put an end to the state of anarchy and disorder which prevails in several of the states.' He considered 'the whole subject one of the greatest importance' which required the 'immediate and earnest attention' of the new Governor.

On 20th September, the day he left London for Singapore, Clarke received instructions which were to lead to far-reaching effects on the future of the peninsula: 'It is an important part of the duties of the Governor of the Straits Settlements to conduct the relations between the British Government and the States of the Malay peninsula which are not tributary to Siam. The anarchy which prevails and appears to be increasing in parts of the peninsula, and the consequent injury to trade and British interests generally, render it necessary to consider seriously whether any step can be taken to improve this condition. . . . Her Majesty's Government have, it need hardly be said, no desire to interfere in the internal affairs of the Malay States. But looking to the long and intimate connection between them and the British Governments and to the well-being of the British Settlements themselves, Her Majesty's Government find it incumbent upon them to employ such influence as they possess with the native princes to rescue, if possible, those fertile and productive countries from the ruin which must befall them if the present disorders continue unchecked. I have to request that you will carefully ascertain, as far as you are able, the actual condition of affairs in each state, and that you will report to me whether there are, in your opinion, any steps which can properly be taken by the Colonial Government to promote the restoration of peace and order, and to secure protection to trade and commerce with the native territories. I should wish you especially to consider whether it would be advisable to appoint a British officer to reside in any of the States. Such an appointment could, of course, only be made with the full consent of the Native Government, and the expenses connected with it would have to be defrayed by the Government of the Straits Settlements.'

The instruction was cautious—'You will carefully ascertain . . .'— but what had caused this departure from a rigid century-old policy? Fear of foreign intervention had influenced the decision, a fear created by reports in London and from the peninsula itself that other western nations might step on to Malay soil. The final piece of evidence came in a letter written by Tengku Kudin, the Viceroy of Selangor, in June 1873 to the promoters of a tin-mining company in Selangor in which he asked them to 'ascertain if the English, or any other government, would interfere in any disturbance that might arise in the territory of Selangor from wicked persons, so that merchants desirous of opening up the country may have security for their property and capital invested'. Lord Kimberley's emphatic reaction to the reports had been, 'It would be impossible for us to consent to any European Power assuming the Protectorate of any State in the Malayan Peninsula. I think we might send this to F.O. (Foreign Office) and enquire whether they would see any objection to Sir A. Clarke being instructed to endeavour to extend the Treaties with Selangor and the other Malay States by a stipulation that they should not enter into any Treaty ceding territory to a Foreign Power or giving such Power any rights or privileges not accorded to us.' Kimberley explained to Mr. Gladstone, the Prime Minister, 'The condition of the Malay Peninsula is becoming very serious. . . . This might go on without any very serious consequences except the stoppage of trade, were it not that European and Chinese capitalists, stimulated by the great riches in tin mines which exist in some of the Malay States, are suggesting to the native Princes that they should seek the aid of Europeans to enable them to put down the disorders which prevail. We are the paramount power on the Peninsula up to the limit of the States tributary to Siam, and looking to the vicinity of India and our whole position in the East I apprehend that it would be a serious matter if any other European Power were to obtain a footing in the Peninsula.'

Clarke was installed Governor on 4th November 1873. Ord had left Singapore unmourned except by his close friend, the Maharajah of Johore. At the very least, Ord could claim that as first Governor he had proved that the Colony could pay its own way; the official statement of accounts for the last year's working showed $240,000 excess of income over expenditure. . . .

The Colonial Office had probably misjudged the character of Clarke, the soldier. Someone in the Office had described him as 'able and cautious', but elsewhere Clarke had had the reputation of being a man of action with a strong dislike of bureaucracy and the way it worked. He was also a fervent imperialist; to him, British traders in every part of the world were the pioneers in building a British empire and they therefore should be assisted, encouraged and protected. In the army, his guiding precept had been, 'Take responsibility; act first and write about it afterwards.' He followed this in the Malay peninsula and it changed the course of history of the Malay States. . . .

Within five weeks of assuming office, Clarke decided there must be intervention in the Malay States, or as he more graphically put it in conversation with Mr. W. H. Read, a non-official member of the Singapore Legislative Council and President of the Singapore Chamber of Commerce which for years had been pressing for a vigorous policy towards the peninsula: he was ready 'at a moment's notice' to take action in Perak provided he could 'get the key to the door'. With alacrity Read accepted this as a cue and replied, 'Give me a fortnight and I will get it for you.' But by then Clarke had himself taken certain action. He called for a report on the situation in Perak where strife raged between rival Chinese miners for the control of a great tin-mining area in Larut, along the coastal belt, and where a feud between rival Malay factions over the succession to the throne threatened civil war. The Chinese struggle in Larut had been going on in violent spasms since 1861 and British interests were concerned because they had invested heavily in the mines. Moreover many of the Chinese mine-owners were British subjects, and although the war was partly of their own making they were demanding their British right to have their troubles sorted out for them.

In the 1840s extensive deposits of tin had been found at the foot of a range of hills at Larut. Malays had never settled here because of its swamps. But when its mud was found to be tin-bearing, Chinese labourers flocked in to it. The Malay minor chief, generally known as the Mentri, who had jurisdiction over Larut, quickly became a very wealthy man. The mines brought him $200,000 in revenue from the $1,000,000 worth produced in a year at its peak period. As they had done elsewhere, the Chinese brought their secret societies with them. Into Larut poured the two great rival factions from Penang, the Ghee Hin, largely Cantonese, and the Hai San, almost entirely Khehs (Hakkas). A traditional hatred existed between these two tribes and they fought each other for the most petty reasons. In 1862 a mere gambling dispute between two men developed into a vicious struggle for exclusive possession of the tinfields that lasted over many years. The losses on both sides were considerable. During one battle in 1872, 1,000 Chinese were reported killed on the first day's fighting alone and the total dead when both sides withdrew were 3,000. Stockades littered the region and tracks between them were constantly under ambush. By 1872 almost every Chinese mining village in Larut had been burned down and almost every mine had ceased to operate. The societies enrolled their fighters in Penang and called to their clans in China for reinforcements. The troops were conveyed from Penang to the Larut coast in armed junks which either did their best to avoid interception by blockading fleets or engaged them in battle. As the blockades prevented food supplies reaching Larut, both sides turned to piracy. Trade between north and south of the peninsula was seriously affected. Clarke was to describe Larut as 'one huge cockpit where nothing but fighting and murder and violence and piracy' was going on.

By 1873 the Chinese troubles had become inextricably mixed with the boiling Malay dispute over claims to the throne. The monarchy in Perak was unique in the peninsula, and for that matter in the world today—three branches of the royal family took it in turn (and still do) to provide the ruler. Under the conditions of the day this system of

rotation of succession inevitably contributed to ferment and frequently strife. It will be recalled that in the closing days of the
Malacca sultanate, Muzaffar Shah, eldest son of Mahmud, the last
ruler, who had been passed over as successor to his father, had gone
to Perak where he had been invited to become ruler. He founded the
modern Perak dynasty. He brought to Perak the trappings and rituals
of the Malacca court and the Malacca system of administration
through major and minor chiefs. The Perak court is still a reflection
of those old days, for the ruler is surrounded by nobles and territorial chiefs bearing ancient lofty titles who come into their own only
at formal ceremonies. The royal regalia used today is said to have
descended from Muzaffar Shah's days. Among them are five articles
which every sultan must wear at his installation—a sword hung from
a chain over the shoulder on which the guardian spirits of the kingdom are said to press during the ceremony, a gold chain, gold arm-
lets fashioned as dragons, a kris in a sheath of gold, and a thunder-
seal worn in the head-dress. The Chief Herald still acclaims the ruler
in the words which hailed Muzaffar Shah: 'Fortunate great king,
smiter of rivals, valorous, whose crown jewels ravish the three worlds,
whose touch dispels suffering, protector, pilot over the ocean of
battle, confuter of opponents, fortunate overlord of kings of
righteousness, supreme lord of the kingdom', and at the moment of
installation he whispers into the royal ear the great State secret, the
real name of the Hindu demigod looked on as the ancestor and
guardian of Perak Royalty.

At the pyramid of Perak's broadbased system of government were
three royal offices—the Ruler, the *Raja Muda* (Heir Apparent) and
the *Raja Bendahara* who was not only Prime Minister and Commander-in-Chief but also had other singular functions. For instance,
as in Malacca, it fell to him to provide a new ruler with a palace.
When the ruler died, he immediately took possession of the regalia,
became regent, and invited the successor to the throne to the palace
to be hailed as new ruler and to receive the regalia which enabled
him to be formally installed in due course. Only when the successor
had been hailed could the dead ruler be buried. The line of succession
moved in turn through the eldest legitimate son of a previous sultan.
In theory, the office of Raja Bendahara was held by the eldest son of
the last ruler and that of Raja Muda by the eldest son of the ruler
before him. The eldest son of the reigning sultan bore the title of
Raja di-Hilir (prince of the lower, or downstream, country of Perak)

and waited for his promotion. Thus, on a ruler's death, the Raja Muda ascended the throne, the Raja Bendahara moved up to Raja Muda, the Raja di-Hilir became Raja Bendahara, and in due time the eldest son of the Sultan was appointed Raja di-Hilir. The chiefs could, of course, by a majority pass over any eldest son if they thought him unfit or unacceptable for office for various reasons, and so other members of the family concerned could be considered. Thus, as Swettenham put it, 'The country was always supposed to secure in its sultan a man of considerable experience, who had held three high offices, who knew the State, its people, its customs, and its needs, and who, if he failed during the period of probation to prove his worth (in other words, if he turned out an irreclaimable scoundrel), would be passed over.'

During the 1850s, civil war virtually broke out in Perak and the Sultan's power broke. Then in 1871 the ruler, Sultan Ali, died and the strife for the succession was renewed. The three claimants were the *Raja Muda*, Raja Abdullah, the *Bendahara*, Raja Ismail, who was not from Perak but from Siak and had been appointed to the office after his marriage to the daughter of Ali's predecessor, and Raja Yusuf, son of a previous ruler. Abdullah had the allegiance of a number of chiefs and might probably have carried the others but for the obstruction of the Mentri of Larut who saw himself as a possible power behind the throne; he threw his financial influence and his armed forces behind the foreigner, Raja Ismail. His support eventually turned the scales against Abdullah. Ismail, as *Bendahara*, had taken possession of the regalia—in anticipation also of his installation as ruler. Abdullah was too frightened to leave his village and travel to Sayong, where the dead ruler lay in his bier waiting for his successor to be announced, to claim his rights as Raja Muda; he knew that he would be ambushed and killed.

He was absent therefore when the chiefs assembled to discuss the succession; they argued long and bitterly. One by one, Abdullah's supporters left Sayong for their homes. A month after Ali's death, the chiefs who had remained in Sayong elected Raja Ismail; only then was Ali buried. Raja Ismail's success precipitated fresh ferment. Raja Abdullah threatened war. He wrote to Ord in Singapore asking for his intervention in the election of Ismail but, of course, Ord could do nothing. Abdullah also invoked armed help from the Ghee Hin and promised them exclusive use of the Larut tinfields if they assisted him to gain the throne. In retaliation, the Mentri of Larut

107

financed the Hai San to fight back. Perak teetered on the verge of a very serious civil war. This was the situation reported to Clarke.

The Malay and Chinese feuds had also resuscitated piracy in an intense form. Coastal trade had all but ceased and, according to report, even fishermen were afraid to put to sea. The British senior naval officer told Clarke that the vessels at his disposal were quite inadequate to deal effectively with piracy. Clarke decided on action. He was no believer in reports to London and then awaiting sanction to carry out his recommendations. He had once said, 'I fear that in some quarters there lurks a belief in the efficacy of reports to cure ills. . . . My own experience of the uses of reports does not tend to a high appreciation of their practical value, and the War Office is at this moment crammed with documents, the majority of which have never been even studied, still less acted upon.' Where Perak was concerned 'reporting alone scarcely seemed to meet the grave urgency of the situation'. He considered it necessary 'to act in the first place, and to report afterwards'.

It is clear that he felt that peace would not come to Perak unless the Chinese and Malay disputes were settled simultaneously. He decided first to find out if the leaders of the secret societies in Penang were prepared for an armistice and if so under what conditions. His reports indicated that although the Hai San had received strong reinforcements from China, and the Ghee Hin were anxiously awaiting theirs, both desperately wanted peace—provided they could save their faces in the traditional Chinese manner. As 1874 opened, Clarke sent Mr. William Alexander Pickering, his adviser on Chinese affairs and the only government official in the Settlements who could speak Chinese (and six dialects at that), to Penang to sound the headmen of the societies about settling their differences through arbitration. If they were in favour, said Clarke, he would meet them at Pangkor Island, off the Larut coast, on 14th January.

Pickering succeeded beyond all expectations. Less than 48 hours after arriving in Penang, he telegraphed Clarke that the societies were ready to cease hostilities and to discuss their dispute with him at Pangkor. The Ghee Hin pleaded that the British Government should 'take the country in hand' and claimed that both societies had been fighting only because 'all they possessed was being ruined by the rapacity of Malay chiefs'. Clarke made his second move. He sent Major McNair, the Colonial Engineer (or Director of Public Works as he would have been known in modern days), and Captain Samuel Dunlop, the Inspector-General, to Perak to invite all the Malay rajas and chiefs to meet him at Pangkor on 14th January for general talks; they were however not to be told that the succession to the throne would be the specific subject for discussion.

On 9th January, two days after McNair and Dunlop had left Singapore for Perak and three weeks after his conversation with Read, Clarke received a letter from Raja Abdullah asking for an inquiry into the Perak disturbances 'so that they shall cease, and be settled properly and with justice'. Abdullah added that once the country was restored to peace 'we desire to settle under the sheltering protection of the English flag. Further we wish to make a new treaty of lasting friendship with the English Government which will benefit both sides, and we, together with our great men, to show our good faith, ask of our friend, Sir Andrew Clarke, for a man of sufficient abilities to live with us in Perak, or at any fit place not far from us, and show us a good system of government for our dominions, so that our country may be opened up and bring profit, and increase the revenues as well as peace and justice. . . .' It transpired that Read, who was legal adviser to Raja Abdullah, had prepared the letter, certain that it would provide the 'key to the door' which Clarke had wanted. The letter must have arrived at a most opportune moment for Clarke because he later asserted in a despatch to the Colonial Office that his actions in Perak had been undertaken at the request of 'certain Chiefs . . . of the Kingdom of Perak'.

On 11th January Clarke sailed to Pangkor in the *Pluto*, accompanied by H.M.S. *Avon* and a steamer loaded with rice for the Chinese in Larut who were reported to be extremely hungry. With Clarke went the Attorney-General, Mr. Thomas Braddell. The parley with 26 Chinese society headmen and mine-owners was quiet but dramatic—and made all the more so when the *Avon* was forced to round up some Ghee Hin war boats which had declined to disarm. The Chinese factions agreed to end hostilities and to disarm their fighters and destroy their stockades. Clarke promised to place a British officer in Larut—he felt that 'one hasty shot' might again plunge the region into war—and to appoint a commission of British officials to settle the dispute over the mines. So the long, cruel, bloody Chinese war in Larut ended.

Clarke's invitation to the Malay princes and chiefs had been accepted by a number of important people, among them Raja Abdullah and a relative, Raja Idris (who was later to rule Perak), the new *Raja Bendahara* appointed by the chiefs when Raja Ismail was proclaimed ruler, and a worried but truculent Mentri of Larut. Raja Ismail and Raja Yusuf were absent. Three days passed in avid discussion about the rightful successor to the throne. Braddell, McNair and Dunlop knew that Clarke, while still in Singapore, had all but decided that Raja Ismail was the best choice. Indeed he had instructed McNair and Dunlop to 'privately sound the Raja Muda as to whether he would peacefully relinquish his claim on receiving a pension, and if so, what pension . . . he would accept'. The two emissaries had however gone into the matter so thoroughly that, in a memorandum, they had urged Clarke to look on Raja Abdullah as the legitimate successor 'by Malay custom and long usage in Perak'. They had singled out the Mentri of Larut as the villain who had persuaded the Ghee Hin to help him 'to carry out what we believe to be his ultimate object, viz., keeping back the Raja Muda from the sovereignty of the country. . . . Up to the death of the late Sultan no question appears to have been raised, as far as we can ascertain, as to his right to succeed as heir apparent, and had it not been for the contrary influence exerted in the country by the Mentri, there can be no doubt that in due course he would have been installed with the general approbation of the people. The reasons assigned by the Mentri and those who have acted, with them, for this departure from the line of proper succession, seem to us to be frivolous.' Braddell described the memorandum as placing matters 'in a clearer light'.

With all the facts in his possession, Clarke employed a certain strategy during the meeting. In its initial phase he gained the agreement of the princes and chiefs to a genealogy of the Perak royal house being drawn up by an accepted expert. This proved that Abdullah had a better claim to the throne than Ismail. On 17th January all the princes and chiefs present gathered aboard the *Pluto* for final talks. The outcome was fairly clear for the majority had begun to indicate acceptance of Abdullah's claims. As princes of the State, Raja Abdullah, the *Bendahara* and Raja Idris sat on chairs while the chiefs sat cross-legged on the floor. The drama was heightened by an incident when the Mentri of Larut, arriving late, demanded a chair for himself as 'independent ruler' of Larut, but was forced to take the deck. When the decisive moment for voting came, all but the Mentri voted for Abdullah. They also agreed that Raja Ismail should be deposed but be compensated with a pension and a title. The Mentri's only remark was, 'If the people like it, I have no place. I, of course, follow them.'

Out of further discussions on Raja Abdullah's request for a 'treaty of lasting friendship' came the Pangkor Treaty which brought British influence—by way of protection and advice rather than annexation—directly into the peninsula through Perak. The document was the forerunner of other treaties signed with the remaining Malay States over the next few decades. Clarke said later, 'I offered them advisers who would restore order from chaos without curtailing their sovereignty.' In place 'of anarchy and irregular revenues, I held out the prospects of peace and plenty'. He was certain that the real interests of the more responsible chiefs were peace, trade, and the opening up of their State. The Pangkor Treaty initiated indirect rule through a British Resident. One article provided specifically that the Sultan should 'receive and provide a suitable residence' for the British Resident 'whose advice must be asked and acted upon on all questions other than those touching Malay religion and custom'. Another article laid it down that the Resident would regulate 'the collection and control of all revenues and the general administration of the country'.

The Treaty was signed and sealed on Tuesday, 20th January, when Raja Abdullah was also formally acknowledged the new Sultan and the British vessels saluted him with guns. A letter was despatched to Raja Ismail informing him that he was deposed and should give up the royal regalia in preparation for Abdullah's installation in a month's time. Finally, the chiefs refused to recognize the Mentri as 'independent' ruler of Larut as he wished to be. He had the added mortification of being told that an Assistant Resident would be assigned to his district in keeping with Clarke's promise to the Chinese miners.

On his return to Singapore, Clarke received the plaudits of the merchant community for having finally brought Britain into the affairs of the Malay States—but everyone, including Clarke himself, must have wondered what the Colonial Office would say about the Pangkor Treaty. In despatches to London, Clarke frankly admitted to the Secretary of State that he was 'perfectly aware' he had 'acted beyond my instructions and that nothing but very urgent circumstances would justify in the eyes of H.M. Government the steps I have taken, but I have confidence that your Lordship will feel that

111

the circumstances at the time, the utter stoppage of all trade, the daily loss of life by the piratical attacks on even peaceful traders and by the fighting of the factions themselves, and the imminent peril of the disturbances spreading to the Chinese in our own Settlements justified me in assuming the responsibility I have taken'. In his second despatch he contended that he had arbitrated rather than intervened. Having achieved settlement in each affair he had felt it imperative to embody the terms in formal documents and to provide for British officers to reside in Perak in order to supervise their execution particularly in Larut where the Chinese factions still faced each other with the risk of fresh fighting breaking out. Clarke assured the Secretary of State that he had in no way bound the Government to any particular course and that it was 'perfectly possible now to withdraw from the position I have temporarily assumed'. 'But', he added, 'the time has arrived when, as a nation, we shall be neglecting a great and paramount duty if we any longer delay that intervention which the causes of civilization and good order now so loudly demand.'

In a private letter to Mr. Hugh Childers, a personal friend who had been First Lord of the Admiralty and Chancellor of the Duchy of Lancaster, Clarke elaborated on his actions in Pangkor: 'The only chance of success I had was to do what I did rapidly so that not a soul knew my plans until I had almost pulled them through. The Chinese were moving and had no idea who was moving them. I had got hold of the heads of both parties and neither knew that I knew the other. I sent a steamer for the Malay chiefs, telling them to come and see me, giving them no time to hesitate, nor telling them what I wanted them for, nor affording them time to send for their lawyers. . . . I was assured I could not get them together under six weeks or two months. I collected them in a week. . . .'

Privately the Colonial Office expressed approval of Clarke's course of action although, after certain experiences in Africa, it had uneasy feelings that the arrangement in Perak might not work smoothly. As the Head of the Eastern Department expressed it, 'We must not keep out of sight that for some unforeseen cause we may possibly be called upon to take steps to prevent some attempted violation of the Agreement, or to enforce an adherence to some of its provisions.' It was not until May, however, when the House of Lords was debating a motion calling on the Government to disapprove Clarke's policy, that the Secretary of State was forced to express publicly his confidence in Clarke and to assert that some form of intervention had been necessary in Perak. However, in a private letter, the Secretary of State, the Earl of Carnarvon, warned Clarke, 'for the great interests which are at stake in the matter and which would easily be jeopardised by precipitancy or immature ambition, to exercise now as much caution and forbearance as you have shown energy and decision'.

CHAPTER 12

A British Resident Murdered

Sir Andrew Clarke turned his attention to Selangor before selecting the men to introduce the unique 'Residential system' of administration in Perak. Presumably he felt like striking while the situation was hot. Conditions in Selangor had not changed very much since Anson's intervention in 1871. The Selangor princes and chiefs were still pirating in the Straits of Malacca as fiercely as they feuded on land. It was a particularly 'atrocious case of piracy' which made Clarke decide to visit Sultan Abdul Samad 'in the hope, not merely of being able to check actual present piracy but to be enabled to exercise a strong influence on the Sultan'.

Malay pirates disguised as fishermen had killed eight of nine people aboard a Malacca boat at the estuary to the Langat River. The attack had occurred within hailing distance of a fort occupied by Raja Yaacob, third son of the Sultan, and evidence later proved that the pirates had been among his followers. Very soon afterwards eight Malays who put into Malacca in the stolen craft were arrested by the police. Two months later, on 11th January 1874—the day Clarke left Singapore on his journey to Pangkor—pirates who paid obeisance to another Selangor prince, Raja Mahmood, attacked a lighthouse at Cape Rachado but were driven off by the lighthouse keeper. 'These attacks,' said Clarke, 'have at last reached a point when they are threatening the peaceful navigation of the Straits, the great highway between Europe and China.' On 7th February, the *Pluto* took him up the Langat River to the Royal village of Langat where the Sultan lived. With him went Braddell—and six warships. Three of these lay in the river out of sight of Langat while the others waited at the mouth of the river.

What occurred next is best described in Clarke's own words in a letter to his friend, Hugh Childers: 'I laid the *Pluto* close alongside

114

the principal fort, and went with all my party to breakfast on deck where we could look up the muzzles of some big guns which were within a few feet of us. The fort itself, both inside and outside, was covered with some hundreds of very villainous-looking Malays armed to the teeth. After breakfast I sent a letter to the Sultan telling him what I had come about and asking him to come and see me. I sent the letter by Major McNair, my Surveyor-General. He was taken to the palace and saw the Sultan who said he had never left his country and could not break through etiquette and come on board to see me. After some three hours' waiting, he said he would come down and look at me and the steamer from the shore. This he did, but someone telling him the day was unlucky, he quickly disappeared. Braddell then landed alone, smoking a cigar as if for a stroll, lounged through the bazaar and town, passing the sentries, and stepped quietly into the Sultan's palace. Braddell speaks Malay better than a Malay and knows their customs. It ended in his getting at the Sultan who at last consented to come on board, provided the steamer was attached to the shore by ropes, and that he might walk on board over a temporary jetty which was improvised on the spot, and on board he came with several hundred fellows.'

Clarke found the Sultan a 'jolly' and 'good-natured' individual who told him, 'Piracy is the affair of the boys, my sons', and added he himself had 'nothing to do with it'. After this enlightening introductory meeting, Clarke returned the Sultan's call and 'told him how much better for him, his family and country it would be if he would support his son-in-law, the Viceroy, against the pirates, and that I wanted to settle matters peacefully without asking the Admiral to step in'. After two days' talks the Sultan issued an order to try all offenders, and agreed that Tengku Kudin should try the alleged pirates. Seven of the accused were sentenced to death and the eighth reprieved because of his youth. The condemned men were executed immediately, the Sultan providing the kris for stabbing them to death according to local custom. A footnote to this affair was written much later by Swettenham who said that during his service with the Sultan he had 'ascertained without much doubt that none of those executed had had any hand in the piracy, but the lesson was made thereby all the more forcible'. Apparently the deterrent had lain in the fact that 'there is nothing so impressive (in Selangor) as the incontinent execution of a few innocent persons; it is a warning not only to the naughtily-inclined but also to the quite, quite good.'

115

Clarke also persuaded Sultan Abdul Samad to accept a British officer to assist him in administering his State. This was a purely verbal arrangement. In August Frank Swettenham was attached to him in an informal capacity. To Swettenham, the Sultan, a thin, wizened man, was 'a delightful potentate' with a strong sense of humour and fond of a good story. To the sharp, intelligent grey-haired ruler, Swettenham was (as he once wrote to Clarke) 'very clever in gaining the hearts of Rajas and sons of Rajas with soft words, delicate and sweet, so that all men rejoice in him as in the perfume of an opened flower'. Within a few weeks (on 3rd October) the Sultan wrote to Clarke again saying, 'As regards our friend's intention of having us enter into an engagement so that our friend will collect the revenue of our country, we feel very glad of it, provided our friend will put to right our country. . . .'

Clarke brought a third, smaller, State under British influence that year. Between Selangor and Malacca ranged a few small provinces formed largely of settlers from Minangkabau, in eastern Sumatra, who had brought with them their tribal systems, their matriarchal laws of inheritance and their enlightened form of democracy. The people elected their tribal elders and over all were the four *Undang-Undang* (law-givers). Once the vassals of the Malacca sultanate, they had, as the influence of the successor-kingdom of Johore waned, looked for one of their race to lead them. In 1775, they invited Raja Melewar, of an ancient Minangkabau royal family in Sumatra, to become their head with the title of *Yang di-Pertuan*, but they gave him no overall authority. Only around his home, beautiful Sri Menanti, the 'Motherland of Royalty' as it is known to the people, was he supreme. The *Undang* of the three major provinces of Rembau, Sungei Ujong and Johol, who were descendants of the *Bendahara* families of Malacca and Johore, remained independent although they genuflected to the *Yang di-Pertuan* on ceremonial occasions. Otherwise they considered themselves his equals. As elsewhere in the peninsula, disunity led to feuds over the succession to leaderships. And the possession of rights to tinfields and the collection of duties on tin played no small part in generating local wars.

Tin in quantity had been found particularly in Sungei Ujong through which ran the Linggi River, the highway for floating the ore to the estuary which today forms part of the Negri Sembilan boundary with Malacca. By the 1870s, 10,000 Chinese miners were digging in Sungei Ujong. The Undang, Dato Klana Putra ('the victorious and princely'), had a considerable problem: the chief of Rembau and other dignitaries were collecting taxes on the tin extracted from Sungei Ujong as it moved along a 20-mile stretch of the Linggi River that flowed through their domains. He had another great rival in his own State, the Dato Bandar, an irascible 80-year-old warrior, who also insisted on collecting dues from the ore coming down the Linggi. By tradition, the Dato Klana Putra ruled the land and the Dato Bandar 'ruled the water' in Sungei Ujong, so the latter felt justified in taking his share.

Over the years the British authorities in neighbouring Malacca had intervened several times in favour of the Dato Klana Putra in his disputes with the Dato Bandar and other chiefs, principally because the Straits tin trade was being affected. For instance, in 1855 the Governor had prohibited the erection of stockades along the Linggi and Rembau rivers; 11 years later he threatened to send a gunboat periodically to ensure that the order was obeyed. . . . A close interest in the region was also being taken by Tengku Kudin of Selangor because a part of the Linggi provided a backdoor to his State and he was having trouble with rebellious chiefs.

Towards the end of 1872 the Dato Klana Putra died and was succeeded by a young and ambitious man who continued the feud with the Dato Bandar with added vigour. The old chief of Rembau died also and fighting broke out over the succession to his chieftaincy. The flow of tin along the Rembau stretch of the Linggi ceased; inevitably the merchants in Malacca pleaded for intervention. Sir Andrew Clarke, fresh from his successes in Pangkor and Selangor, invited the chiefs concerned in all the disputes to put their cases before him. On 21st April 1874 he signed an agreement with the Dato Klana Putra promising him protection in Sungei Ujong; the Dato on his part agreed to keep the river open to traders, to levy only reasonable tolls, and to do his best to stop illegal tax-gathering. As proof that the chief had British support, Clarke sent British naval craft up the Linggi River to destroy stockades put up by his rivals. The Dato Klana's agreement with the British, coupled with, let it be added, the young man's subsequent deliberate acts of provocation, stung the Dato Bandar into action. One day his followers prevented the Dato Klana from his custom of hoisting the British flag every day in the front of his house in Ampangan (now a suburb of the capital town of Seremban). The Dato Klana promptly called for British protection.

Clarke was averse to involving Britain in a local squabble so he sent Pickering (who had been such a successful emissary to the Chinese secret society leaders in Penang over the Larut wars) to Sungei Ujong with the dual task of cautioning the Dato Bandar and also urging the Chinese headmen in the tinfields not to become involved in the local Malay troubles. (Clarke obviously feared the possibility of more trouble of the Larut type in Sungei Ujong.) From the Dato Bandar, Pickering received a written assurance that he had no intention of outright war against the Dato Klana—and on the strength of this the young chief erected a flagstaff 'as large as a schooner's main-mast' outside his house and hoisted the Jack to a salute of 21 guns while the Dato Bandar's followers stood by in anger and frustration. . . .

While the Dato Bandar appeared to have no intention of warring against his rival, he continued to contend that by tradition he was the co-equal of the Dato Klana, had every right to share revenue, and should have been consulted before the Dato Klana signed the agreement with Clarke. Pickering was sent to Sungei Ujong again to try to sort out this constitutional point, but the impetuous Dato Klana decided on action. His forces overwhelmed his rival's stockades at Rasa and Rahang and were marching towards a third strong point at Kepayang when they found the Dato Bandar's forces augmented by those of Raja Mahmood, a redoubtable Selangor rebel. The Klana's men promptly panicked and fled; the Klana equally promptly appealed to Pickering for military assistance. Pickering sent an urgent message to Malacca and Singapore for troops and about 200 marines, soldiers and police arrived. While they were on their way Pickering had taken the offensive with his own small escort of trained police. Raja Mahmood and the Dato Bandar began a withdrawal which turned into a rout when the relieving forces arrived. The Dato Bandar and Raja Mahmood surrendered and were restricted to residence in Singapore for a year. In Sungei Ujong, the Dato Klana resumed ruling the State he had so nearly brought to serious war by his own precipitate aggression. With him however was an Assistant Resident, Captain W. T. Tatham, R.A., attached in an informal capacity.

Although Clarke had received the authority of the Secretary of State in September to appoint Residents to Perak and Selangor it was not until 14th December, after peace had come to Sungei Ujong, that he was able to announce the formal appointments of Mr. J. W. W. Birch, his Colonial Secretary, as Resident at Perak, Captain T. C. Speedy as Assistant Resident in Larut, Mr. J. G. Davidson, a lawyer with a considerable practice in Singapore and with close associations in Selangor, as Resident attached to Tengku Kudin, in Selangor, Mr. F. A. Swettenham as assistant Resident with the Sultan of Selangor, and Captain Tatham as Assistant Resident in Sungei Ujong. The old soldier was irrepressibly optimistic about the future. On 31st December he wrote to the Secretary of State, 'I have every reason to believe that an appeal to force is not likely to occur again for many a long day to come, either in Sungei Ujong or in any of the States where we have intervened in their affairs.' Within a year however, Birch was to be murdered and British troops were to occupy Perak, and in action in another of the Minangkabau States a British officer was to win the Victoria Cross.

Clarke left the Straits Settlements in the middle of May 1875, earlier than he should have done; but he had accepted the high appointment of Member of the Council of the Viceroy of India and Minister of Public Works. Clarke perhaps did not fully appreciate the fact that he had made a niche for himself in the history of the peninsula as the man who began the process which converted a war-ridden jungle-covered peninsula into a peaceful, flourishing and wealthy country.

In his last few months in Singapore he had begun to suspect that Birch was perhaps plunging himself into deep trouble in Perak by attempting to force a strange new order upon a ruler and chiefs who, although they had signed the Pangkor Treaty, suspected the British of a plot to take over their country, pocket their revenues, and upset their traditions and customs. Birch seemed to have little tact; he appeared insensitive to Malay customs and feelings, and his unbending attitude was reflected in a report in which he said, 'It really concerns us little what were the old customs of the country, nor do I consider they are worthy of any consideration in dealing with the present taxation of the country.' He considered affairs in Perak 'of such an irregular character as to require immediate alteration'. Clarke was undoubtedly worried about what he described as the 'head-over-heels way' in which Birch was carrying out his duties and cautioned him to 'have patience' with the people.

Clarke was succeeded by Major-General Sir William Francis Drummond Jervois, the third successive Governor to belong to the

Corps of Royal Engineers. Jervois was always a professional soldier who, given half the chance, would have annexed the Malay States. Within a few days of his installation, he was pitchforked into problems in Perak raised principally by Birch's own tactlessness and by Sultan Abdullah's consequent refusal to take the advice of his Resident, which was imperative under the terms of the Pangkor Treaty. Abdullah had really never been given a chance to understand the functions of the Resident and his purpose. For example, he never appreciated the fact that neither he nor any of his chiefs was any longer free to collect taxes as of old and he resented the proposed appointment of official collectors. He also resented Birch's intention to abolish debt-slavery. This was a common institution in Malay States but practised in severe form in Perak. Theoretically, a debtor became the slave of his creditor if he was unable to settle his debts. In practice the creditor also enslaved the debtor's wife and children. Speedy, in Larut, estimated that 75 per cent of the Perak Malays were slave-debtors to the other 25 per cent. To the ruler and chiefs Birch appeared to be planning to usurp all their prerogatives.

Sultan Abdullah thrice refused to sign proclamations drawn up by Birch bringing into effect his proposals to appoint tax collectors, to punish illegal tax-gatherers, and to end debt-slavery. On the third refusal in June 1875 Birch peremptorily threatened to recommend to the British Government that Abdullah be deposed unless he changed his mind by 20th July. The threat sealed Birch's fate. Abdullah summoned his major chiefs and discussed ways to kill him. The Maharajah Lela, a major chief whose prerogative was to execute the ruler's enemies and who was therefore above the law according to Malay custom, undertook to arrange Birch's death. The chiefs also discussed the possibility of driving the British out of the State. One or two later erected stockades in their villages 'to resist the white people'.

On 24th July, Sultan Abdullah, with a show of doing so under duress, signed a proclamation which authorized the Resident and the Malay *Shahbandar* (Controller of Imports and Exports) to control the levying and collection of all taxes and dues. The depth of Abdullah's hatred of Birch may be gauged by the fact that very soon afterwards he summoned the State *bomoh* (witch doctor) to hold a seance into whether the guardian jinns of Perak would destroy Birch. Abdullah himself was one of the mediums and, according to reliable reports, repeatedly stabbed an effigy of Birch of rice dough, and forecast, 'In a month Mr. Birch will be dead.'

Around this time Jervois decided to visit Perak and meet the ruler and other chiefs. He had become convinced that neither Abdullah nor any of the princes in line of succession was 'fit' to rule. He was also strongly of the opinion that 'government by advice' was impossible in the Malay States. Jervois had his own solution: it was a step short of outright annexation. He suggested to Abdullah that he and his major chiefs should hand over the government of the State to the British in return for liberal pensions. (Jervois explained in a despatch, 'My proposal is to govern the country in the name of the Sultan by means of officers to be styled Queen's Commissioners. I consider it very desirable that the change of policy from one of mere advice to one of control should be marked by a change in the titles of the British officers.') Abdullah asked for a fortnight in which to consult his chiefs. Birch, who felt extremely frustrated by the Malay resistance to advice, exerted great pressure on Abdullah and also continued his threats, and on 1st October Abdullah signed a letter agreeing to hand Perak to the British Crown on promise of a pension of $2,000 a month, while the British agreed to surrender all debt-slaves who had been given refuge in the Residency, pending an inquiry into the whole question of debt-slavery.

Jervois by now had decided for political reasons to switch Birch with Davidson but he postponed the change as he thought the Malays might consider it a sign of weakness. And neither he nor Birch apparently took seriously reports of a plot to kill the Resident. Birch himself had retorted once, 'If one Mr. Birch is killed, ten Mr. Birches will take his place.' And in spite of the undertaking to give up debt-slaves, Birch on 12th October assisted five of them—who included two belonging to the Sultan—to escape by disguising them as boatmen on his own craft. Birch thus signed his own death warrant for Abdullah and the chiefs became certain that he would never cease interfering with Malay custom. On 15th October the chiefs met again, this time under the chairmanship of Raja Ismail, and decided that Birch should be 'executed' the next time he visited the Maharajah Lela's village of Pasir Salak.

On 27th October Birch began posting up proclamations announcing, among other things, that 'Her Britannic Majesty's Government have determined to administer the Government of Perak in the name of the Sultan.' He arranged to journey up the Perak River to post similar notices at major villages. Four days later, Abdullah sent a royal kris to the Maharajah Lela; it represented his *titah* (order) to

121

execute Birch, his enemy. Birch arrived at Pasir Salak on the night of 1st November. He was killed the next morning as he was bathing in a floating bath-house tied to his boat. A Malay named Pandak Indut thrust a spear into him. As Birch fell, another Malay, Sepetum, hacked him with a sword. Birch's body splashed into the river. In Pasir Salak there was feasting for two days.

News of Birch's murder reached the Lieutenant-Governor of Penang on the evening of 3rd November and he organized an immediate expedition to Perak. Jervois, in Singapore, cabled India for reinforcements as he interpreted the murder as the signal for an uprising against the British. He personally left for Perak with 150 men. On 15th November British forces captured Pasir Salak. Raja Ismail and the Maharajah Lela became fugitives. Abdullah and the major chiefs were surprised by the intensity of the British reaction to Birch's death; to them, the assassination of Birch was a just retribution for an infidel and a foreigner who had insisted on trying to uproot their life and customs and who presumed to usurp the hereditary powers of the ruler and chiefs. They least expected British soldiers and sailors to appear, and stay, in their jungles as avengers.

Perak was occupied as 1,200 men arrived from Calcutta and others came from Hong Kong. A naval brigade also landed. Eighteen months passed before this occupation ceased. It was not until the middle of 1876 that all those who had been arrested for implication in Birch's murder were tried. The Maharajah Lela, Pandak Indut, Sepetum, and another Malay were hanged in Larut in January 1877. Sultan Abdullah and three major chiefs—the *Laksmana*, the *Shahbandar*, and the Mentri of Larut—were exiled in the Seychelles Islands. Others were sentenced to imprisonment for life. Raja Ismail had taken refuge in Kedah but was persuaded by the ruler to give himself up in Penang. He had with him some of the Perak royal regalia. As he had never signed the Pangkor Treaty, he could not be accused of treason but he was 'exiled' to Singapore where Jervois placed him under the care of the Maharajah of Johore. Ismail died there in 1889. Raja Yusuf, who had not been implicated in the conspiracy against Birch, was recognized by Jervois as Regent of Perak but he was not elevated to Sultan for many years.

Jervois found a reason for using the troops from India and Hong Kong when trouble broke out again in the Minangkabau States south of Selangor just as Perak was coming under control. The Dato

Klana Putra of Sungei Ujong had again incurred local hostility over his refusal to vote for the election of Tunku Antah of Sri Menanti, son of a former *Yang di-Pertuan*, to the office of head of state which had been vacant since 1869. The other Undang retaliated by 'deposing' him and recognizing as his successor another chief who readily produced the unanimity necessary for Tunku Antah's elevation to the throne. The Dato Klana refused to be ousted. The dogs of war were let slip between him and Tunku Antah ostensibly over rights to the district of Terrachi, which lies between Sungei Ujong and Sri Menanti. An innocent visit to Terrachi paid by the assistant Resident, Commander P. J. Murray, R.N., and a survey party escorted by 50 troops and police, on 26th November, precipitated an attack by about 200 followers of Tunku Antah who a week later invaded Sungei Ujong.

Exaggerated reports of the enemy's strength led Jervois to divert nearly 600 troops from Perak to Sungei Ujong. It became essential to capture the Bukit Putus pass leading to Terrachi which was controlled by Tunku Antah's men, and nearly 400 troops began a frontal approach, moving behind a scouting section of about 50 Gurkhas led by Captain Channer who later split them into two patrols. Channer with 25 men suddenly found himself in front of a strongly-built stockade—and there was no look-out. He attacked and was the first into the stockade which was occupied by 25 or 30 men, who resisted very stubbornly until they withdrew. One Gurkha was killed, another seriously wounded, and two others were slightly wounded in this engagement for which Channer received the Victoria Cross. The pass was won.

By the middle of January, the British forces were in control of the disputed territory. Tunku Antah fled but surrendered in Johore. In November 1876 Jervois succeeded in persuading the senior chiefs of the Minangkabau States to form a confederacy comprising Sri Menanti, Ulu Muar, Jempol and Johol, and the districts of Terrachi, Gunong Pasir and Inas under a *Yam Tuan* (head of state) who would reside in Sri Menanti. They agreed too to accept Tunku Antah as *Yam Tuan*. To complete the story of these Minangkabau States: in 1889, Tampin and Rembau joined the confederacy. Nine years later, all of them united under the name of 'Negri Sembilan' and under one *Yang di-Pertuan Besar*, Tuanku Muhammad, of Sri Menanti, who as a point of modern historical interest was the father of independent Malaya's first elected Paramount Ruler. As another point of interest, the first British Resident of the Negri Sembilan confederation was Mr. E. W. W. Birch, son of James Birch who had been murdered in Perak.

What had been the reaction of the Secretary of State to Jervois's proposal that the Residential system should be superseded by direct rule through Queen's Commissioners? Jervois, in presenting the Secretary of State with the customary *fait accompli*, had added the usual assurance that 'should the policy which I have adopted not be approved, it will be possible, without difficulty, either to recede or to advance, according as your Lordship may desire'. His Lordship however did not desire and said so—'I will not say that the time may not be at hand when such a step may not become necessary. . . . But I am clearly of the opinion that this time, whether it be near or less near, has not yet come.' He wanted the system of Residents to be given a thorough trial. A month later, he emphasized again: 'Neither annexation nor government of the country by British officials in the name of the Sultan can be allowed.' A bitter controversy on paper followed between the Secretary of State and Jervois who finally apologized and withdrew.

CHAPTER 13

Federated and Unfederated States

The tragedy of Birch—the missionary-like zeal with which he had plunged into his self-dedicated task of 'cleaning up' Perak, and then his murder—almost compromised the essay in indirect rule in a country where (as Swettenham put it) 'white men were unknown; where everything that could be wrong was wrong; where almost every man was a law unto himself; where there was hardly any trade, no development of any kind, no roads, no police, or other means of maintaining order; and where two or three individuals claimed to be supreme'. Certainly an almost impossible background for a complex experiment, at first largely in human relationships, which had to be undertaken by lone British officers with no precedents, or instructions, to guide them. Their task had no exact parallel in any other English-administered territory. And yet slowly it was done and peace and government, law and justice began to develop.

It was purely through understanding, tact, a certain degree of firmness and trial and error that the early British Residents and their officers gained the goodwill of rulers and chiefs. Basically they realized that they would 'get nowhere very fast' unless they first understood the Malay people themselves and their customs and reached the closest possible terms of relationship with the rulers and the hereditary chiefs. The conditions of life in the Malay States in the nineteenth century closely resembled those of medieval Britain and Europe of the tenth and eleventh centuries, when the peasants were under the tyrannical yoke of the barons and there was degradation of body and spirit. The peasants never rebelled against their lot for their immediate world consisted solely of the ruling class and themselves and they knew nothing else. To them it was their *nasib* (fate, destiny) to be thus and their attitude could be summed up in the Malay saying,

'*Apa boleh buat, sudah untong nasib*' (It is fated and what can one do?).

Introducing British 'influence' meant thrusting British officers into strange and unknown territory with little assurance that a ruler or a chief would hold himself responsible for their safety. Gaining the friendship of the rulers and chiefs was therefore a slow and heart-breaking process. Swettenham, himself a successful pioneer in those early experiments in making Malay friends and influencing them, said once that 'the great difficulty was to establish really friendly relations with the ruler and to either conciliate or overawe the chiefs, many of whom were powerful enough to at least covertly disregard the orders of the ruler'. The Resident therefore joined the ruler in his amusements, went hunting game and shooting snipe with him, and took every opportunity to assure him that the actions of the British were governed only by their desire to serve the interests of the State. To the chiefs, the Resident patiently explained the reasons for administrative innovations; to the unyielding and unfriendly among them, he showed firmness and determination and where necessary he even went out of his way, as Swettenham put it, to outswagger 'the greatest swaggerer of them all'.

The success of the system initially, therefore, depended almost entirely on the personalities of both sides getting along with each other. The Resident had no executive power, no way of forcing a ruler to accept his advice; he could only use his own powers of persuasion and whatever influence he could derive from them. No attempt had been made by Britain or the rulers to define the questions upon which the Resident's advice was to be followed. The words 'whose advice must be asked and acted upon all questions' covered the widest range of possibilities except for Malay custom and religion, following Britain's custom not to interfere in these spheres more than was absolutely essential. In 1876 the Residents received the following guidance on the broad terms of their duties: '. . . Her Majesty's Government define the functions of the Resident to be the giving of influential and responsible advice to the ruler, the duties of which are well understood in the east. The Residents are not to interfere more frequently or to a greater extent than is necessary with the minor details of government; but their special objects should be the maintenance of peace and law, the initiation of a sound system of taxation, with the consequent development of the resources of the country and the supervision of the collection of the revenue so as to ensure the receipt of funds necessary to carry out the principal engagements of the government and to pay for the cost of the British officers, and whatever establishments may be necessary to support them.'

Whitehall kept a very stern eye on the conduct of each Resident, so much so that in 1878, when one was held to have exceeded his authority, the Secretary of State circulated a reminder that the Residents had been placed in the States 'as advisers and not as rulers, and if they take upon themselves to disregard this principle, they will most assuredly be held responsible if trouble springs out of their neglect of it'. To which the Resident in Perak, Hugh Low, made the comment, 'We must first create the government to be advised and that is what all along I have been trying to do.' It was a tribute to the idealism of those first Residents that they accepted the almost impossible responsibilities imposed on them—and also accepted the primitive living conditions. They had no comforts and found the heat of the pressing jungle appalling. Birch for months lived in a houseboat on the river. Swettenham's first 'home' was an old stockade which had a far from water-tight roof of palm leaves; it stood by a river and twice a day at high tide the mud floor was covered by the tidal waters. At low tide, crocodiles crawled up the banks to bask in the sun, and at night myriads of mosquitoes were only kept at bay by the smoke of a fire blazing inside the 'house'. . . .

Tributes should be paid to the great Residents of the era for their successful pioneering efforts in the unique system of guiding the States by advice: to men like Hugh Low in Perak, Frank Swettenham in Selangor, Hugh Clifford in Pahang, and Martin Lister in Negri Sembilan. They and their numerous successors were men of parts, chosen for their role not only for their intellect and administrative ability but also for their extra-mural interests. They served well and they played well, and whatever the demerits of the system, they—and their British officers in all departments—took the peninsula from anarchism to peace, prosperity and greatness.

Small police forces were formed in each State and trained by non-commissioned officers of the British Army. Courts were established and presided over by British magistrates who administered the Penal Code of the Straits Settlements which had been adapted from the Indian Penal Code. For the peasants the courts were blessed innovations and they thronged them to watch the, to them, strange dispensation of justice. In due course, Malay magistrates sat on the bench.

To simplify administration, each State was divided into districts looked after by British officers who also sat as magistrates. Every district was further subdivided into smaller units known as *mukim* which became the responsibility of Malay *penghulu* (headmen) whose duties ranged from keeping the peace to collecting local revenue, from settling minor disputes to summarily dealing with very minor offences.

Villages within easy distance of each other were connected with bridle paths. Earth roads began to move out from the larger centres of population as these expanded. The population of Perak rose from an estimated 80,000 in 1879 to 214, 254 in 1891 when the first census was taken. Before British influence in Perak, Selangor and Sungei Ujong, the revenue had come from taxation on every article and commodity that had been imported or exported. Taxes hit the peasants principally for high duties were levied on the necessities of life; only the ruling class could enjoy luxuries anyway. The Residents persuaded the rulers to abolish the vexatious taxes; eventually an export duty on tin provided the main source of revenue. At the end of the first year of British guidance, the revenue collected in Perak totalled about $226,233 (equal to about £45,000) and in Selangor $115,651 (£23,000). By 1894, Perak's revenue had risen to $3,542,114 and Selangor's to $3,334,468.

In order to move tin and produce faster to the ports for export, railway lines were laid and so helped to open up the country still further. The first track, opened in 1884, was an eight-mile link from Taiping, the bustling tin town in the heart of Larut, to Port Weld, on the Larut River. Selangor very soon afterwards prided itself on a 22-mile-long track from Kuala Lumpur, a rapidly-growing centre, to Klang on the coast.

In Perak, the path to ordered government and peace was fashioned by Mr. (later Sir) Hugh Low, one of the greatest Residents in the history of the peninsula. He laid a pattern which others were to follow elsewhere in the peninsula. Low arrived in 1877, aged 53, after 30 years' administrative service in the quiet island of Labuan. It was his experience that mattered most for he had learned how to adapt the administrative ways of the West to people whose existence had been ruled by custom and religion. Low soon won trust by his sympathetic approach and by clearly showing his earnest wish to establish good relations with the chiefs and not to interfere with their customs. Four days after arriving in Perak he learned of the 'strong inclination at this Residency to protect runaway slaves which I have no intention

5a. A relic of old Malacca—the Porta de Santiago, gateway to a fort

5b. The Malaysian Houses of Parliament in Kuala Lumpur

6a. The city of Singapore, showing the waterfront, the commercial heart with its tall buildings, and the cathedral in the centre

6b. Evening in Singapore of the 1850s

of following', as he wrote in his diary, adding, 'If I were here long enough I would undertake to abolish every form of slavery in a moderate time with the consent of the chiefs and the people but I shall be of no use here if I do not first thoroughly acquire their confidence and that cannot be done if my first acts be to show that I am determined to prevent or to encourage the breach of (what) is at present so cherished an institution.' Which demonstrated an entirely different attitude from that of Birch. It may be added that Low, step by slow step, persuaded the ruler and chiefs to make it illegal for people to be enslaved. On 31st December 1883 debt-slavery in Perak was abolished and 3,000 men, women and children were set free. Selangor had however taken the lead in ending debt-slavery and in a remarkably few years every State in the peninsula had followed suit.

Low lived in Kuala Kangsar where the Regent, Raja Yusuf, had his palace. His small, Malay-style bungalow stood on a hillside and had a magnificent panorama over and beyond the Perak River. His house was open to any visitor. Mrs. Isabella Bird, who once stayed with him, wrote that Malays had 'free access to him during all hours of daylight and as I sit writing or reading, a Malay shadow constantly falls across my paper, and a Malay with silent, catlike tread glides up the steps and appears unannounced in the verandah, on which Mr. Low at once lays aside whatever he is doing and quietly gives himself to the business in hand. The reigning Prince and Raja Dris are daily visitors.'

Low introduced a State Council to discuss and implement policy. The ruler presided over a membership consisting of the Resident, the major Malay chiefs, and some Chinese miners and businessmen. The Council passed legislation, fixed the appointments and salaries of all Malay chiefs and headmen, discussed the annual estimates of revenue and expenditure, and either confirmed or commuted death sentences. The meetings were conducted in Malay and although, inevitably, they were dominated by the Resident, the discussions on policies and problems gave the Malay and Chinese members insight into the running of government. A seat on the Council became 'much coveted and highly prized'. The Perak Council was the forerunner of similar institutions which were to be established in every State in the peninsula.

The Governor at the time was Sir Frederick Weld, statesman and administrator, who saw a brilliant future for the States. He so immersed himself in Malay affairs that he left the running of the Straits Settlements to his Colonial Secretary and to the Lieutenant-Governor of Penang. He visited the States as often as he could; he treated the sultans with the courtesy due to them as rulers. The plumes on his hat were not the insignia of a master. There is a characteristic story of how, during a visit to Pahang, Weld was content to wait for several hours in his boat on the Pahang River 'before anyone could persuade the Sultan of Pahang to leave a game of chance in which he was engaged with a Chinese in order to grant an interview to His Excellency'. Weld, one of Malaya's great servants, began the close friendship and understanding that was in time built up and strengthened between all the Malay rulers, their people and the British, which faltered only once and then not until 1946.

In 1880, the first year of his governorship, Weld said in a despatch that he did not think the mass of people in Perak, Selangor and Sungei Ujong would be interested in overthrowing British rule. 'Unless we are prepared to evacuate, the country must continue working on the same lines in the future,' he declared, and he gave three possible courses for pursuit: prepare for a gradual retirement, annex all the States, or extend British influence over every State not under the control of the Siamese. Withdrawal he discarded because he thought it would result in worse anarchy. Annexation he described as out of the question (and in this regard, there is a record that certain chiefs of the little States in what is now Negri Sembilan refused to allow Europeans to pass through their territory because of 'dread of British annexation'). Weld strongly advocated the extension of the Residential system as opportunity offered, a policy that fitted in with Colonial Office thinking.

The next opportunity for this did not come until 1888 and it involved Pahang, described then as an 'unregenerate' State. It was still ruled by Ahmad who had assumed the title of 'Sultan' in 1882. He held undisputed and despotic sway over about 50,000 Malays and a few hundred Chinese. In 1885, Swettenham had been sent to Pekan to try to persuade him to agree to the appointment of a British Agent who would watch the interests of British subjects engaged in trade and commerce. He failed and the following year Weld himself visited Pekan but was unsuccessful too. In March 1887 another effort was made through a young cadet, Hugh Clifford. His stay in Pekan coincided with a visit by the Prime Minister of Johore who had sufficient influence to be able to persuade Sultan Ahmad to agree to receive a consular agent. Clifford became Britain's man in Pekan but, although his duties were purely consular, he considered it part of his mission to try to influence the Sultan into introducing law and order and a form of administration in his State.

Clifford has left vivid pictures of life in Pahang in those days. The four major chiefs had the power of life and death over all the people residing in their respective territories. The Sultan had a bodyguard known as the *Budak Raja* (King's Youths), drawn from the nobility; they dressed magnificently in brilliant coloured silks, were armed with dagger, sword and spear, and passed most of their time 'in making love and in playing games of chance'. They guarded the ruler on his walks, they rowed his boat, hunted game with him and snared turtle-doves for him, carried his messages, levied fines on his behalf (and theirs), killed those who offended him (and them), seized property which he (or they) wanted, and abducted women for his household (or theirs). They represented the only force by which the State—really the capital—was policed. The average peasant possessed no rights and, said Clifford once, 'he and his were always and completely at the mercy of those of their neighbours who were more powerful than themselves'. But then, as Clifford himself pointed out, 'the Malays, in common with other more civilised folk, had worked out for themselves unaided a theory of government on feudal lines which bears a startling resemblance to the European models of a long-passed epoch. But here they had halted. To live in independent Malaya is to live in the Europe of the thirteenth century.'

One night in February 1888, Go Hui, a Chinese shopkeeper in Pekan, a British subject, was stabbed near the ruler's palace. He died a few weeks later. Rumours said he had been attacked on the orders of the Sultan who had coveted his wife. Clifford, as British Consul, asked the ruler to offer a reward for the capture of the assailant. The ruler posted a cynically-worded proclamation offering $100 for the identity of the person—'man, spirit or Satan'—responsible for the 'accident' to the shopkeeper. Evidence incriminating the ruler had become so strong that the new Governor of the Straits Settlements, Sir Cecil Clementi Smith, a former Colonial Secretary, demanded satisfaction from Sultan Ahmad under the threat of serious consequences. It was perhaps the first time in the history of the State that a foreigner had intervened on behalf of a local citizen. Sultan Ahmad, on the adjurations of the Maharajah of Johore, a close friend, wrote to the Governor on 24th August 1888, acknowledging 'our responsibility for the murder of Go Hui'. He went on, 'We hope that no more will be said about this matter and that Her Majesty the Queen will be satisfied with out expression of regret for what has occurred.' He asked that 'the Queen should send us a British officer in order that he may assist us in matters relating to the Government of our country, on a similar system to that existing in the Malay States under English protection'.

In October that year, Mr. John Pickersgill Rodger was appointed first Resident with Clifford as his assistant. Rodger served in Pahang for eight years. His most urgent problems were the same as those of the other Residents—the suppression of slavery, withdrawing from the chiefs their customary privileges of taxation and instituting a more regular collection of taxes and duties, regulating land tenure, and fixing the political allowances of the ruler and the chiefs. The last however provided the major reason behind a rebellion which broke out in 1891. It was initiated by a disgruntled chief, the *Orang Kaya* of Semantan, in central Pahang, who claimed that he had not been given an allowance befitting his rank. The uprising spread and quelling it became a long, arduous and expensive task for the Straits Settlements Government. Sultan Ahmad himself took command of an expedition into Semantan and Rodger reported how impressed he had been by the way in which the ruler had 'arranged his scouting and attacking parties, by the facility of organizing transport and commissariat services, and by the excellence of his men as guerrilla soldiers when fighting in dense jungle'. British warships which cruised off Pahang helped to prevent the trouble from spreading along the coastal districts.

In October 1892 the Sultan proclaimed a general amnesty for all except the Orang Kaya and another rebel leader, but both declined to surrender. They withdrew into Trengganu from where two years later they resumed their revolt. In January 1895 Clifford led an expedition against the two chiefs and carried out an incredible chase after them through Trengganu and beyond into Kelantan. He came near to capturing them twice but they escaped with the assistance of local supporters. After three months, Clifford received orders to return to Pahang. In November, however, the two rebels surrendered to the Siamese in Trengganu and were taken to Bangkok. The Pahang rebellion proved to be the last local civil war to be fought in the peninsula.

In 1895, Perak, Selangor, Pahang and the States that formed Negri Sembilan agreed to federate. The idea of federation had sprung from the fertile mind of Swettenham after he became Resident of Perak, the most senior of the four States. He presented his proposals to Clementi Smith in 1893. There were obvious administrative advantages in unifying the divergent systems of the four territories. The Residents, who may have wished to go in the same direction, had no opportunity for consultation among themselves, and Singapore concentrated almost exclusively on the problems of the Straits Settlements. Thus the four States had been left largely to their own devices and were developing individually instead of co-ordinating their plans and co-operating to mutual benefit. The Secretary of State accepted the principle of federation but no further action was taken until Clementi Smith's successor, Sir Charles Mitchell, brought the subject up again. Mitchell recommended the appointment of a Resident-General based in Kuala Lumpur, as chief executive officer to co-ordinate policy in the Malay States under the Governor who would also be High Commissioner of the 'Federated Malay States'. Each Government department would have a Federal head who would ensure uniformity of policy. A unified civil service would be established. Legislation would be the responsibility of the State Councils and each State would be financially autonomous.

The rulers had to be won over to the idea first and Swettenham was sent to each of them to explain the advantages and implications of 'federation'. Hugh Clifford once paid a tribute to the way in which Swettenham succeeded in his certainly difficult task. Clifford spoke of the 'numerous and sensitive' interests which 'had to be placated', how Swettenham's tact quietened the suspicions of the rulers and their chiefs. 'It is necessary', said Clifford, 'to understand the jealousies, rivalries and mutual distrust bred in the various rulers by centuries of open strife or veiled hostility in order that the difficulty of the work performed by Swettenham may be rightly appreciated.'

The rulers eventually agreed to federation, and a clause in the new treaty assured them that it was 'not intended to curtail any of the powers of authority now held by any of the . . . Rulers in their respective States'. Indeed, one of the deliberate intentions of federation, as Swettenham was to write later, was to strengthen the status of the rulers who 'would be stronger, more important, their views more likely to receive consideration should a day come when those views happened to be at variance with the supreme authority, be it

High Commissioner at Singapore or Secretary of State in England'.

The rulers accepted the right of the Resident-General based in Kuala Lumpur to exercise extensive control in the affairs of each State in all matters of administration other than those touching the Muslim religion. Almost benevolently perhaps, the rulers of the two richer States of Perak and Selangor accepted the implication that federation would also mean the use of their revenues in developing Pahang (then 'crippled for want of money') and Negri Sembilan.

The 'Federated Malay States'—this was never its official title (which was 'Protected Malay States') but was adopted by popular usage—came into being on 1st July 1896. Kuala Lumpur became its capital and Frank Swettenham its first Resident-General. Constitutional experts have pointed to the 'glaring inconsistencies' of the 'federation'. They contended it was never a constitutional federation for the agreement did not define the powers and functions of the federal government or of each state government; the federation would perhaps better have been described as a union for it only unified or amalgamated the four States. While the powers of the rulers were not specifically curtailed—those of the Residents were—the real authority and power came to rest with the Resident-General, the agent of the High Commissioner. Federation certainly produced a highly centralized bureaucracy in Kuala Lumpur. In the centre of a complete secretariat sat the all-powerful figure of the Resident-General who made all the major decisions and to whom came every minute detail of administration—even if it was a request from the Sultan of Pahang for a higher rice allowance for his bearers. . . . The Resident-General may in theory have been subordinate to the High Commissioner but in practice he was supreme in his domain. Indeed the thought had once crossed Swettenham's mind that 'it would be more to the advantage of the F.M.S. that the Resident-General should communicate direct with the Colonial Office rather than with a Governor or High Commissioner who knew nothing of the special conditions of the Malay States but who being so close must feel it necessary to exercise some sort of control'. Around the Resident-General orbited a Legal Adviser, a Secretary for Chinese Affairs, a Financial Commissioner, a Judicial Commissioner, a Commissioner of Police, and a Director of Public Works, and later a Director of Education. There was even a General Manager of Railways who had the initial responsibility of connecting all the existing railways and joining them to a main line which would run from the Prai River, in

Province Wellesley, through the agricultural and mining areas of Perak and Selangor, down to Seremban, the new capital of Negri Sembilan (a work completed in July 1903). Federation resulted in a considerable influx of British officials as departments expanded. Into the four States came for the first time a common outlook and unity of purpose. Engineers, doctors, educationists and others worked for the group rather than an individual State. Development was planned on a wider basis, and initially tin provided all the revenue that was needed for the building of roads, the railway, public offices, hospitals and schools.

An exceptional political innovation occurred in 1897 when the four rulers met in Kuala Kangsar for a durbar arranged so that they and their people would feel that federation was a reality. It was also the year of Queen Victoria's Diamond Jubilee. The durbar was an unprecedented event in the history of the peninsula. As Swettenham proudly declared in a report on the occasion, 'Never in the history of Malaya has any such assemblage been even imagined. I doubt whether anybody has ever heard of one Ruler of a State making a ceremonial visit to another; but to have been able to collect together, in one place, the Sultans of Perak, Selangor, Pahang and the Negri Sembilan is a feat that might well have been regarded as impossible.' Several rulers had made long and tedious journeys to Kuala Kangsar. The deeper significance of the gathering however lay in the fact that it provided evidence of the peace and changed conditions of life which British influence had brought. Here were men who 'of old had loved war exceedingly', meeting in amity to discuss common interests and policies which would lead to the welfare of their peoples who never before had been accorded this privilege.

The durbar was 'an unqualified success'. It was the progenitor of regular gatherings of all the nine rulers in the peninsula that took place from 1948 after the birth of the 'Federation of Malaya'. The opening ceremony was a most colourful affair with the rulers dressed in their richest costumes, their major chiefs in their own splendour, and the royal attendants bearing the necessary equipage, the regalias of lances, tufted spears, swords and krises. The Sultan of Selangor invited the High Commissioner, Sir Charles Mitchell, resplendent in plumed helmet and colonial governor's uniform, to preside. The proceedings were in Malay and the discussions ranged from the constitution of the federation to matters concerning Islam and Malay customs and questions relating to the well-being of the Malays.

There was apparently frank speaking for, according to Swettenham's report, the ruler of Perak raised the subject of 'British protection which he did not hesitate to describe as control. . . .'

The next durbar was held in Kuala Lumpur in 1903. By then the strides made in extending communications enabled the rulers of Perak and Negri Sembilan to journey to Kuala Lumpur by train as did the host, the Sultan of Selangor, from Klang. The Sultan of Pahang came by sea. Two sensitive subjects appeared on the agenda. The first was the question of Malay participation in government. The High Commissioner, Sir Frank Swettenham, expressed regret that the national characteristics of the Malays made it 'difficult, though not impossible, for them to take full advantage of the opportunities which now come begging to their doors', a reference to the fact that the British had been invited into the Malay States in order to teach the Malays a better form of administration. If the conference, he said, could devise any means 'of awakening the dormant energies of the Malays and can persuade them to devote themselves to any sustained effort in the way of work, it will render a signal service to the Malay people and these States'. However no suggestions were forthcoming, and the Sultan of Perak expressed regret that no way had been found of handing over to Malays any considerable portion of the administration. This was to be a perennial complaint until the future 'Federation of Malaya' began moving towards independence.

There was also a royal debate on 'over-centralization' in the F.M.S. and this brought from the Sultan of Perak a forthright demand for a 'loosening' of the federation. He said he had not quite been able to understand the nature of the union; recalling a Malay proverb that there could not be two masters in one vessel, he added, 'Neither can there be four Rulers over one country.' The Pangkor Treaty, he went on, provided that only the Residents, and not the Resident-General, should advise the Sultans, and he expressed the hope 'that the affairs of each State may be managed by its own officers so that the governments may be separate entities'. His protest undoubtedly had some result in reforms that were introduced in 1909.

The State Councils suffered from the grip of centralization in Kuala Lumpur. Never potent legislatures before federation, they became little more than bodies advising the Resident on State matters. Sir George Maxwell, a brilliant civil servant who had joined the Perak service in 1891, pertinently commented once, 'If anyone believes that the State Councils of that time (pre-Federation days) played any part in the administration of the States let him note that not one of the Rulers consulted his State Council before consenting to federation.' The industrialists and the merchants in the prospering federation began agitating for representation in the Federal and State legislatures. The *Malay Mail* newspaper, published in Kuala Lumpur, continually criticized the Federal Government for what is called its 'rule in the dark'.

The principal complaint was that the control of public affairs in all States had passed into the hands of the Resident-General. A remedy was not forthcoming until 1909 during the High Commissionership of Sir John Anderson who had succeeded Sir Frank Swettenham in 1904. Sir John, who had come straight from the Colonial Office, was a particularly broad-minded and far-sighted individual. He realized that federation had entirely altered the positions of the Sultans, the High Commissioner and the Residents, and that by the treaty the rulers had undertaken a further obligation to follow the advice of the Resident-General in all matters of administration other than those touching Muslim religion and Malay custom.

Thus the Residents had become, as an official Federal Government paper published in 1925 put it, 'the mouthpiece not of the High Commissioner but of the Resident-General who had not even an Executive Council to advise him and was subject only to a vague and undefined control by the High Commissioner'. Anderson thought that to bring the High Commissioner directly into the administration and to associate the rulers and the Residents with him would provide the cure. So he created a Federal Council and changed the Resident-General into a 'Chief Secretary'. In his speech inaugurating the Federal Council at Kuala Kangsar on 11th December 1909, he assured the rulers that Britain had never had any intention of bringing about British rule as distinct from British advice.

However, the Federal Council had its anomalies, too. It was under the presidency of the High Commissioner and not of the rulers—whose Council it was supposed to be. This fact later raised the question of whether the representative of the British Crown should preside over a council of independent and protected Malay States instead of guiding and advising from without. Again, the High Commissioner and not the rulers nominated the members of the Council. Its principal members consisted of the Chief Secretary, the four Residents, the four rulers (in that order of precedence) and four unofficial members nominated by the High Commissioner with the

137

approval of the British Crown. If the High Commissioner wished to bring into the Council the head of a federal department he could do so with the approval of the Crown—and not the rulers, who therefore found themselves reduced to the level of ordinary members. (In 1927 the then Sultan of Perak was to declare in great exasperation, 'I have sat in this Council for long and weary hours, as far as I can see without profit.')

Again, as the 1925 Federal paper remarked very frankly, Sir John had hoped that the changes he had introduced 'would restore to the Rulers and Residents the fuller powers and responsibilities which they exercised before Federation. In this respect his hopes were not realized'. Administration became more and more centralized in the office of the Chief Secretary; the process may have been 'partly unconscious', to quote the same Federal document, 'but whatever the cause, the result is clear. The powers and influence of the State Councils and the Residents gradually diminished'; increasing efficiency and uniformity under the central government had been 'purchased at the price of the individuality and legitimate independence of the states'.

Sir John Anderson's era (1904–11) was most eventful for the Settlements and the Malay States, and not only because of the creation of the Federal Council. In 1906, the Governor also became the High Commissioner for Brunei after a request from its Sultan for British protection. The following year, Labuan, an island off North Borneo, which had had a varied constitutional existence since its cession to the British in 1846, was annexed and became part of the Colony of Singapore. But the most significant changes affected the Siamese-controlled Malay States of Kedah, Perlis and Kelantan as well as Trengganu. They came under British control when the Siamese transferred to Britain their 'suzerainty, protection, administration, and control' under the Anglo-Siamese Treaty of 1909. The records are not very clear on the reasons for this transfer but undoubtedly one was to forestall any possibility of foreign interference in them.

The four States refused, however, to become members of the Federated Malay States and remained jealous of their independence right up to the day in 1948 when their rulers signed the agreement which created a Federation of the nine Malay States and the two British Settlements. They also declined to have a British Resident because this meant the acceptance of foreign advice—and this was not in accord with their interpretation of 'independence'. They had also noticed the gradual loss of power of their brother-rulers in the F.M.S. . . . Although under the Anglo-Siam Treaty Britain possessed suzerainty over the States, it made no attempt to impose its will on them over the question of Residents. Times and circumstances had changed; by the twentieth century, some machinery of government existed in the northern and eastern states as a contrast to the early days of Perak, Selangor, Negri Sembilan and Pahang. So British 'Advisers' were accepted by Kedah, Perlis, Kelantan and Trengganu. Their functions were purely to advise and they were employed by the State Governments solely in that capacity.

CHAPTER 14

Phenomenal Expansion

B y the end of 1909 therefore the whole of the Malay peninsula, and Singapore, Labuan and the three Borneo territories, were either under direct British rule or under British influence and protection. Singapore and the territories in the peninsula were split into the Colony of the Straits Settlements, and the protectorates of the Federated Malay States and the Unfederated Malay States. The single co-ordinating authority for all of them sat in Singapore, a man with 'two hats' : he was Governor of the Straits Settlements and High Commissioner of the Malay States. In the latter he exercised his authority through the British Resident or the Adviser, and in federal matters in the Federated Malay States through the Chief Secretary. It was cumbersome and complex machinery for such a small peninsula, but in spite of this the development of the Straits Settlements and the Federated Malay States over the next 30 years was phenomenal and a tribute to the British administration. Of the unfederated States, Johore and Kedah also moved into the main streams of economic progress and prosperity, principally because of their proximity to the flourishing ports of Singapore and Penang respectively. Kelantan and Trengganu, isolated by the lack of communications, moved along at the pace of the *kerbau*, the bulls, which ploughed the ricefields.

The west coast of the peninsula blossomed with a railway that ran from Penang to Singapore and also thrust itself into the east coast. Excellent roads led out in many directions from towns to villages. Tin, rubber, copra and other products were shipped to all parts of the world. By the 1920s, the country had achieved an enviable standard of living which by 1939, when World War II broke out, had become the highest in South-East Asia. Political progress may not have matched economic development but then there were no 'demands' for it; the Malays were content with the way of life and the other communities were largely prepared to let the situation lie.

The Malayan prosperity was made possible by an economic revolution during the first 20 years of the twentieth century. There was a world demand for two commodities which Malaya was able to supply in great quantities—tin and rubber. Tin had been there through the centuries waiting to be won by the shovelful. Rubber on the other hand was introduced by the British and grew into the country's second great industry. Its introduction changed the face of the country and led to development in practically every public service.

To tin first. The peace that followed British intervention in the Malay States provided the essential conditions for the more organized production of the ore. It was wanted by the western world for the manufacture of tinplate, and production soared until by 1883 the peninsula emerged as the world's largest tin-producing centre, jumping from fourth place to ahead of Australia, Britain and Indonesia. It was a wholly Chinese industry. The Chinese used ingenious but primitive methods to extract ore—apart from engaging Malay *pawang* to find tin-bearing land for them. The *pawang* worked on almost the same principles as the water-diviners of the West; the Chinese miners followed their advice with great confidence, and often with eminently satisfying financial results. In 1896 the first European tin-mining companies were floated. Soon after the turn of the century British mining engineers introduced the mechanical marvels of the day, the ugly ponderous dredges whose endless chains of buckets gulped their way through tin-bearing fields faster and deeper than Chinese labour *en masse* could do. This more sophisticated method of mining soon brought the industry into European control.

The exports of tin rose from 26,000 tons in 1889 to 51,733 tons in 1904 and to just under 70,000 tons in 1929. Two years later an International Tin Restriction Scheme kept a tight rein on Malayan production but Malaya still continued to be the largest single producer of the ore in the world.

Rubber is the greater money-earner but it has had its violent fluctuations in booms and slumps. In the early 1930s, for instance, a catastrophic world slump produced the unfortunate spectacle of some British rubber planters begging for alms in the streets of Singapore, Kuala Lumpur and other towns. Rubber was unknown in the

141

peninsula before 1876. The inspiration for its choice as a crop to enhance the natural resources of Malaya (and of other British colonies
in the tropics) belonged to Mr. (later Sir) Joseph Hooker, the Director of the Royal Botanic Gardens at Kew. The best rubber then came
chiefly from the *Hevea Brasiliensis* trees growing in the great rubber
'forests' of the Central Amazon basin. Hooker commissioned Mr.
(later Sir) Henry A. Wickham to collect *Hevea* seeds from the
Amazon. About 70,000 arrived in Kew in June 1876. The following
year 22 seedlings were despatched to Singapore where some were
successfully established in the Botanic Gardens. Nine seedlings were
replanted on the bank of the river at Kuala Kangsar where they were
carefully nursed by that ardent naturalist and botanist and successful
British Resident, Hugh Low, but the government really had little
faith in the possibilities of rubber in the country.

Then in 1888 Mr. H. N. Ridley arrived in Singapore as the new
Director of the Botanic Gardens; and it was his enthusiasm and his
research that led to the development of rubber as a great plantation
crop. Ridley also evolved the best method for tapping the tree's
valuable latex. Rubber as an industry was perhaps slow to take root;
in 1897 only 345 acres were under rubber and in 1905 the acreage was
a mere 50,000. On to the world scene came Mr. Henry Ford and his
motor-car for the masses and the more important invention, to
Malaya, of pneumatic tyres. The world wanted to travel on wheels
and the demand for rubber soared. Companies floated in London
easily obtained land for rubber-growing in the peninsula. Malay
peasants were offered fabulous sums for their smallholdings. Rubber
was on its way to its first boom of 1910–12. By 1914 Malayan estates
supplied rubber to the New York market at prices lower than that
asked for by the great South American growers. Today more than
$3\frac{1}{2}$ million acres of land in Malaya are growing rubber and about
2,000,000 people are directly or indirectly dependent on the industry
for their livelihood. The annual production is about 750,000 tons and
the exports represent about 55 per cent of Malaysia's export earn-
ings. Every one of the hundreds of millions of rubber trees grown in
the peninsula since 1877 has been the progeny of the seeds from Kew.
... And Singapore throve as the port of export for Malaya's tin and
rubber and as a trading centre.

The social services had also been expanded considerably. Large
hospitals were built in Singapore, Penang, Malacca, Kuala Lumpur,
Ipoh and other towns. Infant welfare and maternity clinics had begun

the long and slow process of trying to overcome old prejudices and superstitions in efforts to reduce the high infant mortality rate. Malaria, which had killed thousands, was slowly being eradicated in the towns and around the vital mines and estates after Dr. (later Sir) Malcolm Watson, a Government District Surgeon in Klang, had laid a pattern for effective malaria control following Sir Ronald Ross's discovery that the mosquito carried the disease.

In education, the early initiative of missionary societies and organizations set a pattern for the Government which built schools for English and vernacular education. Primary education became compulsory and free for Malay children; Chinese and Indian schools were given grants-in-aid. The demand for English education did not manifest itself until the late 1930s, so for most children—particularly the Malays—education was confined to the primary vernacular schools. For the Chinese and Indian schools, teachers were imported from China and India. From China already came many who were ardent communists and who enthusiastically began inculcating communism upon their boy and girl pupils. In 1905 there had opened in Singapore the first advanced educational institution—the King Edward VII College of Medicine—and from it there slowly began to pour qualified local doctors and dentists. In 1929 Raffles College came into existence and offered degrees in arts and science. After the Japanese War the two colleges formed the initial faculties for a new University of Malaya.

Swamps, coastal marshes and jungle were converted into ricefields. A Drainage and Irrigation Department introduced scientific irrigation facilities and thus improved existing *padi*-lands and developed new areas for rice-growing. A Veterinary Department helped to improve animal stock and poultry. A Forestry Department was charged with the management of the country's forests which had valuable merchantable timber. Co-operative enterprises were introduced and received encouraging response.

Malaya was therefore a happy, prospering, and almost contented country. Law and order prevailed and there was a sense of security and peace. The Malays worked their smallholdings, ricefields and fruit orchards, formed the backbone of the police forces, worked in the forest, survey and other outdoor Government departments, and were also happy to be domestic servants, chauffeurs, and gardeners. Their sons who had had English education formed a large section in the Government administrative service and the time came when the

Government established a special 'Malay Administrative Service' and later opened the ranks of the Malayan Civil Service to Malays of ability. The Chinese worked industriously to save enough money to return to their homeland in pleasant retirement for the rest of their days. There appeared to be no conflicting interests among the communities; their preoccupations were limited to the material things of life. Their motto very largely was 'Live and let live.' The British were the rulers—an 'unquestioned authority'—who could be depended upon to look after the interests of each race.

Political consciousness was the prerogative of the rulers, the Malay aristocracy, and certain intellectual leaders among Chinese who had been born in the country. There were of course the external political influences, particularly the Chinese Kuomintang, founded by Dr. Sun Yat Sen, the father of the Chinese Republic, which had a large following among the middle- and merchant-class immigrant Chinese, and the Malayan Communist Party which drew its supporters largely from the Chinese working class. The Indians were affected by the pace of nationalism in India.

But within the purely local sphere, none of the races appeared anxious for the kind of political progress which would have altered the bureaucratic system of government and placed more responsibility into their hands. On the other hand dissatisfactions over the system of government existed among the rulers and those very closely connected with it in all spheres of activity. The rulers themselves had long been disturbed by the minor roles to which federation had relegated them. They contended that they were ruled by the High Commissioner, that indeed they were subordinate to the Chief Secretary—and they looked jealously towards the unfettered glory of their brother-rulers in the unfederated States who were far from being impotent sovereigns.

This then was the scene in the Malaya of the 1920s. The Great War of 1914–18 had passed Malaya by. The rulers marked their anxiety over the far-away war and their loyalty to Britain, their protector, by presenting a battleship, H.M.S. *Malaya*. In 1920, a new Governor and High Commissioner, Sir Laurence Guillemard, arrived with instructions from the Colonial Office to introduce reforms in Malaya, perhaps the decentralization of authority. Guillemard, after examining the situation, found among the rulers what he was to describe later as 'a feeling of disquiet, a very real disquiet. There was no failure

7a. Early morning along the east coast of Malaya sees groups of fisherfolk drawing up their nets

7b. Tin is one of the staple industries of Malaysia. It is obtained by various processes—dredging and gravel pumping and hydraulizing, and by the oldest and simplest method of panning either in a sluiceway or in a stream as the three Chinese women in the picture are doing

8a. This was Kuching and the Sarawak River in the early days of James Brooke's era as Rajah

8b. One of James Brooke's early problems was the suppression of piracy around Sarawak waters. The Royal Navy came to his assistance and warcraft penetrated the uncharted rivers of the country in order to destroy pirate strongholds

in loyalty but a desire for a change in the conditions.' The Federal Government, he wrote, had grown into 'a highly organized and most efficient bureaucracy which however had tended to over-centralize and possessed too rigid and detailed control of the administration in the four States'. The Malay rulers were apprehensive that federal encroachment might grow worse. Guillemard began considering the question of the transfer of power from the Federal to the State Governments and eventually in 1925 proposed a policy of 'decentralization' which would give each of the federated States greater control over internal affairs. This included the gradual abolition of the powers of the Chief Secretary, a proposal which appeared to have originated from a memorandum sent to the Colonial Office by the Sultan of Perak who desired 'that the original treaty be followed in its exact form' and suggested that the proper policy for the States was one under which 'the ruler should be treated as a Ruler and the Resident carry out, on his behalf and with his co-operation, the policy arrived at by them in consultation with the more powerful State Council'.

Guillemard laid his sweeping proposals before the Federal Council on 14th December 1925 when he expressed his conviction that 'the only effective decentralization and the only cure for the dissatisfaction of the Rulers lie in such gradual devolution of the Chief Secretary's powers to State Councils, Residents, and if necessary, to Federal Heads of Department as will in effect amount to abolition of the post of the Chief Secretary as at present constituted'. This proposal received the concentrated opposition not only of the European and Chinese members of the Federal Council but also of practically the whole commercial community, who genuinely feared that the reduction of the Chief Secretary's powers would release the State Governments and the Residents from the control of the federal authority and would result in financial instability in the States, which would also come under the 'fetters of Singapore', as it was put.

Nevertheless the first stage in the policy of decentralization came into effect with the conclusion on 24th April 1927 of a new Agreement between the British Government and the four rulers for the reconstitution of the Federal Council. Under it the rulers withdrew from active membership of the Council though retaining the right to be present at any meeting if they wished. In the future they were to appear in the Council in formal state on every Budget Day, seated on thrones on a dais behind the High Commissioner. They also gave

K   145

formal assent to legislation approved by the Council, a procedure that had not been necessary when they had been members of the Council. Finally they were to meet at annual durbars at which they, their Residents, the Chief Secretary and the High Commissioner discussed in Malay the affairs of the Federation.

The new Agreement also enlarged the unofficial membership of the Federal Council to give it a more representative character and clearly defined its legislative and financial responsibility. The State Councils were given control over purely domestic expenditure. But unintentionally nothing was done about reducing the powers of the Chief Secretary.

Guillemard was succeeded in 1927 by Sir Hugh Clifford, of Pahang fame, who took no further steps towards giving effect to the decentralization policy but opened his three-year term with a major speech which again clearly set out British policy towards the Malay States. He said: 'The States were, when the British Government was invited by their Rulers and Chiefs to set their troubled houses in order, Muhammadan monarchies; such they are today, and such they must continue to be. No mandate has ever been extended to us by Rajas, Chiefs or people to vary the system of government which has existed in these territories from time immemorial; and in these days when democratic and socialist theories and doctrines are spreading like an infection, bringing with them, too often, not peace but a sword, I feel it incumbent upon me to emphasize, thus early in my allotted term of office, the utter inapplicability of any form of democratic or popular government to the circumstances of these States. The adoption of any kind of government by majority would forthwith entail the complete submersion of the indigenous population, who would find themselves hopelessly outnumbered by folk of other races, and this would produce a situation which would amount to the betrayal of the trust which the Malays of these States, from the highest to the lowest, have been taught to repose in His Majestys' Government.' So, until circumstances brought a change in 1953, it remained the cardinal point in British policy that the position, authority and prestige of the Malay rulers should be maintained and that members of the Federal and State Councils should be appointed rather than elected.

Clifford's successor, Sir Cecil Clementi, resurrected the decentralization issues in 1930, and he wanted to take them further. He not only proposed the transfer to the State Governments of the control of certain departments, the strengthening of the State Councils and an extension of their powers and the abolition of the post of Chief Secretary, but also the establishment of a common Customs union. He put his proposals before a rulers' durbar in Sri Menanti, Negri Sembilan, on 18th August 1931 and in the course of his speech hinted at the need for a union of all the Malay States on the ground that a country almost as large as England had no fewer than ten administrative units which functioned 'with little collaboration or co-ordination, existing (as it were) in watertight compartments'.

Clementi must have expected some opposition to his proposals, but not the vehemence, bitterness and hostility which assailed him from the whole European, Chinese and Indian business community for his intention to abolish the Chief Secretaryship; the reasons were similar to those given when Guillemard first projected his plan. The rulers themselves formally approved the proposals at their next durbar in Pekan, in Pahang, on 28th April 1932, but the public controversy ran on so furiously that the Colonial Office sent Brigadier-General Sir Samuel Wilson, Permanent Under-Secretary of State for the Colonies, to assess the situation on the spot. Wilson agreed that from a purely economic point of view it would be advisable to have one central government administering the whole of Malaya, but he considered there was a strong case on political grounds for giving the rulers of the federated States control of their own domestic affairs. The closer assimilation of the position of the rulers of the F.M.S. to that of the rulers of the unfederated States was obviously an essential preliminary to any scheme for promoting co-operation on matters of common interest between the constituent parts of Malaya as a whole, but he found it evident that the latter would be reluctant 'at the present time' to agree to any closer form of co-operation. Wilson considered there was a strong case for adopting a policy of decentralization and for gradually substituting in the F.M.S. a genuine federal system in place of the 'amalgamation' that existed. He recommended that the changes involved by the adoption of the decentralization policy should be carried out 'very gradually'.

The British Government introduced a measure of decentralization in 1933 through Clementi's successor, Sir Shenton Thomas. The Chief Secretary, for instance, was replaced by a Federal Secretary who was given a reduced status—he was more of a co-ordinating officer—and few powers. In precedence he followed the Residents, and a piquant and symbolic sidelight occurred when the Federal

147

Secretary and the British Resident of Selangor exchanged residences in accordance with their altered status. The British Resident became the High Commissioner's representative in the State he served. Perhaps the most significant political reform lay in the restoration of autonomous powers to the State Councils. The State Governments could draw up their own budgets but financial control remained with the Federal Council which made an annual grant to each State.

The rulers in the federated States appeared much more satisfied with the changes—while those in the unfederated States found their own satisfactions in the assurance given them by Wilson that His Majesty's Government had 'no intention of requiring' any of them to 'enter against his will into any kind of Malayan league or union'.

It was the controversies over decentralization that brought the first stirrings of Malay nationalism—Malay fears of Chinese domination. At the same time non-Malays showed their anxiety over the greater power that would be placed in Malay hands. They had begun to hear a cry of 'Malaya for the Malays' since decentralization was first mooted. Those who had been born in Malaya or whose children had been born there, feared discrimination and criticized the preferential treatment given to the Malays—for instance in appointments to the public service and in the reservation of land.

Until then Malaya had prided itself on the utter racial harmony among its peoples. It was perhaps a false picture simply because outside business in town and country there was little or no social intermingling between the races who moved in their own communities. Their paths seldom crossed, and the Malays and Chinese were as indifferent to each other as the Malays themselves were to their own kin in neighbouring States. Between the Malays and the non-Malays had stood that pillar of strength and trust, the British Government, which watched the interests and privileges of the Malays as assiduously and faithfully as it encouraged the non-Malays to help in the development of the peninsula. As someone said, it was *Pax Britannica* at its best.

The Malay concern over the continuing large-scale immigration of 'foreigners', particularly the Chinese, could well be understood. In 1800, the Malays formed 90 per cent of the population. In 1911 the first all-Malayan census showed that they made up only 51 per cent of the whole. The Government met the situation in 1929 by introducing an Immigration Restriction Ordinance (replaced in 1933 by a tighter Aliens Ordinance) which certainly reduced the influx considerably. The Chinese were the most affected by these restrictions on immigration. Then Chinese voices began to talk of the need of unity among the communities and chided the Government for its policy of 'Malaya for the Malays'. (Indeed, as far back as 1926, a Chinese member of the Legislative Council of the Straits Settlements, Mr. Tan Cheng Lock (later Sir Cheng-Lock Tan), a shrewd and far-sighted leader of his community, a son of Malacca, had declared: 'Our ultimate political goal should be a united self-governing British Malaya with a Federal Government and Parliament for the whole of it, functioning at a convenient centre—say Kuala Lumpur. I think it is high time that we commenced to take action towards forging the surest and strongest link of that united Malaya by fostering and creating a true Malayan spirit and consciousness among its people to the complete elimination of racial and communal feeling.' Tan was the first of the political prophets; in 1955, as the leader of the Malayan Chinese Association, he saw independence come to a united Malaya and felt the stirrings of 'a true Malayan spirit'. . . .)

The proposed decentralization policy was never carried to its ultimate conclusion. First the grievous slump of the mid-1930s, and then the need for severe retrenchment in the Government as the economy of the country declined, and finally the onslaught of war left the proposals in the pigeon-holes of the Secretariat.

By 1939 when the Second World War broke out in Europe, Malaya was a comfortable place to live and work in although the Malayan Communists were posing a serious problem. The Federated Malay States had returned to boom times and after Britain's declaration of war against Nazi Germany had willingly undertaken to increase the output of rubber and tin for the war effort. Singapore boomed too, not only as one of the greatest ports in the world but also in its new stature as an Imperial bastion. Malaya and Singapore had become militarily important. (And between 1919 and 1939 Malaya had demonstrated its loyalty to Britain with contributions totalling over £20,000,000 to the cost of Imperial defence—offerings which had been made voluntarily.) A giant naval base had been carved out of swamps and old rubber land in the north-east of Singapore and three Royal Air Force aerodromes also existed on the island. British and Commonwealth forces were stationed in Singapore and in other parts of the peninsula. More R.A.F. aerodromes were to be found at Butterworth, opposite Penang, and in Kedah, Kelantan, Selangor and Johore.

The possibility of the extension of the war to the Far East was as distant in the minds of the people as was Japan beyond the eastern horizon. However, they thought, if there was war it would only be a short and sharp one for Malaya and Singapore placed the greatest confidence in the strength of the naval base, the 15-inch guns mounted on Singapore's southern coast, and on the garrisons dotted in several parts of Malaya. They also thought that reinforcements would quickly be sent from Europe.

CHAPTER 15

The Japanese Invasion

The war clouds in the Far East began to gather strongly in mid-1940. In Europe, France collapsed to the Germans in June. In Japan, on the other side of the world, in July a new government dominated by a sabre-rattling army took over power and, in the light of the events in the West, began to draw up detailed plans for expansion in South-East Asia.

For Japan, the creation of an empire in South-East Asia had its genesis in November 1936 when an Anti-Communist Pact with Germany was signed. Japan seemed intent on war with Russia for Soviet-Japanese relations were tense; they continued to be unfriendly for years. In July 1937, Japan took advantage of a minor incident near Peking to launch an undeclared and full-scale war on China. On 21st August 1939, Germany and Russia signed a Non-Aggression Pact which took Japan by surprise and later made it cautious about becoming involved in the European war which broke out a fortnight later. Germany's *blitzkrieg* tactics in May 1940 led to the capitulation of Holland, Belgium and France, and the Japanese decided that 'it was the sacred duty of Japan to profit from this situation'; the rich French and Dutch possessions in the Far East were poorly defended and waiting to be plucked.

Under pressure from Berlin the puppet Vichy government in France permitted Japan to use ports, cities and airports in Indo-China for troop movements. This enabled Japan, still at war with China, to seal off one vital supply route to the retreating Chinese Government. It also brought Japanese forces on the fringe of South-East Asia. In September 1940 Japan took the final plunge by signing a military alliance with Germany and Italy, both of which formally recognized 'the leadership of Japan in the establishment of a new order in greater east Asia'. Japan's next step—with the intention of clearing the field of any opposing European power—was to persuade Russia that it had no designs on its possessions in Asia, and to negotiate a neutrality pact with Russia in April 1941 with the approval of Germany—who however did not inform Japan of its plans to attack Russia in a few weeks in spite of the treaty of friendship existing between them. The German invasion of Russia consequently took Japan by surprise; nevertheless it pressed on with its preparations for war, not on Siberia in support of the Germans as Hitler had proposed, but to the south for its own aggrandisement. In July 1941 Japanese troops occupied the whole of Indo-China.

This caused a complete review by Britain of its plans for the defence of Malaya and the naval base of Singapore which was obviously Japan's prize target. Japan now had a naval base within 700 miles of Singapore and an air base within 600 miles. Reinforcements began to arrive in Malaya from October onwards to augment the British, Australian, Indian and Malayan brigades already in defence positions from the Siamese frontier in the north down to Singapore, and already in training for an expected Japanese invasion. Lieutenant-General A. E. Percival, the General Officer Commanding in Malaya, time and again in despatches stressed the lack of any fighting experience whatever of his troops who were expected to hold a country considered most vital to the Allies because of its increasing production of rubber and tin.

The day after Japan announced its establishment of a 'protectorate' over Indo-China, President Franklin D. Roosevelt of the United States froze all Japanese assets in the United States. The British and Dutch Governments took similar action. This meant that Japan no longer had access to raw materials and particularly to all its sources of oil supplies. Japan either had to come to an agreement with the United States—which would have meant withdrawing from Indo-China and possibly from all occupied parts of China—or to fight for the countries which held the supplies it needed. Japan was not completely ready for war and America did not want war, so diplomatic negotiations opened in Washington in efforts to settle the impasse. On 6th September 1941 the Japanese Supreme War Council, sitting under the chairmanship of the Emperor, decided that, 'if by the early part of October there is no reasonable hope of having our demands agreed to . . . we will immediately make up our minds to get ready for war against America, England and Holland'. The negotiations failed. The question was, when would this new war be launched?

On 2nd December a British battle fleet comprising the new battle-ship, *Prince of Wales*, the battle-cruiser *Repulse* and four destroyers arrived in Singapore. They presented a majestic and comforting spectacle as they steamed through the Singapore Straits and then turned into the Straits of Johore to anchor at the naval base. They had been sent in an eleventh-hour effort to deter the Japanese from going to war. Four days later, a British long-range reconnaissance aircraft spied a Japanese fleet of a battleship, 7 cruisers and 14 destroyers escorting 43 merchant ships in the Gulf of Siam and steaming westward in the direction of Singgora in Southern Siam. Was Japan invading Southern Siam as a prelude to thrusting southwards into Malaya?

Just after one o'clock on the morning of Monday, 8th December, Japanese warships suddenly began shelling the beaches near Kota Bahru, the capital of Kelantan, and Japanese troops began landings. At 4.30, two waves of Japanese bombers droned over a sleeping Singapore and dropped bombs on the harbour, airfields, and in the heart of the city. That same day several thousand miles away, Japanese torpedo-bombers attacked the American naval base at Pearl Harbour, in Hawaii, and sank or heavily damaged 18 battleships, aircraft carriers, cruisers and destroyers of the Pacific Fleet and killed 2,400 men. America came into the war against Germany and Japan.

As the days passed in grim battle in Malaya, the Japanese emerged superior in numbers in all spheres. The Royal Air Force, with only 141 aircraft of various descriptions in the peninsula and Singapore, were outclassed by the Japanese bombers and fighters which very soon flew nonchalantly on their missions. Japanese troops with experience of war in China began moving into Kedah after landing at Singgora and crossing the isthmus. Japanese tanks—of which the army in Malaya had none—began rumbling down the roads. On 10th December came calamity. The *Prince of Wales* and *Repulse* and their four destroyers were off the coast at Kuantan investigating reports of Japanese landings when Japanese reconnaissance aircraft picked them up. Very soon a Japanese striking force of high-level bombers and torpedo-bombers began an attack and sank the two great ships. About 2,080 out of 2,921 officers and men were picked out of the water by the destroyers. It was Britain's greatest naval disaster since war had begun in 1939. Mr. Winston Churchill, the British Prime Minister, has described in his history of the Second World War how the news affected him: 'In all the war I never received a more direct

153

shock. . . . As I turned over and twisted in bed the full horror of the news sank in upon me. There were no British or American capital ships in the Indian Ocean or the Pacific except the American survivors of Pearl Harbour. . . . Over all this vast expanse of waters Japan was supreme, and we everywhere were weak and naked.'

The rest of the story of the war in Malaya may swiftly be told. The Japanese army swept irresistibly down the peninsula. On the night of 30th–31st January 1942 the defending troops made the final withdrawal across the causeway linking the peninsula and Singapore. They breached the causeway, but rather ineffectively as it proved later. The battle of Malaya had ended and the battle of Singapore was about to begin. Singapore was already facing a grave danger of water shortage. Most of its water supplies came by pipeline across the causeway from a catchment reservoir in Johore which was now in enemy hands. Air bombing and artillery shelling had burst watermains; drastic water rationing had already been imposed. The water levels in the three reservoirs on the island were lower than usual. Refugees from the peninsula had swollen the population in the city to over one million. . . .

The battle for Singapore opened on 8th February with a massive artillery barrage from Japanese guns firing from rubber estates behind Johore Bahru. That night Japanese assault troops swarmed across the narrow straits and before dawn 13,000 had landed. They were followed at daylight by another 10,000 who were followed by other divisions. . . . On 12th January the naval base was evacuated and its defences destroyed. Then for three days the Japanese Air Force concentrated its fury on the city continuously in daylight. Japanese artillery pounded the city. Civilian casualties were considerable every day. More water-mains were broken. From the harbour little ships tried to sail away with civilians, nurses, and officers and men of the armed forces intent on escape but most of them were bombed and sunk for all the seas around had become a vast Japanese lake. A funeral pall of smoke from innumerable fires hid the sky over Singapore even to the horizon to the south.

On the afternoon of Sunday, 15th February, everything in that insufferably overcrowded city seemed to be still except for the monotonous whine of shells and the explosion of bombs dropped by lazily circling Japanese aircraft. At 4.30 p.m. a lull in the bombing and shelling became apparent; an hour later the Japanese attacks ceased. An uncanny silence began to reign over the city which had gone through its savage physical Gehenna for three days and nights. General Percival was at the headquarters of the Japanese Commander-in-Chief, General Tomoyuki Yamashita,[1] discussing surrender terms, for the water situation had become grievous—and the population had also to be saved from the agonies of a final assault by the Japanese. So Singapore—so often described as the 'impregnable citadel' and 'formidable bastion' because of its £63,000,000 naval base—surrendered. In the silence of that night it presented a nightmare spectacle of an anguished, conquered city burning from hundreds of fires.

The Japanese occupation of Malaya, Singapore, and the British Borneo territories lasted for 3½ years. The Japanese took over people who were stunned by the completeness of the defeat of the British and also gripped by fear of savagery at the hands of the conquerors. Stories of the barbaric brutality which had followed Japanese victories in Chinese towns were fresh in the memories of the people, and the Chinese particularly waited with typical stoicism and fatalism for vengeance to be wreaked on them. This came after the entire British administration and all the European population who had stayed in the country either because they had wished to or because (and this only concerned a minority) they had not been able to escape, had been sent into internment camps. The Japanese indulged in an orgy of executions of Chinese in the name of 'anti-Communism'. Their reign of terror lasted for about six months. They killed thousands of Chinese, most of whom were innocent of the allegations against them; also killed were people whom they accused of being 'British sympathizers'. Thousands of others were flung into gaols where they were inhumanly tortured by the Japanese Kempeitai.

Then the Japanese made efforts at appeasement, but the fear they had generated nullified any possibility of their gaining the slightest co-operation from the people in their plans for creating an 'Asia for the Asians', the banner they unfurled after their blood-letting had ceased. Had they adopted different tactics from the outset of their occupation and in this way gained the trust of most of the people,

[1] On 7th December 1946 a United States Army War Crimes Commission found General Yamashita, who at the end of the war was Commander-in-Chief in the Philippines, guilty of being a war criminal. He was hanged on 23rd February 1947. In Malaya and Singapore, War Crimes courts meted out sentences of death or rigorous imprisonment to more than 1,000 officers and other ranks of the Japanese forces and Kempeitai (secret police) for atrocities in both territories.

there is little doubt that Malaya's history might have followed a different course, because sections of the population, bitter over the failure of Britain to defend them, had been ready to give the Japanese a trial as the successors of the British.

The Japanese continued the general pattern of the administration with, of course, their own governors in control in each State and settlement and a governor-general based in Singapore. They also severed Sumatra from the administration of Java and placed it under the jurisdiction of Malaya but this proved a failure; in 1944 Sumatra operated under its own government—a taste of 'independence' which still affects its relations with the Indonesian central government today.

Within the peninsula, the Japanese 'returned' Kedah, Perlis, Kelantan and Trengganu to the Siamese who placed a governor in each State and left the Malay administrations to run themselves until the return of the British. The Japanese claimed to recognize the full status of the rulers but actually stripped them of many rights and privileges without disturbing their positions as heads of religion. Advisory councils composed mostly of Malays and Japanese replaced state and legislative councils; these were intended to appease the Malays and gain their support and friendship but, to quote a comment in a post-war Japanese document, the proceedings were so 'one-sided (that) it was natural that people were thrown into despair and came to lose enthusiasm'. The Indians were 'invited' to join the 'Indian National Army' which had been formed to 'co-operate' with the Japanese in destroying British power in India but the vast majority were suspicious and disinclined to join or support this 'nationalist' movement.

Life, industry, and business in Malaya slowly ran down as the months passed and the Japanese found more and more difficulty—as their lines of communication began to be interrupted by the Allies— in importing food and other essential products. The tin industry almost came to a standstill principally because the Japanese were unable to replace the dredges and other mining machinery which had been 'scorched' by the British during their withdrawal down the peninsula and because they themselves shipped much of it to Japan as scrap iron to be turned into armaments. The rubber estates were all but denuded of Indian labourers as the Japanese transferred thousands of them to Siam to work as forced labour—with Allied prisoners-of-war—on a 'strategic' railway link between Siam and Burma. (The Japanese ripped up the Malayan railway line to the east coast and sent the rails to Siam.) A considerable number of men of other races in Malaya were also sent to work in Borneo and other parts of Asia.

For all practical purposes secondary education ceased in the country although rural schools remained open with some form of teaching. The ranks of teachers were thinned as the Japanese either killed or imprisoned what they called 'dangerous elements' among them; North Borneo lost a fearful number of teachers—and local civil servants—through indiscriminate executions. In the schools which functioned, the Japanese language replaced English on the syllabus. Public health measures almost ceased, too, and malaria once again became a fatal disease as controls disappeared. Hospitals were poorly supplied with drugs after the stores left by the British at the end of the war had been used up. Rice production dropped by one-third and tapioca was grown as an unattractive substitute.

The end result was massive unemployment, an acute shortage of food, and spiralling inflation. There was little the people could buy with the currency which the Japanese printed by the millions and which was scathingly dubbed 'banana dollars'. (At the end of the war Japanese currency in circulation was computed at $4,000 million against a pre-war average circulation of just over $200 million.) Moral standards disintegrated in the fight for survival. But, despite its miseries, the country gave itself solace in the confidence that the war would end in victory for Britain and its allies. Those in the know placed quiet hopes in the ability of guerrilla units inside the jungle to wreak havoc among the Japanese forces when the signal came from the Allies.

When the battle for Singapore began, 'stay-behind' parties of British and Chinese had been dispersing into the jungles for the long-term task of harassing the Japanese. The Chinese were almost all members of the Malayan Communist Party which, until the outbreak of the Japanese war, had been an outlawed organization and a serious menace to the Government. The Party's co-operation with the British in the war was however convenient politics because Japan was a common enemy and Russia was Britain's ally against Germany. It was a temporary truce in a local struggle which had already lasted more than 20 years.

In March 1919 the Russian revolutionists who styled themselves 'The Third Internationale of the Soviet Republic' decided to establish communism throughout the world, if necessary by force. In China, four years later, a Communist Party was formed which 26 years afterwards conquered Nationalist China and emerged as the greatest communist force outside Russia. Singapore and Malaya came into Chinese communist designs in 1924 when agents arrived from Shanghai to infuse Marxism into the overseas Chinese and other races. These agents found the Malays too satisfied with their lot to want 'freedom' and 'liberation' by revolution but groups of southern Chinese proved susceptible to their gospel. The 'Malayan Communist Party' was established in Singapore in April 1930 with the long-term objective of the establishment of a republic in Malaya. Chinese schools and organization of labourers became the communist nurseries and breeding-grounds and, because the mass of communism's supporters came from the lower working class, the British Government appeared sceptical of the Party's power and indeed of its connection with Chinese Communist headquarters in Shanghai. Mr. R. H. de S. Onraet, Inspector-General of Police, who spent half his career in Singapore and Malaya fighting the communists, wrote later, 'Those in high places judged the potential menace of revolutionary communism not by the brains that organised the movement but by the poor quality of the coolie masses used to implement it.' But then the potential force of communism was hardly recognized anywhere else in the world.

The police Special Branches of the island and the peninsula waged a relentless campaign against the Party as it promoted strikes and labour troubles on rubber estates and in all other industries. The communists were all but successful in their trials of strength in the mid-thirties; in 1937 the Inspector-General of Police in the Federated Malay States admitted in a report, 'The Federated Malay States passed through the most serious crisis of its history. It was within an ace of dissolving into temporary chaos as a result of communist intrigue.' The Japanese war against China gave the Party an impetus and it shrewdly set into motion 'anti-Japanese' movements under the cloak of patriotism. Then when Russia signed its Non-Aggression Pact with Germany in August 1939, the Party launched a violent anti-British campaign. Its known membership by that time was about 37,000, at least half of which was in Singapore. The possibility of Russia entering World War II on the side of Germany gave the Party further incentive for arranging waves of strikes which all but brought the vital production of rubber and tin to a standstill.

Although the German attack on Russia in June 1941 threw the Party into confusion, it obeyed a Moscow order to co-operate with Britain. The Party ceased calling strikes and fomenting labour troubles. A few days after the Japanese attack on Malaya, the Secretary-General of the Party sent a message to the Government offering unconditional co-operation against the common enemy. The nettle was unwillingly grasped; the Government could not do otherwise in view of the new relationship between Britain and Russia. It accepted the Party's offer to use its members as a resistance force behind the Japanese lines. About 200 communists were trained at a secret training school which had been set up in Singapore early in 1941 to train British and Asian troops and civilians in guerrilla warfare in Far Eastern countries in the event of war with Japan. However, the speed of the Japanese race down the peninsula prevented the 'stay behind' units from being satisfactorily equipped with explosives and with wireless transmitters for communication with Allied Headquarters—wherever it was to be.

During the occupation, the communist guerrillas called themselves the 'Malayan Peoples' Anti-Japanese Army'. They grew in strength as hundreds of young Chinese rubber tappers, miners, vegetable gardeners, woodcutters, barbers, shop assistants and house servants joined them in order to fight the Japanese. Hundreds of thousands of Chinese in the towns and villages willingly supplied the guerrillas with food, medicines and other supplies and also spied on the Japanese. The M.P.A.J.A. units were never a serious menace to the Japanese—they were too ill-equipped—but they had considerable nuisance value; they attacked small Japanese units and kidnapped and executed Japanese supporters and informers.

News from the outside world indicated that in Europe the tide was turning against the Germans and that Japan had been pushed on to the defensive. In 1943 the executive of the Malayan Communist Party, confident now that the war would end in favour of the Allies, drew up plans for establishing a Soviet republic in Malaya immediately after Japan's defeat. The ready-made M.P.A.J.A. would become the 'national army of liberation'. A Party order instructed commanders to expand their units and prepare them for the 'liberation' of the 'oppressed' people of Malaya by 'direct action' against the British at the end of the Japanese war.

From May 1943 a considerable number of Allied guerrillas were parachuted into Malaya or landed by submarine from India and

Ceylon in preparation for an Allied invasion. With them came supplies of the latest weapons. They joined Chinese guerrilla units, trained them in the art of ambush, attack and jungle warfare, and equipped them with weapons. Once again the Communist executive must have felt that they were being favoured by some Marxist destiny because into their hands were coming badly-wanted arms and ammunition for the revolt they planned. After large canisters of arms and ammunition had been parachuted into Malaya by Allied aircraft, Chinese guerrilla recovery teams invariably reported a number 'lost'; the contents of these were concealed in secret dumps. By the beginning of August 1945, the M.P.A.J.A. was believed to be about 7,000 strong.

On 6th August 1945 the Americans dropped an atomic bomb on Hiroshima in Japan, and three days later another on Nagasaki. On 14th August Japan suddenly surrendered. A great armada of allied warcraft which had been assembled in Indian waters for the invasion of Malaya, set sail, but now on a mission of liberation. It was therefore some time before Allied troops could be deployed to all parts of the country. During this period, the troops of the M.P.A.J.A., wearing British uniforms, emerged from their jungle camps and accepted tribute as the 'glorious anti-Japanese Army'. They took control of villages and towns. They raised their three-starred flags and terrorized the people. When officers of the British Military Administration eventually arrived they had to use considerable firmness in many regions before they could install themselves as the real authority.

Only the presence of three divisions of Allied troops stopped the Malayan Communist Party from launching an immediate revolt against the British. Outwardly the Communist executive accepted the British order for the disbandment of the M.P.A.J.A. Also to orders, they returned every weapon that had been registered as having been given to their troops; they said nothing of course about either an armed secret force waiting in the jungle camps under orders or about their caches or weapons. The Party formed an 'M.P.A.J.A. Ex-Services Comrades' Association' with branches in every town and village and all demobilized guerrillas were instructed to become members so that they were not lost sight of. The association's funds were used to feed, clothe and maintain the secret force which at the end of 1945 was believed to number about 4,000.

As Russia was still a friendly nation, the British Military Administration and later the civil government had to permit the Malayan Communist Party to function as a political organization—in spite of available evidence that it intended to try to create a Soviet republic in the country. A contingent of ex-guerrillas readily travelled to London to participate in the great Victory parade. The communist tiger was content to play for a while at being friends with the British bulldog.

CHAPTER 16

Liberation Brings Political Development

Malaya and Singapore were fortunate. The Japanese surrender meant they had escaped the considerable devastation they would have suffered had the Allies had to reconquer them by force as they had Burma and the Borneo territories. The recapture of the latter began in June 1945 when Allied forces landed in North Borneo and Brunei. Jesselton, the capital of North Borneo, and other towns were flattened. In Brunei the withdrawing Japanese set fire to the oilfields at Seria. In both countries they also carried out last-minute executions of people imprisoned for suspected activities against them. . . .

For Malaya and Singapore the peace that followed the surrender was to prove very much an uneasy peace. The tranquillity of the pre-war years was a thing of the past, a moment in history. The people—and those in Sarawak, Brunei and North Borneo—suffered the difficulties of physical and moral rehabilitation against a background of food shortages, universal malnutrition, the neglect of nearly four years, labour unrest and unemployment. Almost primitive living standards prevailed in the rural districts. The exhilaration, exuberance and joy with which Malayans had welcomed Britain back in September 1945, had been a sincere tribute to the strength of old relationships and old friendships and not just a floodtide of reaction and relief that the Japanese occupation had ended. Something different, however, had intruded. While respect for him still remained, the European had lost his prestige because of his military failures in Malaya and around South-East Asia and because of his public degradation as a prisoner-of-war.

In Malaya, the police under the influence and example of the Japanese had indulged in barbarities and succumbed to corruption, and were now a demoralized force, frightened of reprisals and con-

162

sequently unnerved by fear. It was inefficient and very much under strength. Consequently the country became gripped by unparalleled violent crime. Armed robbery and murder were common as young unemployed men used the weapons and ammunition they had acquired from dumps lying scattered all over the country after the Japanese surrender. In certain parts of the country blood feuds occurred between Malays and Chinese as 'reprisals' for collaboration with the Japanese during the occupation. In some places, the Malays were the aggressors, in others the Chinese, and many people lost their lives. Fortunately, these racial passions blazed in isolated areas and were extinguished before they got out of hand and engulfed more people. But the pre-war racial harmony had disappeared.

As the Government and industries struggled to restore services and production, labour, influenced by the Malayan Communist Party, called strikes which aggravated the difficulties still further. 'Caught in a maelstrom' was an understatement if applied to Malaya and Singapore in the long months that followed the end of the war.

There was hardly peace, either, on the political front. In the declining months of the Japanese occupation, the seeds of political consciousness had been planted in the minds of young Malays. The banner of nationalism was waving lustily and aggressively in the Dutch East Indies and in French Indo-China. The intense nationalistic currents that flowed through Java and Sumatra were felt in Malaya. Indonesian politicians of two categories—the sincere and the dangerous opportunists—crossed into Malaya surreptitiously during the last months of the Japanese occupation to sound Malay leaders about establishing after the war a Malay republic consisting of Sumatra, Java, Malaya, the whole of Borneo and the other islands in the archipelago. Among those to whom the Indonesians talked was Onn bin Ja'afar, member of a leading Malay family in Johore, who was destined after the war to become the national leader of Malaya's Malays. Onn listened but made no promise nor gave any encouragement to his visitors. Privately, and as a Malay nationalist himself, he envisaged nothing but trouble, if not disaster, for Malaya if it became part of a gigantic Indonesian republic. But young Malays of Indonesian stock were swept into fervour and formed the Malay Nationalist Party. They found little support among Malays who declined to be associated with any Indonesian-inspired movement. *Merdeka* (freedom) was not yet in Malay thoughts; if it had been they would probably have preferred *merdeka* by evolution and not by revolution.

In Kedah, other young Malays, in whom *merdeka* struck a receptive chord, formed the *Saberkas* (Unity) Party, socialistic in theory but extremist in ideas. They wanted outright opposition, even violence, against the British Government upon its return. *Saberkas* had as its patron a scion of the ruling Kedah house, a young prince named Tunku Abdul Rahman, whose own personal concern at the time however was not the overthrow of the British Government but a matter of greater import to him, the establishment of a 'more democratic' form of government in Kedah, one in which the British Adviser and British civil servants would not wield as much 'authority' as they had done before the war. Thus destiny touched two men at extreme points in Malaya for the commanding roles they were each to play in the next decades of Malayan history—Onn bin Ja'afar in Johore Bahru in the south, and Tunku Abdul Rahman in Alor Star in the north. The latter was to take over the mantle of national leadership from the former at a critical stage in Malay politics and in a rapid five years to lead the country to independence.

In October 1945, the British Government announced a bold decision to end indirect rule in the peninsula by uniting the States into a 'Malayan Union' under a Governor with full executive powers. It proposed also to institute a Malayan form of citizenship which would give equal citizenship rights to 'those who can claim Malaya to be their homeland'. Penang and Malacca although forming parts of the proposed union would remain British settlements.

Singapore was to remain a separate colony, a decision which met with considerable criticism because its economy was so much bound up with that of the States in the peninsula with which it also shared many common problems. The separation was perhaps a reflection of Singapore's importance in post-war British strategy in the Far East and also of the different problems and outlooks created by its predominantly Chinese population. The Government considered that the Malay States, with their predominantly Malay population, would have a better chance of political development on their own and if Singapore was, at the outset, a separate administrative unit. It was, however, made clear that the door for Singapore's eventual union with the new federation lay open; the British Government declared in a White Paper that it was 'no part of the policy of His Majesty's Government to preclude or prejudice in any way the fusion of Singapore and the Malayan Union in a wider union at a later date should it be considered that such a course was desirable'.

The Malayan Union and Singapore would therefore have separate governors and their individual Executive and Legislative Councils, while a Governor-General, based in Singapore, would co-ordinate policy not only in the two territories but also in Sarawak and North Borneo although he would have no executive powers. (Did this presage thoughts of an eventual grand union of all these territories?)

In the Malayan Union, the rulers as 'traditional and spiritual leaders of the Malay people' would each in his State preside over a a Malay Advisory Council which would mainly be concerned with religious matters. They would also be members of a Central Advisory Council under the chairmanship of the Governor which would review legislation affecting the Muslim religion and also discuss other subjects 'at the Governor's discretion'. Finally, the proposals envisaged the British Crown as providing the common link to draw all the communities together. To make it possible to put these proposals into effect, the rulers would be asked to sign new treaties which would give the British Crown jurisdiction in their States.

The idea behind the 'Malayan Union' was sound—indeed it was the genesis of the future federation—but the Malays saw the proposals as converting the protected Malay States into colonies by terminating the autonomy of the rulers and relegating them to the positions of exalted religious advisers. Much more serious to them were the citizenship proposals, which they saw as threats to their special position, which had been protected and guarded for decades under the existing treaties. Citizenship would become easily available to all non-Malays who could claim to belong to the country through birth or domicile for 10 years out of the previous 15. It could also be acquired after five years' continuous residence. To the Malays, these simple qualifications would give the Chinese unwarranted political power.

These constitutional proposals actually represented a complete change of policy by the British Government. The Malay States had never been British territory; the peninsula may have been marked red on the map of the 'British Empire' but Britain had always meticulously described the States as protectorates. The positions and authority of the rulers had never been questioned, and indeed their prestige had been built up by the British. Basically 'Malayan Union' may have been intended to make government less complicated but the decision to impose it (for that was what it was) without local consultations—followed later by the methods adopted for gaining the 'agreement' of the rulers—alienated the Malays, who came very close to revolting against the British.

The day after the Government's announcement, Sir Harold MacMichael arrived in Kuala Lumpur to 'negotiate' the new treaties with the rulers. He expressed the view that these would take two to six months but he was in Malaya less than two months. Within a fortnight, however, every ruler had abdicated his sovereign rights and powers to the British Crown. They later claimed that they had signed the new treaty under protest or under duress. Every ruler claimed to have questioned MacMichael over the need for haste and to have asserted that he needed time to consult his advisers and chiefs as he was bound to do by custom and tradition. MacMichael was alleged to have used varying forms of persuasion to get the rulers' signatures. Some evidence of this emerged in the House of Commons a few weeks later when, during a vigorous debate on the Malayan Union proposals, a member read extracts from personal letters written by rulers who had taken the unprecedented royal step of publicizing their strong feelings. Sultan Abdul Aziz of Perak, a man of wisdom, learning, and great loyalty to Britain, wrote: 'One cannot help regretting the necessity for extreme speed in deciding the destiny of a nation when a little delay would have been conducive to wiser counsel. I signed because I was caught in an atmosphere of haste and because I was engrossed in my unshaken loyalty to the British Crown, with full confidence that my rights and the rights of my people would not be disturbed. It cannot be said I have agreed to the serious implications in the proposed Malayan Union.' Sultan Badlishah of Kedah, who had read economics at Wadham College, Oxford, wrote: 'I was presented with a verbal ultimatum with a time limit, and in the event of refusing to sign what I call the instrument of surrender, my successor who would sign would be appointed. Members of the State Council were compelled to sign, undertaking they would advise me to sign. I was told the matter was personal and confidential, and I was not allowed to tell my people what had taken place.'

MacMichael, in a report which was made public, claimed that only in Negri Sembilan and Kedah had he been conscious of any preliminary undercurrent of antagonism to the proposals and that 'with these qualifications it may fairly be said that every ruler and every responsible councillor left me with the impression that he was genuinely convinced that the new policy was a wise and just one, calculated to serve the long-term interests of the country as a whole'. But there appeared to be no answer to the Malay contentions that the people themselves had not been consulted before the rulers signed away the States.

Malays throughout the country raised their voices in protest. They reacted in what one observer correctly described as 'an uncharacteristically aggressive manner'. Political parties and associations blossomed in order to 'fight' the Malayan Union proposals which were to come into effect on 1st April 1946, when civil government was to be restored. The British Government never appeared to appreciate fully or accept local reports about the intense feelings of the Malays and of the lengths to which they were prepared to go to restore constitutional rights to their rulers and to recover their own birthright— and to survive politically in their own country. Onn bin Ja'afar, whose father and grandfather had been *Mentri Besar* (Prime Minister) of Johore (and who was destined in two years' time to become the third member of his family to hold that distinguished office), formed the 'National Movement of Peninsular Malays'. It gathered a quick membership which reached 110,000 in Johore alone. Inspired by the response, he publicly suggested the amalgamation of all Malay political associations into a 'United Malays' Organization' which would give Malays considerable political strength. On 1st March 1946, representatives from 41 Malay associations formed not the 'United Malays' Organization' but more significantly the 'United Malays' National Organization'; the emphasis was on the nationalistic nature of the association. Onn was elected first president which made him the acknowledged leader of over 2,000,000 Malays; at that time the Malays could be said to have been more united over a single purpose than they were ever to be afterwards.

That meeting of Malay associations provided the spearhead for deep and spreading Malay opposition to the Malayan Union. This Malay unity was a new force to the British—and also to the Chinese —and its granite-like quality also made a pronounced impression on the Malay rulers who were witnessing the spectacle of their subjects taking action to control their own destinies. The U.M.N.O. passed a resolution declaring that the agreements signed by the Sultans had not been executed in accordance with the constitution, traditions, customs and usages of their respective states and were therefore 'null and void'; that, executed without the knowledge of the Sultan's subjects, they were 'contrary to democratic principles; that they amounted to outright annexation; and that by ending the existence of the nine sovereign Malay States they 'violated the principle of the sanctity of treaties'.

However the Malayan Union inexorably came into being on the due date. The peninsula and Singapore, which for so many years had been a single political unit, were separated. A Governor was installed in Singapore where also Mr. Malcolm MacDonald, a son of a former British Prime Minister, Mr. Ramsay MacDonald, took up his appointment as Governor-General. In the Malayan Union, the Governor, Sir Edward Gent, of the Colonial Office, who was taking up his first overseas appointment, was ceremonially installed before a half-empty Legislative Council chamber. None of the Malay rulers was present, nor were any Malays who had been nominated as members of the Council. The rulers had actually arrived in Kuala Lumpur for Gent's installation but they had received a message from Onn saying that it was 'the desire' of 'your peoples' that they should not attend. They obeyed for they sensed the power and the mood of the Malays. The U.M.N.O. had called a boycott of the administration (which was to last until the Malayan Union was revoked two years later) by ordering Malays not to serve on any council or committee formed by the Government.

Proud and dignified, the Malays waited for the first move by the British Government. It eventually came in the form of an invitation to the rulers and Onn to present counter-proposals for the future of their country. On 2nd May the rulers met Gent for what was officially described as an 'informal' and a 'friendly' discussion on a possible new constitution. Later that month two British Members of Parliament, Captain L. D. Gammans (Conservative) and Lieutenant-Colonel D. R. Rees-Williams (Labour), arrived on a mission to ascertain the views of the rulers and the people. Both men had worked in Malaya before the war, Gammans in the Co-operative Department before he resigned to enter politics in Britain, and Rees-Williams as a lawyer in Penang. (He is now Lord Ogmore.) Gammans and Rees-Williams toured the country talking to Malays and other races. They eventually arrived in Kuala Kangsar, the capital and royal town of Perak, to meet the rulers and Onn and the Executive Committee of the U.M.N.O.

The Malays had staged 'protest rallies' in every town and village which the two M.P.s had visited but they kept the full force of their demonstrations and feelings for Kuala Kangsar. Past Gammans and Rees-Williams and the rulers moved a mile-long procession of Malay men and women who carried banners calling for the 'death' of the Malayan Union and the abrogation of the MacMichael treaties, and shouted the battle-cry of the day—'*Hidup Melayu*' (Long live the Malays). Perhaps the most significant feature was the dominant, challenging, vehement part played by Malay women who had left their ricefields, kitchens and children to participate in this demonstration. At their head walked the wife of the Sultan of Perak—an unprecedented role for a ruler's wife. All this made an impact on Gammans and Rees-Williams. Their first meeting afterwards with the rulers was, as expected, a difficult one and it said much for their efforts to restore the friendliest possible relations that the atmosphere at the second and final three-hour-long meeting was very much more relaxed. Gammans and Rees-Williams returned to London with proposals from the rulers and the U.M.N.O. which they were sure, if accepted, would lead to the restoration of the *status quo ante* between Malaya and Britain.

On 1st June Mr. MacDonald arrived in Kuala Lumpur. The following day he attended a conference of rulers and of delegations from the Government and the U.M.N.O., to discuss the Malay proposals which had received the consideration of the British Government. The meeting created optimism that a solution would be found to the impasse. The initial broad agreements reached were disclosed on 4th July—that a 'federation' of the nine Malay States and two Settlements would replace the Union and that a 'High Commissioner' would be the Crown's representative and not a governor. On 25th July, it was announced that a working committee of six Malays and five British officials under the chairmanship of Mr. MacDonald would consider the details of a proposed new agreement that would be signed by Britain and the rulers, and that citizenship would be one subject to be examined.

Four months later, the committee produced its recommendations and also a draft agreement for revoking the Malayan Union and creating a federation with clearly defined powers. Both the British Government and the rulers had conditionally approved the committee's report and recommendations and the draft agreement subject to views expressed by all other interested communities. A consultative committee, composed mainly of men of influence and standing among the non-Malay communities, was formed to receive the reactions of the non-Malay communities to the new proposals and to make its recommendations. As a result, modifications were made in the draft proposals with the agreement of the rulers and the U.M.N.O.

In July 1947 a White Paper detailing the proposed constitution for a federation was published. Under it the rulers were to be reinvested with their powers, prerogatives and privileges. The States and Settlements would retain their autonomy over matters of regional concern but they would be united under a strong central government to which they surrendered certain major functions and whose authority was clearly defined. Penang and Malacca would remain British territory. A High Commissioner would replace the Governor; his Executive Council would be composed of members chosen from the various races. The Legislative Council would consist of 15 official members and 61 non-officials nominated by the High Commissioner. It would be the first legislature on which every State and Settlement was to be represented, and here the two points of major political significance were that the Malay unofficial members would have a majority of one over those of other races and—a reflection of the changing times—the European representatives of trade, commerce and the rubber and mining industries would no longer wield the considerable influence they had in the pre-war councils.

The rulers would retain reserve powers of fundamental importance which they would use in a Conference of Rulers which would meet from time to time. For instance, no legislation making changes in the constitution could be introduced without the consent of the Conference of Rulers who also had to be consulted about proposed changes in immigration policy. Incorporated in a new treaty which each ruler would sign with Britain would be the old understanding that they would accept British advice in all matters save those of Malay religion and custom. This apparently was a mere formality considered necessary to enable the British Government to resume its role as the protecting power. There was also emphasis on the point that the Malays would have special rights and privileges in the Federation.

The rules covering citizenship were tightened, although not as much as the Malays would have wished them to be. A common federal citizenship was to be established over and above state citizenships. Apart from Malays, only second-generation Chinese, Indians and other races would automatically qualify for federal citizenship. Immigrants could obtain papers on proof of 15 years' continuous residence out of the previous 25 in the Federation and on passing a 'simple' Malay language test. The consensus of opinion was that the rules would make a Chinese political majority impossible for many years. But the rules allowed opportunities for non-Malays to make Malaya their home. Finally, the proposed 'Federation of Malaya Agreement'—which the rulers later signed—pledged the 'early introduction of elections' with self-government as the goal.

Chinese and Indians erupted into bitter hostility over the new qualifications for citizenship. However, throughout the negotiations for the new agreement, the Chinese community had remained strangely quiet; and one observer of the Chinese scene in Malaya was to write later that 'this was an omission for which the Chinese leaders have since expressed regret'. Citizenship—and Malay privileges—became the whetstones on which the Chinese particularly were to grind their racial dissatisfactions for some years to come.

The Federation of Malaya came into being on 1st February 1948. That day the Malays ended their boycott of the government. In Kuala Lumpur, the rulers and Malay members of the Executive and Legislative Councils, full of pride and self-satisfaction, watched Sir Edward Gent being formally installed as 'High Commissioner'. The cleavage between Britain and the Malays no longer existed, but it was to be some time before Malay trust was restored too. How much real harm had been created by the 'Malayan Union'? Properly the comment should come from a Malayan source and the Government of the independent State of Malaya declared in 1961, in its first official year book, 'In the event little damage was done.' Significantly, although the opportunity had been given during the discussions over the future constitution of the peninsula to reconsider the question of union with Singapore, the point was never taken. . . .

With the new Federation came written constitutions for every Malay State. Perlis, Kedah, Perak, Selangor, Pahang, Kelantan and Negri Sembilan were thus given their first-ever constitutions. (Johore and Trengganu already possessed these but supplements brought them into conformity with the other States.) The Malay rulers became constitutional monarchs and the succession to each Malay throne and the royal prerogatives were defined in writing—where for so many of them it had existed only in *adat* (custom). The executive head of each State was the *Mentri Besar* (Chief Minister) appointed by the ruler. Kedah, Perlis, Perak, Selangor, Pahang and Negri Sembilan made fresh history for themselves for they had never had such an official before.

A British Adviser was attached to each State (the 'British Resident' disappeared) and his functions were severely confined to advising. In the new spirit of the times, the inevitable happened during the first few months of the Federation—most of the State Governments sought no advice from the patiently-waiting British Adviser who received no State papers for comment, or even for information. . . . But this proved a passing phase.

The Federation and State Agreements were the foundations on which Malaya was to become independent and upon which Malaysia was also built.

The Federation had hardly had time to settle down before it was plunged into mortal combat with the Malayan communists. Any thoughts of a measured tread towards elections and eventual self-government were swept away as desperate defensive measures had to be taken to frustrate the determination of the Malayan Communist Party to establish a 'People's Republic'. Officially the communist revolt was called an 'Emergency', but this 'emergency' was to last 12 years.

CHAPTER 17

War Against Communists

The Malayan Communist Party's fateful decision to embark on murder, arson and terrorism in Malaya had probably developed from a conference of Asian and Australian communists in Calcutta. There Russia disclosed its plans for violent communist action in South-East Asian countries. Western experts in communist affairs believe that from this conference stemmed the communist revolts that occurred in Burma and the Philippines and the fiery militancy of the communists in India and in Indonesia. In Malaya, the number of strikes, armed robberies, and murders rose alarmingly. Instigated by the Malayan Communist Party, intimidation and terror on plantations and tin mines became widespread. The Government seemed disinclined to take firm measures against the Malayan Communist Party without the necessary authority from Whitehall.

In spite of the fact that the Commissioner of Police admitted that the organizations 'were prepared to go to extreme lengths', Sir Edward Gent described the situation as 'a war of nerves' by 'forces of disorder'. Five days later, however, Mr. Malcolm MacDonald said in a broadcast that the communists were 'making a desperate effort to impose the rule of the knife and the gun in plantations, mines and factories,' and that, as a consequence of communist reverses in Europe, an offensive in Asia might be expected.

The murders continued as the days moved on. Gurkha troops were sent into Johore to help the police on troubled rubber estates. Finally, on 16th June the murder of three British and two Chinese planters forced a decision on Sir Edward Gent. That afternoon he declared an 'Emergency' to exist in certain districts of Perak and Johore, the two States worst afflicted by terrorism. About a fortnight later Gent was recalled to London ostensibly for consultations. Four days later he was killed when his aircraft collided with another over London. It was not until September that the British Government announced the name of his successor, Sir Henry Lovell Goldsworthy Gurney, aged 50, former Chief Secretary of the Palestine Government.

On 12th July the Officer Administering the Government, Sir Alec Newboult, issued a proclamation declaring a 'state of emergency' to exist everywhere in the Federation. The Malayan Communist Party and its front organizations were banned—but by this time, every important communist had escaped to pre-arranged camps in the jungle. The British Army accepted a request to assist the civil power and to issue weapons and ammunition to the ill-equipped police. In the House of Commons, the Government conceded that Malaya was faced with an armed revolt which aimed at terminating British rule in Malaya and substituting a Soviet government. In due course military operations reached a scale never anticipated; at one time there were no fewer than 25 battalions of Malayan, British, Australian, New Zealand, Fijian and East African troops, 67,000 police, and 350,000 Home Guards engaged against the communist armed forces, which at their peak were believed never to have been higher than 10,000 at any one time, although for at least six or seven years their casualties were replaced by willing recruits from the towns and villages.

The communist force which had been kept in trim in secret in the jungle since 1945 emerged as 'The Malayan Peoples' Anti-British Army'; later it was renamed 'The Malayan Races' Liberation Army' (M.R.L.A.) when the Party claimed that the revolt had switched to a 'struggle against colonialism'. However even this failed to influence 'the masses' who were clearly against evolution through terrorism which was aimed principally at them. As the weeks passed the pattern of the communist strategy became clear. They attempted to paralyse the rubber and tin industries by attacking estates and mines in great strength, sometimes using up to 300 men. They planned to create so much chaos that the Government would be forced to admit defeat.

The communists had all the advantages of surprise, initiative and strength they desired for successful assaults on estates, mines, villages and police stations, and these they exploited to the full. Fortunately the estates and mines stood firm, however unprepared they were when they took the first severe blows. In a belated tribute expressed some years afterwards, the Government admitted, 'If it had not been for the indomitable determination of planters and miners to stand

174

fast during the early months of the Emergency and the loyal support they received from their staff and labourers, large areas of the country might have fallen under communist control and so made possible the establishment of small communist republics—one of the terrorists' declared aims.' The destruction of the Malayan economy remained the major communist aim until 1951, when the tactics switched to appeasement of the population in the hope of winning them over to a 'united front' against the Government—but by then it was too late.

At the beginning of the Emergency the communist terrorists were believed to number not more than 5,000, almost all of them Chinese, and were organized into 'regiments', companies, platoons and sections. They had all the weapons and ammunition necessary for quick hit-and-run attacks on villages, police stations, estates and mines. They operated from extensive camps strategically sited in jungle and well away from beaten tracks; many of these had obviously been constructed between 1946 and 1948. They were well screened from the air, had defences in depth (the first line of sentry posts stood more than a quarter of a mile out) and escape routes, a parade ground, an administrative office, separate huts for officers, and kitchens and latrines. Some camps could accommodate 600 men; a great number had room for 300. Political education was a predominant feature in the camps in the first three years, before the Government's security forces, at last suitably girded for offence, began moving into the jungle. Then camp life became insecure, and later impossible.

A most valuable arm of the M.R.L.A. was the *Min Yuen*, the supply organization formed of men and women in towns and villages and in the isolated settlements of vegetable gardeners generally called 'squatters', who collected clothes, medicines, and recruits, and also spied on the army and police. This corps covered the whole country; its numbers were once computed to be about half-a-million but this was a very conservative estimate for the *Min Yuen* drew its willing, and unwilling, members from the rich down to the squatter on the jungle fringe.

The people in the smaller towns and in the villages away from the main roads lived abnormal lives in which fear predominated and liberty was restricted. Rubber estates and tin mines, factories, police stations, and the homes of planters and tin miners and those of their staffs, became armed camps surrounded by high wire fences and barbed-wire entanglements. At night spotlights beamed outwards.

European planters and miners slept with revolvers under their pillows, carbines within reach, and grenades ready on tables in the lounge. They drove to and from work in motor-cars and trucks which were converted into armoured vehicles; they were invariably accompanied by heavily-armed escorts. Travellers risked ambushes on the winding roads every curve of which provided the terrorists with excellent points for attacks on motor-cars, buses, food-carrying trucks, and military and police vehicles. Literally no stretch of road in the country could be guaranteed safe from ambush. The trains, too, were targets and derailments became a hazard along isolated sections of line where terrorists could move lengths of track without fear of interruption.

Slowly, however, the industries built up their static defence corps through a Special Constabulary formed mostly of raw countrymen from the *kampong* (and, also ne'er-do-wells from the towns). The police, so much under strength for the grim role thrust upon it, was reinforced by several hundred British sergeants demobilized from Palestine where Britain had given up its sovereignty, and was also expanded; but for too long a time it was without proper equipment. In Britain, the Government approved the further despatch of more and more troops to Malaya. The Royal Air Force was augmented for reconnoitring over the jungle and bombing camps. The Navy patrolled the coasts in case communist reinforcements were landed on isolated beaches or attempts made to smuggle in arms and ammunition. Slowly Britain fastened on Malaya's armour, but it was not until 1953 that a great fighting machine swung from the defensive to the offensive and took the fight into the deep jungle camps of the terrorists.

The Government equipped itself with wide-ranging powers over life generally and the liberty of the individual. The police could detain suspects for periods up to two years without trial (although every detainee had a right to have his detention reviewed by a High Court judge assisted by a panel of local assessors), control the movement of traffic and food along the roads and on the railway, impose 24-hour curfews, and search without warrants. A much-criticized measure enabled the Government to fling into detention the residents of an entire village, area or district on merely satisfactory evidence of aiding, abetting or consorting with the terrorists. Inevitably innocent people suffered as communities were moved into detention camps but, after 1950, the Government never used this form of punishment.

176

Sir Henry Gurney took over the reins of government in September 1948. Malayan history is certain to describe him as a visionary. From the very beginning he asserted that the communists could only be successfully fought if there was to be parallel political and economic advancement for the people. Pure police and military action would never defeat the communists; the people had to be convinced that democracy was better than communism. There was, of course, little hope then of political reforms or developments in the social and economic fields. It was far more crucial to keep the terrorists at bay.

It was also obvious that the war had to be prosecuted by men versed in war and not by civil administrators. In March 1950, Lieutenant-General Sir Harold Briggs, a veteran of the Western Desert and of Burma where he had commanded the famous Fifth Indian Division during the Japanese war, arrived to be 'Director of Operations' under Gurney. A most fortuitous combination of talent developed, for between them Gurney and Briggs laid the foundation for eventual victory and political progress that came much sooner than anyone expected.

Gurney sought ways and means to commit the people to the side of the Government and his most important move in this direction was constitutional advance—the introduction of a 'Member' system of government—on 9th April 1951. Political and community leaders who were in the Executive Council were given ministerial status (and called 'Member') and entrusted with the executive control of certain government departments. While they were responsible to the High Commissioner, they were answerable also to the people through the nominated representatives in the Legislative Council for the manner in which their departments were administered. The Executive Council henceforth functioned as an embryonic Cabinet, as it were. So the Government began its initiation into political control and Malayans received their first taste of the running of government.

Within a fortnight of arriving in Kuala Lumpur, Briggs issued what turned out to be the master-plan for the defeat of the communists. Simple and direct, it meant in essence, 'Protect the populated areas, cut the enemy lines of communication, prevent food and other supplies getting to him and force him out to battle.' The army would be the striking force and the police would protect villages in 'bad areas' (dominated by terrorists) and bring confidence back to the people. Briggs formed a Federal War Council consisting of the top Government, police, army and air force officers to plan general war policy. 'War Executive Committees' were established at State and District levels to co-ordinate operational plans within their boundaries and to build up local intelligence about communist units and supporters. Joint police-army 'operations rooms' were established in every administrative district.

Finally, there was the master-stroke, the resettlement of all Chinese squatters and Malays living beyond government protection on the jungle fringes where they had been under the domination of local terrorists. Moving them away would deprive the terrorists of a vital source of supplies and information. But resettlement meant transferring more than half-a-million people into newly set-up villages— and it became one of the most significant social experiments carried out by any government in the free world. It posed enormous physical, and financial, problems. Questions of economy, road links and security governed the choice of sites for the 'New Villages'. When resettlement began on a large scale in 1951, the haste to get the squatters away from the communist zones of influence gave no time for town-planning in the New Villages. Slums developed, security was poor, and the reactions of the unhappy villagers were intensely anti-Government; local authorities were forced to carry out 're-resettlement'. Fortunately, there were very few such failures.

Into each New Village whenever possible went a Chinese-speaking British administrative officer who was later replaced by trained Chinese officers. These Britons and Chinese were the first of the new type of administrative pioneers in the Malaya of the second half of the twentieth century. They led lonely, dangerous lives for many of them lived among people who were apparently exemplary villagers by day but either terrorists or communist supporters by night. They had not only to win the confidence of the villagers but also to persuade them that democracy was preferable to communism. Quite a number were murdered.

The communists did everything possible to wreck the process of resettlement. They attacked villages in order to frighten the inhabitants and killed selected residents. The terrorists were forced to try to re-establish their food lines. To block these efforts, the Government introduced sweeping regulations controlling the sale and movement of every kind of food, raw and tinned, and of supplies like paper, printing materials, cloth and shoes. Villages and small towns, and labourers' homes in estates and mines, became guarded food larders.

Shopkeepers were forced to keep records of customers and their purchases.

Early in 1949 an important political development had occurred among the Chinese. Their reluctance to side openly with the Government against the communists principally because of insecurity, their failure to demonstrate even moral resistance, brought an unhealthy change in their relations with the other communities, particularly the Malays. Chinese leaders sought desperately for a solution to this serious situation. Gurney understood their dilemma and quietly suggested to their leaders that they should form an organization which would look after their communal interests and also hold out the hand of friendship to the Malays. In February 1949 the 'Malayan Chinese Association' was formed. Its president was Tan Cheng Lock. In his inaugural speech, Tan declared that the M.C.A. looked to the day when the Chinese, Malays and other races would unite 'to make this land one country and one nation'.

The M.C.A. management committee consisted principally of influential and wealthy Chinese, conservative in their political outlook and fervently anxious to knit the community and to close the wide gap between the wealthy and the extensive middle-class Chinese section. The communists immediately vilified the M.C.A. It earmarked its leaders for assassination, and once nearly succeeded in killing Tan Cheng Lock with a hand-grenade thrown into a meeting of the association. The M.C.A. might have welded the Chinese and brought them to co-operation with the Government against the communists sooner than was expected but for Mao Tse-Tung's victory in China in 1949, and the subsequent recognition of the Chinese People's Government by the British Government in January 1950. Perhaps this diplomatic recognition was inevitable but in Malaya it did not help the war against the communists. It had two serious effects: first it gave a tremendous boost to the morale of the Malayan Communist Party, and there was an upsurge of attacks on villages, police stations, estates, mines, trains and transport generally. Secondly, as a government report of the day declared, the Chinese became 'more disposed to insure themselves with the other side, for they feared that if they openly sided with the Government in Malaya their relatives or their property, or both, in China, would suffer at the hands of the Communist Government'. It took more than two years to get many Chinese off the fence and on to the side of democracy. Malaya can perhaps be thankful that the Chinese did not slide down the communist side of the fence; had they done so, the country might have become a communist satellite.

Sir Henry Gurney was assassinated in an ambush on the morning of Saturday, 7th October 1951, as he drove with Lady Gurney from Kuala Lumpur to Fraser's Hill, a resort 60 miles to the north. It was later established that the ambush had not been laid specifically for him; a terrorist group had been waiting on a bank overlooking the road for two days waiting for a suitable target, and the Union Jack which always fluttered from the bonnet of Gurney's car attracted their attention. In his three years as High Commissioner, Gurney had won respect for courage and statesmanship. He had travelled fearlessly through the country to see things for himself; he had identified himself closely with the aspirations of the people. He had devoted his time to expanding the social services, and to encouraging the growth of a responsible trade union movement. He had in effect planted the seeds of a national, rather than a communal, thinking as he introduced schemes for political, social and economic advancement.

Sir Henry's murder released feelings of unsurpassed bitterness against the terrorists, but nothing really positive resulted simply because the tragedy had shattered public morale. Then early in November Briggs left Malaya, tired and critical of his lack of executive power. Towards the end of the month, the Secretary of State for the Colonies, Mr. Oliver Lyttelton (later Lord Chandos), arrived in Malaya to ascertain the situation and heard very forthright talking from British planters and miners and the community leaders, who asked for a ruthless campaign against the terrorists. In January 1952, General Sir Gerald Walter Robert Templer, Commander-in-Chief of Eastern Command in Britain, arrived in Malaya as High Commissioner with 'full and direct responsibility for the Emergency'. He was assisted by a Deputy High Commissioner, Mr. (later Sir) Donald MacGillivray, former Colonial Secretary in Jamaica, who would concentrate on administration. The British Government had broken modern Colonial precedent by placing a soldier in charge of delicate and complex political problems—but Malaya was a country demanding a break with tradition for it was in fact waging two wars: one against the communists and the other against racialism. The multi-racial problem in Malaya was as unprecedented in Colonial history as the communist campaign.

180

CHAPTER 18

The Political Road Resumed

G eneral Templer had a directive which reassured Malaya that the war against the communists would be conducted relentlessly and that terrorism would provide no excuse for delay in political progress. The directive declared categorically that the policy of the British Government was 'that Malaya should in due course become a fully self-governing nation'. Templer's primary task was the restoration of law and order so that the communist 'barrier to progress' might be removed. A main objective on the political front was the welding of a united Malayan nation, the ideal of which did not 'involve sacrifice by any community of its traditions and culture and customs'. It was to be Templer's duty 'to guide the peoples of Malaya towards the attainment of this objective and to promote such political progress in the country as will, without prejudice to the campaign against the terrorists, further our democratic aims for Malaya'.

History will credit Templer with bringing the real turning-point to the challenge presented by the communist terrorists. His was a dynamic leadership. The High Commissionership of Malaya was the toughest job any British administrator had been given in modern history—and Templer was prepared to use his full authority without reference to Whitehall.

His approach was twofold: the first, an intensified military campaign, and the second a parallel battle for what he called 'the hearts and minds of the people' by progressively introducing further political, social and economic programmes which would pave the way to self-government. He began by streamlining the war and administrative machines. Wanting no government with a 'split personality', he merged the Federal War Council with the Executive Council so that there was only one instrument of policy. He told government officers,

'Any idea that the business of normal civil Government and the business of the Emergency are two separate entities must be killed for good and all. The two activities are completely and utterly inter-related.' He told the people that they too were in the front line, for the Emergency was 'a thread that runs through the pattern of all our lives, whether we are employed in the Government, in commerce, in industry, in our own business, or in winning a livelihood from the soil'. He reiterated time and again that the communists had to be defeated first before there could even be talk of self-government and that only through the combined efforts of the security forces and the people could a new 'Malayan way of life' be created.

Templer's priorities were first, improving public morale and keeping the people fully informed of the Government's plans through an increased information service which even reached isolated areas; next, the reorganization of the intelligence services. He brought from Britain experts with fresh minds to carry out all his programmes. For instance, a senior officer of the City of London police had the task of reverting the paramilitary force which the police had become, to plain policemen carrying out their more normal watch-and-ward duties in villages and towns and so regaining the trust of the people.

A research unit studied every conceivable problem concerned with working out new jungle warfare techniques and improving old ones, as the campaign had reached the stage where the terrorists had to be 'winkled out' of the depths of the jungle into which they had withdrawn in accordance with planned strategy. Templer demanded and got military reinforcements; battalions came from Fiji, East Africa, Australia and New Zealand. Bombers and other aircraft also came from Australia and New Zealand, and helicopters were introduced into jungle warfare for the first time in military history, thus setting a pattern for similar future operations. Fortunately Malaya's coffers were in excellent state thanks (paradoxically enough) to the boom that resulted from the Korean War. Templer's plans cost a lot of money, as did the high priority he gave to completing the resettlement of squatters and to providing their villages with excellent social services. At the end of 1953 when resettlement ended, the names of about 300 new villages appeared on the map of Malaya.

Templer also turned his attention to winning over an estimated 10,000 aborigines who were being used by the terrorists for growing food, spying on security forces, and guiding M.R.L.A. units through untracked jungle. Briggs had conceived 'jungle forts' placed strategically amidst the aborigines' tribal and hunting grounds. Templer began to build them and man them with paramilitary police units which were also specially trained in watch-and-ward duties in the jungle. Their main function was to spread a sense of security among the aborigines by frequent patrols through their areas, and so eventually to gain their confidence. It was a very slow progress but in time almost every aboriginal who had been dominated by the terrorists was on the government side. Into this deep jungle battle to win over the aborigines went British troops, particularly the 22nd Special Air Service Regiment which had the very special role of utterly destroying the extensive and complex links the communists had in the jungle. The time was to come too when the Malayan Government formed the *Senoi Praak*, a fighting unit consisting solely of aborigines which operated successfully in the jungles of Kelantan, Perak and Pahang. It was the first aboriginal military unit to be established anywhere in the world; it still exists as a useful arm of the Malayan forces.

The Home Guard, consisting of all races, was given the responsible role of defending their own villages and this enabled army and police units to be released for other vital duties. Handing this responsibility to the Home Guard was considered by many people to be an unjustified risk because of the danger of arms and ammunition finding their way to the terrorists, or because *kampong* and villages would become the special targets of terrorists who wished to fill the gaps in their arsenals. Templer, however, seemed less concerned with the possible risks than with the importance of instilling an offensive spirit into the people and uniting them as defenders of their homes and families. In this—and in other ways such as forming a Federation Regiment as a national multi-racial unit—Templer tried to drive home the point that the Emergency was not a British war but a Malayan peoples' war.

Slowly the reorganized intelligence services built up most detailed dossiers on every communist group in the country. (In the end Malaya could boast of having one of the best-informed Special Branches in the world.) The information formed the basis for new techniques aimed at isolating the terrorists and starving them out. Into a selected operational area went army and police units, intelligence agents, psychological warfare groups, and men trained in food control. They began a 'squeeze' which had as its ultimate objects the disruption of communist links, the arrest of supporters, and the disorganization of the groups inside the jungle. The army sought the terrorists' trails and lairs acting almost entirely on information obtained by agents. Artillery and mortars carried out periodic barrages at night on suspected terrorist camping spots; this kept the terrorists on the move and sapped their morale. Meanwhile a rigid watch on food in the villages in the area reduced supplies into the jungle. This combined operation was often continued relentlessly for months. Slowly, but very slowly, the communist casualties grew. Areas which had been operationally cleared of terrorists with the help of their inhabitants were given the accolade of being called 'white areas' and were freed of the irksome Emergency restrictions; the people could live normal lives again. Here again there was the risk of terrorists returning to an area after it had been declared 'white'; but not once was the Government forced to withdraw the privilege because villagers had resumed support.

When Templer left in May 1954 the whole Emergency picture had changed. The security forces were on the initiative, the terrorists were falling further into the jungle where they were growing their own food or getting supplies from aborigines. They had lost many experienced leaders who were irreplaceable. In towns and villages there was new confidence and certainly higher morale. The change had been little short of amazing.

From captured documents it became clear that the Central Committee of the Malayan Communist Party had realized in 1951 that the insurrection had failed in its immediate objectives; in 1952 they had switched from a policy of indiscriminate terrorism to attacks only against the security forces in a new effort to win the peasants and the middle classes over to a 'united front' which would 'drive the imperialists out'. But they found they were too late. . . .

The picture in the political world also had changed in the two years of Templer's régime, and had progressed in a way which no one in 1952 would have thought possible. When Templer left, many towns and villages had elected councils, preparations had begun for holding elections to State and Settlement legislatures, and Malaya as a whole stood on the threshold of its first general elections.

Early in 1950, important but controversial reforms had been launched, principally to get the allegiance of the Chinese by assuring them that they had a future as citizens and also to offset the bitter hostility that was being displayed against them. The Chinese themselves wanted a stake in the land. Doubtless under the compelling influence of Templer, the rulers and their governments (and the U.M.N.O.) agreed to relax the qualifications for citizenship by birth and registration. This enabled about 1·25 million Chinese and 220,000 Indians, to say nothing of about 2·7 million Malays, to qualify as citizens. While the Chinese were partially assuaged, the Malays expressed concern—but it was generally accepted as a necessary step forward in the evolution of a united nation.

Equally controversial was an attempt to introduce a national system of education to supersede the 'Malay', 'Chinese' and 'Indian' primary schools in which children were educated communally and in their own mother-tongues until they moved into secondary schools where English was the medium of instruction. It was argued that unity in a plural society could not develop unless reform began in the schools. In 1954, the Federal Government agreed to the principle of introducing 'national' schools but the policy did not become a reality until after Malaya had become independent. Another break with tradition came when the Civil Service was opened to non-Malays who were federal citizens. Templer, announcing this reform, emphasized the need to retain 'the special position of the Malays' in the Government and that recruiting would conform to a ratio of four Malays to one non-Malay. It was some time however before Chinese and Indians applied for vacancies; the 'quota' system is still a subject which rankles with non-Malays.

Politically, the star of Onn bin Ja'afar was on the wane. His downfall had begun after the middle of 1950 when impulsively, and in spite of warnings from friends and supporters, he proposed opening the membership of U.M.N.O. to other races. The vast majority of Malays were not prepared to move so fast politically. In a calculated test of his popularity, Onn announced his resignation as president of the U.M.N.O. but withdrew it after appeals from influential members of the party. At the annual assembly of the U.N.M.O. in August that year he was re-elected president. At this assembly, it was announced that the party's slogan of '*Hidup Melayu*' (Long live the Malays) would be changed to '*Merdeka*' (Freedom, Independence). Confident about his position in the party, Onn once again declared his belief that the U.M.N.O. had reached the stage when it should be put on a 'full national footing' by offering equal membership, rights, and privileges to all races. He envisaged Malays voting for non-Malays at federal, municipal and local elections. Once again his advisers warned him that any attempt to force through his premature plan would split the Malays. Only a very small minority, they said, was ready to accept the change from a 'Malay' to a 'Malayan' nation.

In the middle of August 1951 Onn impetuously threatened to leave U.M.N.O. and form a non-communal party with which he would achieve independence by 1958. How stood his position with the Malays then? When he resigned before the annual assembly of the Party he received no appeals to reconsider his decision. The majority of the Malays had disowned him. Tunku Abdul Rahman, little-known Kedah prince and civil servant, younger brother of the ruler of Kedah, became the new president of the U.M.N.O. He was then 51 years old, had been out of politics for some years, and was a Deputy Public Prosecutor in the Federal Government. His interest in politics had largely centred upon the Kedah branch of the U.M.N.O. from 1946 until 1948. He had been a moderately able District Officer in the Kedah Civil Service but his assets were his sincerity, a rare princely ability to dissemble, his nationalism (a vital asset at that time), and his sense of leadership. A small coterie of friends had pitchforked him into national politics by putting him forward as a candidate for the U.M.N.O. presidency. In his first presidential speech he scored heavily with a fervently nationalistic approach, 'This is a Malay country. . . . The Malays will decide who the "Malayans" should be.' This remained his theme until the day he realized, as Onn had done long before him, that the British Government would only grant Malaya independence if its races were united. Then he worked hard for unity. But in 1951 Tunku Abdul Rahman was striking the right note for the Malays. The U.M.N.O., which had been split widely by Onn's resignation, closed its ranks behind Tunku Abdul Rahman.

Twenty-one days after the U.M.N.O. Assembly, Onn launched his non-communal 'Independence of Malaya Party' (I.M.P.). To the country there seemed nothing unusual about the fact that Tan Cheng Lock, the president of the communal Malayan Chinese Association, should be on the platform to announce the inauguration of the I.M.P., or that Malays were members of both the U.M.N.O. and I.M.P., or that some members of the M.C.A. were also members of the I.M.P. Inevitably, the U.M.N.O. threatened to expel members who were also in I.M.P. Onn must have been disappointed, however, at the small number of Malays who came across to him from the U.M.N.O. As the months passed he also found he was not receiving promised Chinese support. Bitterly, he reverted to nationalism and began to criticize the Chinese; the I.M.P. lost even its small Chinese support.

As 1952 opened attention focussed on the first elections to 12 seats in the Kuala Lumpur Municipal Council. Onn was supremely confident of the I.M.P. winning the majority of the seats. Certainly the chances of other parties were considered small. One morning, however, the local U.M.N.O. and M.C.A. branches jointly declared their intention to fight the elections as allies and enter 12 Malay and Chinese candidates. They explained, 'Inter-racial harmony is a prerequisite to any successful administration.' The unexpected news of the alliance dumbfounded the political world generally and was a source of consternation to the national leaders of the two parties concerned, neither of whom had either been consulted or informed about it. Tan Cheng Lock was in a dilemma for not only was he president of the M.C.A. but also a founder member of the I.M.P., which was opposing the U.M.N.O. in the elections and would now be opposing an U.M.N.O.-M.C.A. combination; he decided to keep silent. Tunku Abdul Rahman made a cautious comment.

On polling day, 16th February, the alliance won nine seats, and the I.M.P. two, while the twelfth seat went to an independent. The alliance polled a total of 10,330 votes against the I.M.P.s 6,630. The result was as confounding as it was dramatic. Not surprisingly, a rash of local Malay-Chinese alliances developed as other elections were held. By the end of 1952, they had won control in four other town councils. The possibility of racial unity through communal organizations had never been contemplated or envisaged. The alliance was described by the cynics and the political opponents as a 'marriage of convenience' which would end in a 'divorce' because of incompatibility. The 'links' were too tenuous for the political issues that would develop. However the 'Alliance' went on from strength to strength. . . . The U.M.N.O. and M.C.A. formally became the 'Alliance Party' in the early months of 1953.

It was significant that at an assembly of the U.M.N.O. in April 1953 Tunku Abdul Rahman changed his theme-song from Malay nationalism to unity among races. It was his first effort to swing the Malays away from racialism. He pointed out that unity was a salient requirement by the British Government before granting independence, and therefore the Chinese and other communities 'must be offered something more than the status of subject people' if they were to 'feel Malayan'. The assembly passed a resolution which called for federal elections 'in 1954', and included a rider that if the Government rejected this proposal 'all representatives' of the U.M.N.O. and the M.C.A. should resign from the Legislative Council.

Discussions between the British Government and the Malay rulers on possible constitutional changes had opened, and in July 1953 the Government appointed an all-party committee of 46 members of the Legislative Council to examine the practical issues involved in introducing legislation for federal elections. An overwhelming majority of its members were either in I.M.P. or supported its policy of independence by the progressive stages usually advocated by the British Government. The rest of the committee were Alliance members and independents. As expected, the committee's report, issued early in 1954, showed sharp conflicts between the two groups. A majority report signed by 'the I.M.P. group' recommended a Federal Council of 92 members 44 of whom, a minority, would be elected. The 'Alliance Group' wanted a Council of 100 with a majority of 60 elected members, and elections not later than November that year, but its opponents considered it would be impracticable to specify a date because of legislative and administrative arrangements. In this regard, it seemed clear that the Alliance was 'playing politics' for it did not appear to have gone thoroughly into the practical difficulties of arranging elections in the time it had set. Apart from legislation having to be drawn up, considered, and approved, constituencies had to be delineated and voters to be registered. Conservative estimates were that elections could be possible only late in 1955 after allowing State and Settlement elections to be held first.

However, the Alliance remained adamant that the pace of political progress could be hastened. It sent a delegation consisting of Tunku Abdul Rahman and Dato Abdul Razak, deputy president of the U.M.N.O., with Mr. T. H. Tan, executive secretary of the M.C.A., to London to seek British Parliamentary, particularly Labour, and public support for its demand for an elected majority and elections that year. They sought a meeting with the Secretary of State for the Colonies, Mr. Oliver Lyttelton, before he announced his decision on federal elections. On 27th April, within a few days of the delegation's arrival in London, the Colonial Office published a White Paper giving an exchange of despatches on the subjects between Mr. Lyttelton and General Templer. These disclosed an agreement with the rulers that the new Federal Legislative Council should have 52 elected and 46 nominated members (giving an elected majority of six) and that the High Commissioner would fill a reserve group of seven seats with people of his own choice. Elections were promised in the second half of 1955, a little over twelve months' time. The White Paper drew attention to the unusual constitutional procedure of a territory moving at once from a wholly nominated council to one with an elected majority. The British Government appeared to be letting Malaya take a bigger constitutional stride towards self-government principally because its normal pace of political progress had been interrupted by the Emergency. The Alliance could claim to have at least gained a point, that of an elected majority.

In London, Lyttelton eventually agreed to see the Alliance delegation which in the meantime had been warned by Labour politicians that it would be embarrassing for the Colonial Secretary to be forced to meet the Alliance demands, since he could not commit a breach of faith with the Malay rulers on the agreements already reached. Lyttelton told Abdul Rahman that he was not anxious that negotiations should break down on the 'small difference' between the number of 52 elected seats agreed to with the Malay rulers and the 60 demanded by the Alliance. Abdul Rahman argued that a single party could not expect to win more than 80 per cent of the seats and would therefore not have a working majority in the kind of House proposed. Lyttelton's final written reply to the delegation was that there was 'no real difference of substance and very little even of degree' between them and repudiated apprehensions that, unless a three-fifths' elected majority existed, the party in power could not function effectively in government since it could not always be sure of substantial support from non-elected members.

A few days after the delegation's return to Kuala Lumpur, Tunku Abdul Rahman presented Templer with an ultimatum, 'If the authorities insist on the implementation of the White Paper, the Alliance with great regret will have no choice but to withdraw all its members from participation in the Government.' Templer was reported on good authority to have exclaimed, 'Well, the pistol is out.' Seven days later, on 1st June, Templer left Malaya to become Chief of the Imperial General Staff. He handed the political crisis over to his deputy, Sir Donald MacGillivray, who was the new High Commissioner. The British Government considered that the Emergency situation had improved so much that it was no longer necessary to have a professional soldier in the dual role of High Commissioner and Commander-in-Chief. The war would be conducted by a separate Director of Operations, while MacGillivray concentrated on moving Malaya on to self-government.

CHAPTER 19

Independence

Within a month of taking over, Sir Donald MacGillivray was faced with a trial of strength from the Alliance. The U.M.N.O. had decided to force an issue on the question of the Legislative Council having a three-fifths' elected majority, and it received the support of the M.C.A. Both instructed all members who had been elected or nominated to the Federal and State legislatures and to every other form of council or were serving on government committees, to resign. This was the sweeping boycott envisaged in the U.M.N.O. resolution passed a year before. At least 1,000 Malay and Chinese men and women obeyed and handed in their resignations from the bodies on which they were serving.

The Alliance was severely criticized for its action, and its boycott twice formed the subject of questions in the House of Commons but Mr. Lyttelton denied that it was over 'small' outstanding differences. However the situation held obvious dangers, particularly against the background of the anti-communist campaign. An early solution was clearly necessary: either the Alliance withdrew its demand and accepted official assurances (given in a Legislative Council debate) that, if an elected majority was not successful, the High Commissioner and the Malay rulers would be asked to take immediate steps to remedy the situation—or an agreeable compromise had to be found.

A group of very senior British civil servants were convinced that a solution could be worked out which would also be acceptable to the other political parties. With MacGillivray's approval, the Attorney-General, Mr. (later Sir) M. J. Hogan, and the acting Chief Secretary, Mr. David Gray, opened informal talks with the leaders of the Alliance with whom they were in extremely friendly relations. These eventually led to Tunku Abdul Rahman and two colleagues being

191

invited to meet MacGillivray aboard the Royal Navy frigate, H.M.S. *Alert*, in the naval base in Singapore on the night of 2nd July. It was perhaps an unduly dramatic venue for talks which it was hoped would lead to conciliation, but MacGillivray had a long time before planned to tour the east coast States and complete his first formal calls as new High Commissioner on the Malay rulers and he was due to leave the following morning. In the intimate atmosphere of the Captain's quarters, the basic principles of a settlement were reached after a couple of hours' discussion. The compromise revolved around the consultations which the High Commissioner would have with the leader of the party commanding a majority in the new Council before he filled the seven seats specially reserved for his nominations. A week later, after MacGillivray had had time, while travelling up the east coast, to receive the approval of the Malay rulers and the Colonial Office to the proposal and to have it explained to the leaders of other parties, there was a public exchange of letters between him and Abdul Rahman. MacGillivray's letter said that the appointments to five of the seats (the other two would be filled by the Secretary for Defence and the Member for Economic Affairs) would only be made in the light of the results of the election, and that the primary purpose of these particular appointed members was to give a voice to any important element which had not found adequate representation in the Council through the electoral process. MacGillivray added that the basic intention of the constitution would be 'more readily and appropriately achieved by filling these seats with representatives . . . who are not likely to find themselves out of harmony with major political opinion in the Council as reflected amongst the elected members'. He intended, therefore, to consult the leader or leaders of the majority party before making appointments. Abdul Rahman replied that the Alliance was satisfied that this arrangement had a 'reasonable prospect of working satisfactorily' and was prepared to resume participation in government at all levels. The following day, 7th July, the Alliance called off its three-weeks-old boycott.

On 18th August, the Legislative Council unanimously passed a Bill which amended the Federation Agreement to allow for federal elections. The Attorney-General gave the assurance that the policy of self-government for Malaya was 'in accord with Great Britain's hopes and her record throughout the world'. When he spoke of the unlikelihood of federal elections being held before the middle of 1955, Abdul Rahman and his colleagues in the Council made no protest. Very

192

soon afterwards, the U.M.N.O. and the M.C.A. proclaimed Tunku Abdul Rahman as 'Leader of the Alliance'. This sealed the political merger. (Early in 1955, the Malayan Indian Congress, the major Indian political party in the country, became the third racial link in the Alliance.) By the end of the year, the Alliance had further demonstrated its formidable strength in elections to two State legislatures. In Johore it won all 16 seats. Onn bin Ja'afar had formed the new Party Negara to 'succeed' the ill-fated I.M.P., but it polled only 9·4 per cent of the votes. Nineteen days later, the Alliance made another clean sweep of the 12 seats in the Trengganu State Council, polling 56,554 votes against the Negara's 7,169. This victorious trend continued for the remaining elections to the State and Settlement legislatures when these were held in the following year.

Early in March 1955, the Government announced that the federal elections would be held on 27th July and that the Legislative Council would be dissolved on 2nd June. Onn resigned as Member for Home Affairs to devote himself to organizing, if not reorganizing, his party. Unfortunately, he again embarked on communalistic campaigning in a vain effort to break the Alliance, and lost valuable votes from Chinese who were unhappy about the M.C.A. partnership with the Malays but who would have been prepared to support an ostensibly non-communal party.

Within the Alliance itself, strains were felt over the question of the racial distribution of candidates for the elections after the voting strengths of the races became known. Of the 1,280,865 registered voters, 1,077,562, or 84·2 per cent, were Malays and only 142,947, or 11·2 per cent, were Chinese; most of the remaining 4·6 per cent were Indians. (It was estimated that about 350,000 Chinese who were eligible to vote had not taken the trouble to register, principally because of apathy and the belief that, in an independent Malaya, the Malays would dominate in government and only tolerate other races in the economic sphere. The U.M.N.O. demanded that on the figures Malay candidates should predominate. This time Abdul Rahman himself threatened to resign if the U.M.N.O. persisted in its demands. He had become converted to the thought that racial unity was vital for Malaya, and was no longer a rabid nationalist. The strength of racial amity in Malaya today owes itself solely to his unceasing efforts to put substance into the shadows of 1955.

The Alliance produced an election manifesto of forty pages entitled *The Road to Independence* which detailed a comprehensive

programme embracing administration, the Emergency, social services, labour, economic and financial policy, local government, political reform, and town and country planning. It was noted, however,
that on the pressing issue of citizenship, which so intimately concerned the Chinese, the manifesto took no positive stand. Since the
formation of the Alliance, the M.C.A. had significantly muted its
strident demands that citizenship should be based on the principle of
jus soli so that everyone born in the country acquired nationality as a
birthright. The manifesto took the safe course of suggesting that the
problem of citizenship should be solved by an independent commission which would review constitutional reform. The Alliance contended that the Emergency could be ended by the offer of a general
amnesty, and if this failed, then 'by mobilizing all our resources and
seeking all foreign aid to increase the vigour and intensity of the fight
against the terrorists'. The Alliance promised independence in four
years, with the future legislature based on the British model, with a
fully elected House of Assembly and an Upper House. The Party
Negara pledged independence in five years in a form which would be
decided by a constituent assembly.

On nomination day, the Alliance proved the only party to put up
52 candidates, offering 35 Malays, 15 Chinese and 2 Indians. The
Party Negara had 30 candidates (29 Malays and 1 Chinese), and four
minor political parties set up 29 candidates; there were 18 independents. It was generally expected that the Alliance would win
the elections. Conservative forecasts gave them between 30 and 35
seats and Negara between 8 and 12. Onn quietly hoped that the
Negara and other anti-Alliance candidates would between them gain
the necessary minimum of 27 seats to enable a coalition to be formed.

The Alliance won 51 seats. The remaining seat went to a candidate
of a new politico-religious Pan-Malayan Islamic Party, then a small
group mostly composed of Malay religious teachers. The Alliance
polled 818,013 votes, or 79·6 per cent of the total cast. The Negara
attracted only 7·6 per cent of the vote. It was a bitter blow for Onn
but, although the result threw him into the political wilderness, he
continued to battle for Party Negara until his death in 1961. There
were several reasons for the overwhelming victory of the Alliance. It
had a powerful party machine backed by considerable funds provided
almost entirely by the Chinese. *Merdeka* provided a resoundingly
successful slogan; it matched the mood of the majority of the people,
especially the Malays. Although it was principally a Malay victory,

all the 17 non-Malay Alliance candidates were elected. Many of them had been placed in predominantly Malay constituencies and Abdul Rahman and leading U.M.N.O. officials worked tirelessly to ensure that there would be no communal voting.

Tunku Abdul Rahman became Chief Minister in the new Government. He formed a Cabinet consisting of five other Malays, three Chinese, and one Indian. In discussions with MacGillivray over the five reserved seats, Abdul Rahman agreed that these should go to three Chinese and two Indians so that the Council would have a more balanced racial representation. The Alliance found that it could count on at least 70 votes in the Council which also comprised three British officials, the nine *Mentri-Mentri Besar* (Chief Ministers) of the Malay States, two representatives from Penang and Malacca, and 32 people nominated by the High Commissioner (22 representing the planting and mining industries, agricultural and commercial interests and the trade unions). The new Executive Council consisted of the High Commissioner, 5 British civil servants (the Chief Secretary, the Attorney-General and the Financial, Defence and Economic Affairs Secretaries), and the 10 Malayan ministers. Tunku Abdul Rahman immediately set his sights on independence in four years, if not sooner.

Further gains had been made in the campaign against the communists, and food denial had become an essential part of every military operation. Some of these operations had begun to be conducted on a massive scale. For instance in July 1954, after Lincoln aircraft had dropped 14,000 lb. of bombs on two points in Perak jungle where a large force of terrorists were reported to be camped, more than 100 paratroopers of the 22nd Special Air Service Regiment jumped into the target area while the battalions ringed the area in the hope of intercepting fleeing terrorists.

Just before the end of 1954, the Government had taken the unusual step of bringing political and community leaders into every War Committee, from the federal level down to the districts, thus intimately associating all sections of the community with the conduct of the campaign. Into the federal policy-planning body came Onn bin Ja'afar, the Member for Home Affairs, and Tunku Abdul Rahman, as president of the U.M.N.O.; Colonel H. S. Lee, a vice-president of the Malayan Chinese Association who was then Member for Transport; an Indian, Mr. V. M. N. Menon, Member for Posts and Telecommunications and a member of Party Negara; and a Briton, Mr. R. B. Carey, the Member for Works. Malays, Chinese, Indians, and British planters and miners were appointed to State or District War Executive Committees and were entrusted with secret information about the communists. Their presence in all these committees made a tremendous impact on the Malayans, who were firmly convinced that the British Government was not fighting in order to retain Malaya but in order to keep international communism out of Malaya.

Four major events affected the course of the Emergency in 1955: in June the Malayan Communist Party offered to negotiate a peace; after the general elections in July an increasing amount of the control over the conduct of the war passed to politicians; in September, the Alliance Government offered the communists an amnesty; at the end of December, Tunku Abdul Rahman met the leader of the Malayan Communist Party, Chan Peng, and bluntly offered him only unconditional surrender which he rejected.

The communist offer to negotiate a settlement had come through a letter signed 'Ng Heng' which was later proved to have been written by Chan Peng. It suggested a 'round-table' conference between himself and the leaders of all those political parties that wished to end the war by negotiation. It was a shrewd move, coming as it did when all the parties were deep in electioneering and when most of them were making 'early end to the Emergency' a main plank in their platforms. Moreover international communism had just begun to preach peaceful co-existence (with increased subversion as an essential by-product) and the Malayan Communist Party wanted to get in line. However, the shock to Chan Peng came when the political parties unanimously rejected negotiation. The communists' anxiety to discontinue the war in some way which would bring advantage to them could well be understood; terrorism had brought them nothing, and the impending federal elections and the approach of self-government, combined with the British promise of independence, had nullified their claim that they were fighting for freedom on behalf of the Malayan peoples.

In September the Alliance Government offered an amnesty and 40 million leaflets instructing terrorists how to surrender were dropped into the jungle by aircraft. The amnesty proved a failure. Then on 17th November Chan Peng addressed a letter personally to Tunku Abdul Rahman offering to meet him to discuss terms for concluding the war. A meeting was arranged for 28th December in the small town of Baling, in Kedah. Tunku Abdul Rahman was accompanied by Dato Tan Cheng Lock, the president of the M.C.A., and Mr. David Marshall, Chief Minister of Singapore, whom he had invited. Chan Peng, stout, pasty-faced from living in the shadows of the jungle, black hair well-brushed, walked from his headquarters somewhere in the Betong salient of South Siam—into which he had withdrawn in 1951—to the Malayan mining village of Klian Intan just inside the border. There he was picked up by waiting Malayan police officers and conducted to Baling. He sought what he described as 'just and reasonable terms' for ending the fighting; his principal condition was recognition of his party as a legal political organization. Abdul Rahman offered only unconditional surrender which, he pointed out, would naturally mean dissolution of the Communist Party. The talks ended the following day when Chan Peng declared that his party would never accept surrender. 'We would prefer to fight to the last man,' he added. He was taken back to the jungle fringe outside Klian Intan, from where he disappeared in the direction of South Siam. Tunku Abdul Rahman permitted himself to say: 'Chan Peng really taught me what Communism was. I had never really understood and appreciated its full meaning. When I was briefed on Communism by the British experts, I always felt that they were interested in making a bad case against the Communists. But in that room Chan Peng taught me that Malaya and Communism can never co-exist.' He has remained resolutely anti-communist ever since.

A couple of days later on 2nd January 1956, Tunku Abdul Rahman and delegations representing the Malay rulers and the Alliance sailed for London to discuss with the British Government the granting of self-government and independence. A few weeks before, MacGillivray had announced to a cheering Legislative Council that the British Government no longer considered the continuation of the Emergency as 'an obstacle to the Federation's advance to self-government'. A subsequent general assembly of the U.M.N.O. passed a resolution that independence 'must be given by 31st August 1957'—two years earlier than the Alliance had originally set. This was the mandate which Tunku Abdul Rahman took with him to London.

The conference in London, which lasted from 18th January to 8th February, was under the chairmanship of the Secretary of State for the Colonies, Mr. Alan Lennox-Boyd (later Lord Boyd). The rulers were anxious that their position, prestige, and rights as constitutional sovereigns should be maintained. They did not wish Malaya on independence to become a republic but that it should have 'a constitutional Ruler' chosen from among themselves who would be a symbol of the unity of the country and to whom federal citizens would bear allegiance.

The talks went well with agreement on all major points. There was to be home rule during a transition period before independence; during this time, the High Commissioner would act in accordance with the advice of the Executive Council except in matters of external affairs and defence; Malayan Ministers would take over the portfolios of internal security and defence, finance, and commerce and industry. Independence within the Commonwealth would be granted by 31st August 1957 'if possible'. It was nothing less than breathtaking, or as the *Straits Times* newspaper, published in Singapore, put it, 'There has been nothing quite like it in the entire history of colonies and dependencies.' The promise of independence had been given a brief six months after the first national elections; self-government was being given to a country with a partially-elected central legislature; in two years the Federation would have moved from the status of a dependency with a fully nominated legislature to a sovereign and independent country having equal status to Britain in the Commonwealth. Perhaps there was little else the British Government could do in the face of two very pertinent facts: first was Tunku Abdul Rahman's insistence that the multi-racial character and strength of his mandate were of a kind which the Colonial Office had never before encountered from any dependent territory. Second, the rulers themselves agreed to independence—and if they had no objection there was little that their good friend and partner, the Queen, could do but accede also.

There were other important decisions. Upon the attainment of independence, Britain and Malaya would enter into a treaty of defence and mutual assistance which would enable British and Commonwealth troops to be kept in Malaya as part of the Commonwealth Strategic Reserve. As far as the conduct of the Emergency was concerned during the period of self-government, the Federal War Executive Council would be replaced by an Emergency Operations Council over which the Malayan Minister for Internal Defence and Security (a portfolio which Tunku Abdul Rahman took when the time came) would preside and in which the Director of Operations would be a member. As it was impossible for British and Commonwealth forces to be under the orders of a Malayan Minister, they would come under the operational command of the Director of Operations and be used in aid of the civil authorities in giving effect to policy laid down by the Emergency Operations Council. Thus the direction of war policy would pass completely into the hands of Malayans.

A decision to appoint a commission with members from Commonwealth countries to make recommendations for a federal constitution, resurrected the old Chinese sores: *jus soli* (the Chinese saw a handsome opportunity for restoring the rights of citizenship taken from them when the Federation supplanted the Malayan Union), education, and the 'special position of the Malays'. These provided the Alliance with a serious testing time for racialism was involved in each subject and racialism could break the Alliance. Both Abdul Rahman and Tan Cheng Lock found it necessary to appeal continuously to the Malays and Chinese to show impartiality and responsibility in considering these controversial problems. Abdul Rahman said that in the changes envisaged under the new constitution 'the Malays are prepared within reason to share their rights with others who owe loyalty to this country. I must, however, ask non-Malays to be fair and considerate, and not to make unreasonable demands. It is well to remember that no natives of any country in the world have given away so much as the Malays have done; no natives have been as friendly to immigrant people as the Malays have been.' He said that the only chance the Malays had of keeping their identity alive was to insist on the retention of inherent rights guaranteed by the Federation Agreement and by treaties made between the British Government and the Malay rulers. Suspicions about Malay insincerity were unjustified. To Malays he said, 'No country in the world has won independence without sacrifices by the people. I have no doubt that you are prepared to make sacrifices and to live up to your reputation of tolerance, hospitality and courtesy.'

Behind the scenes, the Malay and Chinese leaders worked quickly to find solutions which they could present to the Constitutional Commission which was to be under the chairmanship of Lord Reid, a Lord of Appeal in Ordinary, and whose other members were Sir Ivor Jennings, Master of Trinity Hall, Cambridge, an authority on constitutional law: Sir William McKell, a former Governor-General of Australia; Mr. Justice Abdul Hamid, of Pakistan, and Mr. B.

Malik, a former Chief Justice in India. The memorandum eventually produced by the Alliance National Council showed a compromise on citizenship; *jus soli* would apply to all those born in the country after 1957 but not retrospectively. The rules would be modified to admit more Chinese and Indians to the franchise. A federal nationality would replace British and State nationality. An educational policy acceptable to all races would be considered by a special committee of the Legislative Council headed by the Minister for Education. (In the event, this committee drew up a ten-year plan for a national system of primary and secondary education which would foster the development of a united Malayan nation. Chinese and Indian schools could continue but Malay would be a compulsory subject for them as it was intended to be the national language. Malay and English would be compulsory in all secondary schools. Syllabuses common to all schools would be introduced as 'an essential element in the development of a Malayan nation'.)

After six months' work, the Reid Commission published its report in February 1957. Inevitably controversies raged again over some of its recommendations. The special rights proposed for Malays included preferential quotas for admission to the government services and for licences for the operation of certain businesses, particularly transport, and preferences in the awards of scholarships and other forms of educational assistance. The Commission recommended that these rights should continue for 15 years and the legislature should then decide whether to retain, reduce or abolish them. (In the event, no time limit appeared in the constitution.) On citizenship, the Commission accepted the Alliance proposals almost in their entirety but went further by advocating the acceptance of *jus soli*. (It called for considerable tact and persuasion by the Malay leaders in the Alliance to persuade their Chinese and Indian partners later to adhere to the terms of the Alliance memorandum and not to force a point which the U.M.N.O. had not agreed to.) The Commission recommended the election of a Paramount Ruler to be known as the '*Yang di-Pertuan Agong*' from among the rulers every five years. He would be a constitutional monarch and act on the advice of his ministers; he would appoint as Prime Minister the leader of the majority party in the House of Representatives. Parliament would be bicameral, consisting of a wholly elected House of Representatives of 100 members serving for five years and a Senate of 33, serving for six years, two-thirds of whom would be elected by the States and the remaining 11 by the Paramount Ruler. The Upper House would have power to delay legislation. The Commission also recommended that each Malay ruler should become a constitutional ruler and that each *Mentri Besar* should no longer be responsible to the Sultan. Each State would have a legislative assembly with an elected majority. The two settlements of Penang and Malacca would in future be known as 'States' and would each have a Governor as constitutional head of State appointed for four years.

All the Commission's recommendations were accepted, some with modifications, and a constitution was drafted and approved. It also provided that Islam would be the State religion but guaranteed freedom of worship to all creeds. On the point of special rights for the Malays, it became the responsibility of the Yang di-Pertuan Agong to safeguard the special position of the Malays 'and the legitimate interests' of other communities. Malay rights would be reviewed from time to time. With an eye to the possibilities of the future, the constitution permitted Parliament by law to 'admit other States to the Federation'. By the time the Commission's recommendations had been considered and accepted, only six months remained for all the constitutional changes and processes to be carried out if independence by 31st August was to be achieved. With an effort they were completed in time.

On the morning of 31st August the Duke of Gloucester, as the Queen's representative, presented Tunku Abdul Rahman, the first Prime Minister of independent Malaya, with the constitutional instruments that made the Federation a free country. The flag of the new nation was hoisted to the masthead in the presence of the newly-elected Yang di-Pertuan Agong, who had been the Yang di-Pertuan Besar of Negri Sembilan, and the other Malay rulers or their representatives. From Queen Elizabeth came a message, 'I am confident that Malaya will respond worthily to the challenging tasks of independence and that she will continue to show to the world that example of moderation and goodwill between all races that has been so marked a feature of her history.'

A British pledge had been honoured and a new nation born. For Tunku Abdul Rahman particularly, the day had its deep historical significance. Over 170 years before, his great-great-great-grandfather had ceded the island of Penang to Britain and so had given the British their first footing in the country. Proudly he read the Proclamation of Independence, 'I . . . do hereby proclaim and declare that the *Persekutuan Tanah Melayu* (Federation of Malaya) is, and with God's blessing shall be for ever, a sovereign democratic and independent State founded upon the principles of liberty and justice and ever seeking the welfare and happiness of its people and the maintenance of a just peace among all nations.'

CHAPTER 20

Fresh Problems

Two days after the declaration of independence, the constitutional formalities were brought to a picturesque climax with the formal installation of the Yang di-Pertuan Agong as 'King and Ruler of the Federation of Malaya'. The rich and impressive pageantry was a peculiar blending of the ancient and the modern Malay worlds and it culminated in the dramatic moment when the King unsheathed his gold Kris of State, the august emblem of his authority, and kissed its blade in acceptance of his high office.

The Yang di-Pertuan Agong was the symbol of the new Malayan Age and the first monarch of the second independent Malay kingdom. Not surprisingly the thoughts of those concerned with the majesty of the court had travelled back to the first Malay Empire of Malacca. Flanking the throne therefore at the installation were regalia-bearers and attendants who wore costumes matching those that Malay manuscripts described as having been worn in the Malacca court. There was one vital difference however. In this twentieth-century Malayan court, the regalia-bearers and attendants represented the races of Malaya and were not Malays only as they had been in old Malacca. The new regalia incidentally had the Malay counterpart of the Western sceptre and orb. These were two silver maces, the *Chogam Alam*, symbol of the universe, representing temporal power, and the *Chogam Ugama*, representing spiritual power. There were also old Malay swords and long krises, two *chokmar*, a short spikeless mace (unlike its ancient counterpart, which was heavy, spiked, and long-handled), two *sundang* (two-edged heavy-bladed swords once used for close fighting), and two *tombak berambu* (broad-bladed tufted spears). Finally, the *Kris Kerajaan*, the Kris of State, symbol of power and authority, with the coat-of-arms of Malaya and the crests of the 11 States decorating its sheath and hilt, its handle sur-mounted by an 11-pointed star.

Missing from the installation ceremony were the intricate Hindu rituals which had marked the enthronement of the Malacca rulers. Instead, the ceremony was brief, simple, solemn, gracious and digni-fied. Yet the acclamation that greeted the Paramount Ruler after he had taken his oath of office was traditional Malay: a thrice-called *'Daulat Tuanku'* (Long live the King). In ancient Malacca this had been the moment when the Maharajah Lela, one of the major chiefs, had the authority to kill any man in the assembly who did not imme-diately hail the new ruler in full spirit. In modern Malaya, instead, artillery in the grounds outside began a 21-gun salute, ending a cere-mony which had its own political and historical significance—the union for the first time in the peninsula's history of all its peoples under a constitutional sovereign.

The following day, the King opened the new Parliamentary session. The composition of the legislature remained as it had been since 1955 with one notable exception, namely that the last two British *ex officio* members, the Chief Secretary and the Attorney-General, had dis-appeared. (This Parliament was to continue in this form until 1959 when the bicameral legislature—the *Dewan Raayat*, the House of Representatives, completely elected, and the *Dewan Negara*, the Senate, partially elected and partially nominated—was established.) That day also no longer did a British High Commissioner review the past and look to the future as he had done at the opening of every new session of the Legislative Council. Instead the King spoke of, 'My Government and its policy'. He announced, among other things, the offer of new surrender terms, including an amnesty, to the communist terrorists who no longer could claim that they were fighting for the 'liberation' of Malaya from the 'British Imperialists'.

In the anti-communist war, the Government, for political and military reasons, gave the task of bringing the Emergency to an end to a British Director of Emergency Operations who had responsi-bility for the overall co-ordination of the Malayan and Common-wealth forces. He did not command them but they operated under his general direction; he himself was responsible to the Federation Government. The Government had also formally asked the Com-monwealth forces to help in pursuing the campaign as relentlessly as before, since Malaya's own forces were not quite large enough to complete the final stages. So on 12th October 1957, Malaya and

Britain signed a Treaty of Defence and Mutual Assistance. This provided for action by both to resist any armed attack on Malaya or on British territories in the Far East, such as Hong Kong, North Borneo, Sarawak and the British-protected State of Brunei. Any threat to the territories or to peace in the Far East would bring Malaya and Britain into consultation on how the situation should be met. Britain could withdraw forces to deal with any situation but could only take military action from her bases in Malaya by agreement with the Federation Government. This formula enabled Britain to fulfil her obligations under the South-East Asia Treaty Organization, of which Malaya was not a member (or likely to be), without in any way implicating Malaya. Under the Treaty Britain undertook to train and develop Malaya's armed forces.

Assured of its defences and adequate forces to help it in eliminating the remaining communists, the Malayan Government turned its attention to evolving a foreign policy. Tunku Abdul Rahman showed himself as firmly against 'neutralism' as he was resolutely anti-communist. He looked on Communist China as a potential enemy, but the time was to come when he declared his readiness to support its admission into the United Nations on condition that Nationalist China was allowed to continue as a member in the organization representing Formosa. He contended that as Communist China was a world power it should *ipso facto* sit among the nations where it could be directly influenced by world opinion. It should be added that up to well into 1964 Malaysia had no diplomatic connections with either Communist China or Formosa.

It was not without significance that the first official visits Tunku Abdul Rahman should pay as Prime Minister were to countries which were either involved in anti-communist campaigns like South Vietnam, or threatened by communist pressures like Thailand, or had defeated a strong local communist insurrection like the Philippines. He returned from Thailand with a promise of co-operation in combined operations against Malayan terrorists who were in refuge in South Siam where they were being retrained in defended camps. (In the ensuing years there were joint army-police conferences on the problem but Thailand never moved forces of any substance into the border area to help flush out the fugitives, principally because of its own anxieties along its north-eastern border with Vietnam.)

In Baguio in January 1959, Tunku Abdul Rahman suggested in a speech that nations in South-East Asia should join themselves into a regional group to promote economic and cultural co-operation. Many people thought that this perhaps rather vague proposal held an invitation to form a bloc of their own, a South-East Asian counterpart of Western groupings like the Atlantic Pact or the Central European Treaty Organization. He followed this up in October with letters to the heads of State of Indonesia, Thailand, Cambodia, the Philippines, South Vietnam, Burma and Laos, inviting them to become members of an economic and cultural association. Only the Philippines and Thailand responded. In February 1961 the three countries announced the formation of an 'Association of South-East Asia' (A.S.A.—initials which formed a word meaning 'hope' in the Malay, Filipino and Siamese languages) to promote economic and cultural development among themselves. A.S.A. was a sincere attempt at regional co-operation; among its aims were the provision of educational, professional, technical and administrative training and research facilities for students and officials of member countries, the establishment of a common market, and easier shipping and air communications and travel between the member territories; but it never really got off the ground. However, the first rumbles of jealousy and disapprobation came from the direction of Indonesia where President Soekarno saw his aspirations of becoming the acknowledged leader of South-East Asian countries in international affairs upset by the formation of A.S.A.

A different motive lay behind Tunku Abdul Rahman's visit to Japan in May 1957. For years after the Japanese war Malaya had closed its doors to Japanese traders and businessmen but the realities of independence—the need to expand trade, establish new industries, raise loans to help build roads, schools and hospitals, and clear jungle for agriculture and land settlement—brought recognition that old hatreds had to be forgotten. Before the war Japan had, for instance, been Malaya's only market for iron ore; it could become a bigger market for this mineral. Malaya and Japan signed a trade pact and a large amount of Japanese capital has since been invested in the country.

Malaya is a staunch supporter of the Commonwealth and its concepts and it was in support of these that in 1960 it took a forthright stand against the *apartheid* policy pursued by the South African Government. At a meeting of Commonwealth Prime Ministers in London that year Tunku Abdul Rahman condemned the South African policy in an unprecedentedly frank speech when, as Prime

Minister of the newest member-nation, he had to reply to the welcoming words of the host, the British Prime Minister, Mr. Harold MacMillan. At the next meeting of Prime Ministers in 1962 South Africa withdrew its application to remain in the Commonwealth as a republic. In the United Nations, Malaya made its voice heard firmly and strongly, and it was among the first nations to send a battalion of troops to form part of a United Nations peace-keeping force in the Congo. Then later, at a critical stage when several countries began withdrawing their forces from the Congo, Malaya instead announced its intention of reinforcing its contingent, a gesture which received the public thanks of the Secretary-General. With Britain, Malaya continued to be on the most friendly terms. But it was solidly against any suggestions of union with its closest neighbour, Singapore.

On 31st July 1960 the Malayan Government proclaimed the Emergency to be at an end. This had come far earlier than anybody had anticipated. The headway against the communists, particularly after independence, had been little short of astonishing. It had been engendered by a powerful combination of relentless military pressure and the most intense food control in every operational area. The other campaign to win 'the hearts and minds of the people' had very largely succeeded as security brought confidence and they willingly provided information to the Government and ceased material assistance to the terrorists. In the jungle, the communist units had been completely broken up by the tenacious prodding of security forces, by the desertion of aborigines who had then turned hunters, and by the sheer necessity of keeping on the move in order to avoid capture or death and to find food for existence. There was also disillusionment among the ranks and the lower echelons of command, while dissatisfaction over the failure of Chan Peng, safe in the Betong salient of South Siam, to direct the battle had begun to affect the experienced senior commanders.

The fresh surrender terms offered as a *Merdeka* gesture had produced a very slow response. Then suddenly in November 1957 Chan Peng wrote to Tunku Abdul Rahman proposing a meeting 'with the object of obtaining a just and fair agreement in order to end the war'. Tunku Abdul Rahman broadcast a reply saying that he agreed to a meeting since he inferred that Chan Peng had accepted the principle of surrender; he left it to him to propose a time and place. But total surrender appeared again still to be far from the communist leader's mind because he never answered. This seemed to be the psychological moment for pressing home the advantage, and the whole of Malaya's excellent Psychological Warfare Department moved into action at the same time as the army began a systematic drive to try to break the morale of the toughest communist groups, those in Perak and Johore. In several villages the Government set up central kitchens which cooked rice for the whole community and served it to families under supervision, a drastic but most effective measure against food reaching the enemy. It was later used elsewhere. The first cracks came in Perak where more than 100 terrorists surrendered in the course of six weeks. Two months later the Johore organization broke up, and in four months nearly 300 of its terrorists surrendered. By the beginning of 1960 only about 500 communists were known to be left in Malaya—and nearly all of them along the Kedah and Perak frontier with Siam. Confident that these could be contained the Government decided to call an end to the Emergency.

It had been a most expensive 'small war'. The armed services of Malaya and several Commonwealth countries—from Britain, through East Africa, down to Australia and New Zealand and across to far-away Fiji—had been involved. From first to last, a total of 41 British battalions had been engaged in the campaign. So had tens of thousands of Malayan policemen and at one time about 350,000 Home Guards. Over 11,000 men and women had been killed, comprising 1,865 soldiers and police, 2,473 civilians (the majority of them Chinese) and 6,710 communists. Another 801 civilians (almost all Chinese) were listed as 'missing'. These were grim statistics. The campaign had cost the British and Malayan Governments hundreds of millions of Malayan dollars to say nothing of the considerable cost to the rubber industry, which had been put on the defensive when it should have been recovering from the ravages of the Japanese occupation and replacing old uneconomic acres with high-yielding trees in order to meet the growing challenge from synthetic rubber. But international communism had lost its first war since Korea.

The ending of the Emergency did not of course remove the communist threat. Communist plans for internal subversion were known to exist—and still do. The Communist Party had come to the conclusion that in the very long term subversion might succeed where force had not. There was early evidence that they planned to use Chinese school students and youth movements like Old Boys' Associations and musical societies, trade unions and pliable opposition political parties as a cover in open and legal activities. The Alliance Government showed its awareness of the dangers from subversion for it did not run down its vast and splendid Special Branch service. It went further and set up a special department to counter subversion.

After the end of the Emergency the common view in Kuala Lumpur was that the most serious threat to Malaya appeared to lie in Singapore, where a strong communist front organization was openly in existence. After the Japanese war the vigorous Singapore branch of the Malayan Communist Party had gained a great degree of control over trade unions, had planted vigorous cells in Chinese schools, and had insinuated members in left-wing political parties. In the first year of the Malayan Emergency, Singapore had become perhaps the most important supply base for the terrorists on the mainland; ammunition, explosives, food, medicine, clothing and other supplies and considerable sums of money were smuggled over the narrow Strait of Johore and reached terrorist jungle camps by devious means. The Singapore Government introduced 'Emergency Regulations' and rigidly applied them. Its Special Branch kept a very close eye on the situation, and the Federation Special Branch would have been the first to acknowledge its great obligation to its southern counterpart for the effectiveness of its counter-operations, which not only kept a 'shooting war' out of Singapore but also hindered the Singapore communists from sending material support to their comrades on the mainland. The Singapore communists concentrated on gaining strength through subversion and the penetration of political parties.

Opportunity for the latter came in 1954, when new political parties bloomed to contest elections arranged for 1955 which would introduce a new constitution giving Singapore a greater measure of self-government. The new Legislative Assembly would have 32 members, of whom 25 would be elected. The old Colonial-style Executive Council would be replaced by a Council of Ministers composed of the Governor and nine ministers, six of whom would be elected and three would be officials. This Council would be responsible for policy in all matters but those relating to external affairs, internal security, and defence which would continue to lie with Britain. The Governor would have reserved powers—'designed to meet exceptional circumstances'—including withholding assent to bills and legislating by decree.

Three major parties were formed with the single objective of challenging the right wing and non-communal Progressive Party (the majority of its members were Straits Chinese) which since 1951 had held the majority in the partly-elected Legislative Council. They were the Labour Front, a loose amalgamation of small labour groups, the further-to-the-left Peoples' Action Party (P.A.P.) consisting of Chinese and Indian intellectuals and trade unionists and containing some communist elements, and the Democratic Party, formed just two months before the elections by the wealthy and powerful Singapore Chinese Chamber of Commerce. Other contesting parties included the Singapore branches of the Malayan U.M.N.O. and M.C.A. which forged a local alliance with the Singapore Malay Union.

The result of the election which was held on 2nd April 1955 was a surprise victory for the unorganized Labour Front which won ten seats though polling only 26·3 per cent of the votes. The Progressives won four seats, the P.A.P. three of four they had contested, the Alliance three, the Democrats two and independents three. The Labour Front's leader, Mr. David Marshall, a prominent lawyer born in Singapore of Iraqi Jewish extraction, formed a coalition with the Alliance; with the support of two nominated members and the three officials, he had a majority in the Assembly.

This transfer of real power to elected ministers brought in an era of turbulent political strife during which communist front organizations, with the extreme left-wing of the P.A.P. to the forefront, made intense efforts to undermine the Government by defiance and by staging demonstrations which sometimes ended in ugly violence in which people were killed and injured. Marshall's government failed to react strongly; he himself proved to be an excitable, flamboyant and impetuous Chief Minister. In the midst of the troubles, Marshall began attacking the constitution and brought a resolution before the Assembly which declared, 'The time has arrived for the transfer of power from the United Kingdom, and a new constitution providing self-government should be granted immediately'—this after only four months' operation of the existing constitution by his government. He finally succeeded in getting the Secretary of State for the Colonies, Mr. Alan Lennox-Boyd, to agree that an all-party mission should go to London in April 1956, after one year's experience of the constitution, to discuss the demand for self-government.

Marshall led a delegation of 13 to London. The talks with Mr.

Lennox-Boyd lasted from 23rd April to 15th May, but although the British Government was willing to grant a wide measure of self-government it was unwilling to hand over responsibility for internal security, not only because of the danger of a communist take-over of the government but also because of Singapore's considerable strategic importance in the Far East. As Mr. Lennox-Boyd said in his opening address to the delegation, 'We do not intend that Singapore should become an outpost of Communist China and, in fact, a colony of Peking.' He described the threat in Singapore as 'one of subversion by highly organized and powerful groups' and added, 'External defence and internal security are, in Singapore, inevitably intertwined. This responsibility for external defence cannot be dissociated from internal security or called on only when affairs have got largely or completely out of hand.' He pointed out that the British Government was being asked 'to take the irrevocable step of abrogating all rights and powers of any sort in connection with Singapore for all time' at a 'moment in history when there has been no appreciable period of stable democratic government in Singapore, when no political party at present holds a commanding majority, when it is impossible to foresee what the future may bring in internal political development, and when strong subversive forces are known to be at work: and all this in an island State of the greatest strategic importance in the defence of the free world'.

The conference failed, as had been expected, on the question of internal security, a subject which had been kept to the last for discussion. The British Government had accepted almost all other requests by the delegation in the event of full self-government being granted to the colony, such as: its status would be that of a self-governing 'State', its Legislative Assembly would be fully elected with 51 members, a Prime Minister would preside over a fully-elected Council of Ministers, the Queen's representative would be a 'High Commissioner' and not a Governor, and he would govern in accordance with the advice of his ministers except for external affairs and defence, and a separate Singapore citizenship would be introduced.

Any possibility of a compromise on the subject of internal security was also negated because the Singapore delegation had been divided from the day it had left for London and this alone doomed its mission. On 6th June Marshall resigned as Chief Minister and was succeeded by his deputy, Mr. Lim Yew Hock, a trade unionist who was respected in responsible labour circles and who introduced a measure of stability in the running of the government which Singapore had not got from Marshall. But the communist front was out to exploit the failure of the London conference and, as Lim announced his intention, the 'early attainment of complete self-government', the communists inspired fresh strikes and further violent demonstrations which culminated in serious riots in October. Lim showed his determination to enforce law and order and ordered the detention of men known to be behind all the troubles; they included some of the more extremist members of the P.A.P.

A little happier about Lim's unhesitating stand against the extremists, the British Government agreed to reopen the talks which had collapsed under Marshall. In March 1957, Lim led another all-party delegation, which however was limited to five members, to London and after a month reached agreement on 11th April.

Britain agreed to the creation after 1st January 1958 of a self-governing 'State of Singapore' with an enlarged Legislative Assembly of 51 elected members. The Queen would be represented by a Malayan Head of State with the title of *Yang di-Pertuan Negara* while a Commissioner would represent the British Government. The Singapore and British Governments would consult on defence and foreign policies and trade. The previous disagreement over internal security was resolved. It would become the responsibility of the Singapore Government but an Internal Security Council would have the right to intervene effectively in order to safeguard the defence and integrity of the State. It would comprise seven members, three each appointed by the Singapore and British Governments, and the seventh by the Malayan Government. Tunku Abdul Rahman reluctantly agreed to furnish the seventh member but the arrangement on the other hand clearly suited the other two governments. The British may be assumed to have felt it could depend upon the Malayan vote in any decision relating to the suppression of Singapore's communists and to the defence of Malaya, while the Singapore Government was probably equally content to rely on another Malayan casting vote in any issue with the British.

This particular phase of Singapore's history was marked by a close friendship between Tunku Abdul Rahman and Lim Yew Hock. The former publicly supported Lim in his determined forays against the Singapore communists, while Lim Yew Hock was concerned about maintaining the friendliest relations with independent Malaya for he envisaged—as did all thinking people in Singapore—a merger between the two countries as the correct historical, political and economic step, or as he put it in a message to the Federation on its day of Independence, '. . . it is the prime interest of both people to merge into a single political unit within which, as one people with one outlook and purpose, all may share. . . . We of Singapore look forward to that day when our strength will be added to your strength and our separation will be ended. . . .' However, the Federation's response to this hint was cautious, albeit firm. 'My Government', declared the Paramount Ruler in his Speech from the Throne on 3rd September 1957 to the first meeting of the Parliament of independent Malaya, 'will enter into discussions with sympathy towards the special problems of Singapore and with understanding of the difficulties which face the Government.'

But 1958 showed little intention by the Federation Government to facilitate moves towards a union. Indeed, Tunku Abdul Rahman, despite his friendship with Lim, hardened his attitude, once saying that he did not think there was 'any possibility of a merger'—and that he would not even have Singapore as a subordinate unit. The University of Malaya was, at the instance of the Federation Government, split into a Singapore and a Kuala Lumpur division with separate staffs and the Pan-Malayan Department of Broadcasting was also divided into two units. The Royal Malayan Navy was transferred to the Federation.

Elections under the new constitution for the self-governing State of Singapore were fixed for 31st May 1959. The months preceding were full of news and events concerning the P.A.P. There was little doubt by the middle of 1958 that the P.A.P. would be the next party in power; its strength among the Chinese was great and Lim Yew Hock's party had lost considerable ground. But there were conflicts within the P.A.P. and these were bared in August 1957 when the extremist wing made an unsuccessful attempt to overthrow the leader of the party, Mr. Lee Kuan Yew, and his supporters.

On its formation in 1954, the P.A.P. had declared its policy as that of working for an 'independent, democratic, Socialist, non-Communist Malaya' but this failed to convince because of the obvious communist elements in its organization and its instigation of strikes and demonstrations. Lee Kuan Yew, a founder of the party and a lawyer, was a young Chinese born in Singapore and had been a brilliant scholar at Cambridge University. He was to acknowledge later

Map of Singapore

that the P.A.P. had been used as a communist front, and a P.A.P. publication was to say that the party had 'tolerated the communists in its ranks during the struggle for independence' but that 'at no time' did it 'permit the communists to lead it by the nose'. But in the middle of 1957 the communists did try to gain control quite apart from continuing to foment trouble in Singapore.

On the night of 21st August 1957, Lim ordered the detention of 39 known communist leaders; they included five members of the newly-elected executive committee of the P.A.P. and officials of its branches on the island. Lim issued a White Paper which described how the communists had rebuilt their organization and said, 'Communists and their agents are back in key positions, daily increasing their propaganda and power.' It added that the Singapore Government considered it had 'an inescapable duty to step in and frustrate the attempts to create an essentially dictatorial communist state'. Later Lim Yew Hock, perhaps realizing that the Labour Front itself had little chance of winning the elections, formed the Singapore Peoples' Alliance (S.P.A.) which he hoped would attract sufficiently strong support to defeat the P.A.P.

In the event, the P.A.P., after a hard-hitting campaign, won 43 out of the 51 seats in the Legislative Assembly, with 53·4 per cent of the total votes cast. Lim Yew Hock was one of the only four S.P.A. candidates returned out of its 39 contestants. The U.M.N.O.-M.C.A. Alliance won three seats and one constituency went to an independent. Upon being invited to form a government, Lee immediately said his party would not take office until those in prison, who had been closely associated with the party, had been released. The Governor, Sir William Goode, agreed to release the eight men named 'in view of the changed political situation' and 'in order to achieve a swift and smooth introduction of the new constitution'. These prisoners included Lim Chin Siong, described later by the P.A.P. as 'the most important open front man put forward by the communists'; the others were in sympathy with communism in varying degrees. Upon release they subscribed in writing to the non-communist democratic socialist policy as defined by the P.A.P. and were given appointments in the Government as political secretaries, acknowledged later by Lee Kuan Yew as 'a piece of calculated risk meant to contain them where they could do least harm'.

On 3rd June Singapore became a self-governing State. The last Colonial Governor, Sir William Goode, remained for six months as the first Yang di-Pertuan Negara of the new State. When he left in December to become Governor of North Borneo, he was succeeded by a Malay, Inche Yusof bin Ishak, a former editor of a Malay language newspaper published in Malaya. Lee Kuan Yew was Prime Minister of a Cabinet which was notable for its intellectual resources and its youth; its average age was 37 years. He took over the reins of government in a Singapore which, outside the circles of the P.A.P. and the communists' united front and their supporters, was visibly worried and concerned about the new régime. The P.A.P.'s extreme anti-Western electioneering campaign had shaken business confidence and there was some movement of capital and management from Singapore to Kuala Lumpur. Slowly however it became apparent that the P.A.P. Government seemed genuinely determined both to foster Singapore's trade and industry and to contain the communists, just as Lee had once said that the real fight between his party and the communists would begin after the elections.

The battle came over the question of independence for Singapore. The communists and their supporters began agitating for independence for Singapore as a solitary State and through no merger with Malaya. Their intention was obvious: a separate independent Singapore would provide the communists with a stronghold in South-East Asia and with a ready-made entrance to Malaya. Lee and his supporters fought the communists with considerable courage and tenacity—or as one observer described it to the writer, 'His brilliant calculating analysis of the political pluses and minuses and his planning of moves and counter-moves' stretched over months. He won a crushing victory in 1961. He described much of this remarkable story in an extraordinarily frank series of broadcasts in Singapore in September and October 1961 when he related why he and his colleagues had considered it would be necessary to work hand-in-glove with the communists in order to gain self-government, and why, at the same time, it became necessary to prevent the communists taking control of the situation. Lee concluded by saying, 'My colleagues and I in the P.A.P. are one of the few groups that have worked in a united front with the Malayan Communist Party and have not been absorbed.' Nevertheless it was a very near thing. . . .

While Lee was regaining the confidence of business—local and overseas—by demonstrating competence, integrity of purpose and freedom from corruption, Malaya was moving further away from close association with Singapore. An international frontier at the

216

causeway linking the two territories seemed imminent. Certainly Tunku Abdul Rahman threatened to introduce immigration control at Johore Bahru in order to prevent the entry of extreme left-wing Chinese. Lee Kuan Yew, on the other hand, spared no effort to try to ensure continuing relations with Malaya. His aim was to 'bring about conditions favourable to an early reunification with the Federation'. The British Government had made it clear that Singapore's eventual independence rested entirely on unification with a larger territory, preferably Malaya. Quite apart from this political necessity for a merger, Lee personally believed in union and he kept urging it at every opportunity. To him 'whatever the twists and turns of events in the immediate present, the relentless logic of geography and the force of historical ethnic and economic forces must prevail'. He asserted that the Federation could not afford a hostile Singapore because economically Singapore handled 32 per cent of Malaya's exports and 41 per cent of its imports.

Lee's sentiments undoubtedly met with reciprocity among certain members of Tunku Abdul Rahman's Cabinet, who on the other hand realized that Malay-dominated Malaya would never agree to direct merger with Chinese-dominated Singapore as this would make the Malays lose their political ascendancy. Moreover there were deep suspicions in Malaya of Singapore's left-wing Chinese. There is little doubt however that Tunku Abdul Rahman in Kuala Lumpur began to be pressed towards revising his adamant attitude and to realize that what happened in, and to, Singapore was of very important concern to Malaya—particularly if the island and its port should fall into communist hands.

Tunku Abdul Rahman relaxed sufficiently in his relations with Singapore to make his first formal visit to it late in January 1961. One observer interpreted his visit as making merger a 'milestone ahead rather than the mirage described by the supporters of immediate independence for Singapore'. This interpretation was supported by Tunku Abdul Rahman's more amiable comments about Singapore and its P.A.P. leaders on his return to Kuala Lumpur when he said that the barrier to merger was not the predominantly Chinese population because the Singapore Government itself was 'Malayan-minded'. The P.A.P., he added, was as good a Malayan government as the Alliance and the 'real Singaporeans are all right'—but communism among certain Chinese who were 'China-minded' remained the threat.

217

A future historian might pick on the result of a by-election in Singapore on 29th April 1961 as the factor which perhaps forced Tunku Abdul Rahman to change completely his attitude towards Singapore. A candidate of the P.A.P. was decisively beaten in the Hong Lim constituency, once a P.A.P. base in Singapore's Chinatown. The three-to-one extent of the defeat and its implications for Singapore made its impact in Kuala Lumpur. Tunku Abdul Rahman was clearly perturbed and expressed his thoughts at an U.M.N.O. conference on 6th May when he said, 'There is a section of the Chinese in Singapore who do not want a good government which works for the good of the people. What they want is a communist government or a communist-orientated government.'

CHAPTER 21

Wider Horizons

On 26th May 1961, Tunku Abdul Rahman was in Singapore as the guest at lunch of the Foreign Correspondents' Association of South-East Asia. He prefaced his remarks with a disarming 'I have nothing important to tell you'; and his large audience of newspapermen sprinkled with diplomats and business tycoons settled back expecting to hear a general discourse on Malaya's problems, particularly those concerning the Chinese in Singapore. The Tunku ranged from what he described as the natural tendency of the Chinese in Singapore to try to make the island 'a little China' to the dangers from local communism inspired by international communism. As he seemed about to conclude, he began drawing his concept of political and economic co-operation in South-East Asia. Malaya as a nation, he said, realized that she could not stand alone and in isolation. Sooner or later she should 'have an understanding with Britain and the peoples of the territories of Singapore, Borneo, Brunei and Sarawak'. He added, 'It is premature for me to say how this close understanding can be brought about but it is inevitable that we should look ahead to this objective and think of a plan whereby these territories can be brought closer together in political and economic co-operation.' So unexpected was this statement of policy that it was some moments before its significance made its impact on the audience.

Here was the Tunku, hitherto so adamant against merger with Singapore, all but saying that he was ready to embrace the Chinese city-State in a wider political union. If this were so, it would have the most far-reaching consequences in South-East Asia. It was obvious from the start that Britain would approve a merger between Singapore and Malaya; it was good policy apart from the fact that the continued division of these closely-related territories was a 'nonsense'; it was equally obvious that Britain would not stand in the way of North Borneo and Sarawak amalgamating in a wider political union if their peoples wished to do so.

Tunku Abdul Rahman's idea was not new. For years there had been talk of the possibility of the federation of the five territories concerned. For instance in the later 1940's and early 1950's, political circles in Singapore were publicly speaking of a 'dominion of South-East Asia'. Had there not been significance too in the appointment of Mr. Malcolm MacDonald in 1946 as Governor-General over the five territories? And Mr. MacDonald himself had publicly referred to the idea of an eventual 'Greater Malaya' comprising the five countries. It became common knowledge that from 1945 British policy had some such form of association as a long-term object of policy. Then, as late as January 1960, the retiring Governor of North Borneo had spoken of the possibility of 'a great Commonwealth member' emerging from such an association. But in the changing mood of post-war South-East Asia, the communist troubles in Malaya and the turbulences in Singapore, the right opportunity for inter-governmental talks about such a union had not occurred.

However, in Borneo efforts had begun in 1958 to interest the three territories in closer association as a step towards independence as a federation. The governors of North Borneo and Sarawak advocated it in broadcasts and the project was debated in the local legislatures, but the proposal hung fire. Brunei was jealous of its newly-granted internal self-government and suspicious that its oil revenues would be used to finance development in the other two States. North Borneo had an historical antipathy to the Brunei Malays who had been aggressive overlords in the past and was also nervous of the way political parties were developing in Sarawak under Chinese leadership. In both North Borneo and Sarawak, the indigenous peoples generally were conscious of their backwardness and fearful that political and constitutional changes would lead to economic and political power passing to the Chinese.

In these two territories therefore, Tunku Abdul Rahman's statement had the effect of a large rock flung into a placid pool. It roused them to a consciousness of the world and the political dangers around them as only the Japanese invasion had done in 1942. In politics, they were the 'new boys' of South-East Asia. Economically, they were just discovering their potentialities; North Borneo particularly was bursting with promise of wealth from timber and the minerals hidden beneath its vast forests. Politically, Sarawak had moved faster than North Borneo. Initially its transition into a colony in 1946 had caused much more political furore than in North Borneo, and its larger Chinese minority was perhaps an additional indirect reason for earlier political development. On 1st April 1957, it had received a new constitution providing for a legislature of 45 members, 24 of whom would be elected from the advisory councils in its five Administrative Divisions and from the Kuching Municipal Council and the Sibu and Miri District Councils. Thus the local government bodies constituted electoral and sub-electoral colleges within a 'tier' system of central government representation. This was designed as an interim expedient, to initiate the people slowly into the concept of a political system and its attendant responsibilities. The first general elections of representatives to the district councils were held in November and December 1959; the suffrage was based on male heads of household and it was an interesting sidelight that 71 per cent of the electorate cast their vote. The first political party, the Sarawak United Peoples' Party, professedly multi-racial, was formed with official encouragement in June 1959, with a predominantly Chinese leadership. It then split along communal lines. In 1960 appeared the Party Negara Sarawak, consisting of Malays, Ibans, and some Chinese.

In North Borneo, constitutional and political development had been very much slower, principally because the emphasis in the years after the war had been on reconstruction from devastation after the Japanese war, and then development. The normal type of Executive and Legislative Councils had been inaugurated in October 1950. In 1960 a nominated unofficial majority was introduced into the Legislative Council. By May 1961, North Borneo still had no political parties, and elections even on the lowest levels were still below the horizon.

Thus, the initial Bornean reactions to the winds of change wafted by Tunku Abdul Rahman were a mixture of suspicion and anxieties. Both territories, particularly North Borneo, were content, or seemed content, with their quiet and orderly political, economic, social and educational development. They suspected Tunku Abdul Rahman's statement to represent a Malay desire to 'take over' the Borneo territories and they feared that Britain might be coerced into handing them over to Malaya. They also suspected, as a North Borneo politician put it later, that Tunku Abdul Rahman was 'using the Borneo regions' as 'tools to solve the Singapore problem'. There was little

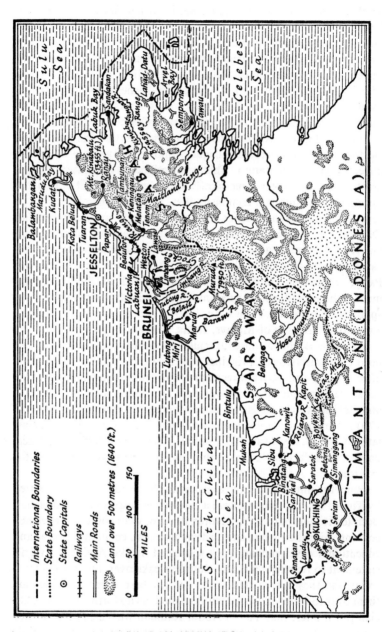

Map of Sarawak and Sabah in Eastern Malaysia

doubt that the political and community leaders in the two Borneo territories felt there would be little, if any, immediate advantage in union with the Malays of Malaya and the Chinese of Singapore; to them this kind of union spelled the exchange of a British form of colonialism for the return of Malay domination.

In Singapore, however, Lee Kuan Yew was quick to respond favourably to Tunku Abdul Rahman's statement. He declared that if merger and independence for Singapore would come sooner and more easily through political integration with the Borneo territories and Malaya, then Singapore would support it. Six days later, Dr. Toh Chin Chye, the Deputy Prime Minister and Chairman of the People's Action Party, declared that the Singapore Government would, in constitutional talks with Britain which were planned for June 1963, seek independence through a merger under conditions which would give Singapore autonomy in education and labour policy. Lee Kuan Yew worked assiduously and with conviction to negotiate with the Federation Government and try to obtain the best bargain he could for Singapore's membership in the proposed Federation. Indeed, he may be said to have battled right up to inauguration day itself. . . .

The first official British Government reaction came on 20th June when the Prime Minister, Mr. Harold Macmillan, replying to a question in the House of Commons, said that the Tunku's idea was 'striking'. Cautiously, he drew attention to the fact that all the territories concerned were in widely different stages of political and economic advance and therefore considerable problems had first to be overcome. Five days later, Sir William Goode, Governor of North Borneo, Sir Alexander Waddell, Governor of Sarawak, and Mr. (later Sir) D. C. White, High Commissioner of Brunei, arrived in Singapore for discussions with Lord Selkirk, the British Commissioner-General in South-East Asia. After their conference they let it be known that they felt that the Borneo territories should bind themselves closer together before joining any wider confederation, because they lagged behind Singapore and Malaya politically and there were obvious difficulties in bringing together countries in such different political and constitutional stages of development.

Early in July, three leaders in the Borneo territories—Mr. Donald Stephens, president of the North Borneo United National Kadazan Organization, and a member of the Executive and Legislative Councils, Mr. Ong Kee Hui, chairman of the Sarawak United Peoples'

Party, and Sheikh A. M. Azahari, president of the Party Rakyat of Brunei—met in Jesselton. After two days' talks they issued a joint statement which described the Tunku's plan as 'totally unacceptable' and added that it was vitally important that constitutional advance in their three territories should be accelerated first; a constitutional link between them was the prime need. The mood of the Borneans then was best summed up by the terms of a letter Stephens wrote to the *Straits Times* very shortly afterwards in which he said, 'Our hope is that the Tunku will let matters rest, that he will not be piqued by our refusal to accept what to him is a big-hearted offer and that he will see to it that the friendship between the Borneo territories and Malaya will remain.'

A turning point in the Bornean antagonism came on 21st July when a regional conference of the Malaya-Borneo group of the Commonwealth Parliamentary Association opened in Singapore. The Malayan and Singapore delegations devoted their lobby efforts towards answering the specific fears and reservations of the Borneans. (Brunei sent observers to the conference.) Stephens in a speech explained these in terms well understood by Asians: 'If it is to be a good marriage we must make sure of the dowry to be paid. We must make sure of the state of health of those who are about to enter into the matrimonial bond. The properties of the parties concerned after marriage and how they are to be managed and so on, must be known beforehand. These are important issues that must be settled before the marriage takes place.' At any rate, at the end of the two-day conference, the Borneans appeared to have been sufficiently converted to agree to a joint statement which said, 'Malaysia can become a reality and a popular movement if the concept can be translated into a concrete plan for the mutual benefit of all the parties concerned. . . . Once the people concerned are agreed as to the shape and contents of a united states of Malaysia, then no outside force can hinder its emergence.' Indeed, the Bornean delegates themselves took the lead in forming a 'Malaysian Solidarity Consultative Committee' composed of representatives from each of the five territories with Stephens as chairman, to examine the plan, assess public opinion upon it, and then develop and shape it into an acceptable formula. The importance of this Consultative Committee needs to be stressed because the end results—the creation of Malaysia and the constitutional pattern it took—had been worked out by the Committee and accepted by the peoples of the territories; they were not therefore tinged by 'Imperialist' or 'Colonialist' thought or actions. Sarawak's and North Borneo's final constitutions as units of Malaysia were based largely on the recommendations hammered out by the Committee.

A milestone was passed on 23rd August 1961 when Tunku Abdul Rahman and Lee Kuan Yew reached agreement in principle on a merger. External affairs, defence and security would be responsibilities of a central government while Singapore would retain autonomy in education and labour policy. The two Prime Ministers appointed a joint working party to go into the overall financial and other implications of a merger based on these principles. By 11th November the basic proposals were accepted by the two governments. Although Singapore would retain autonomy in labour and education policy because of the essentially Chinese bias in these spheres, it was to be at the expense of seats in the national Parliament. Singapore would be represented in the Federal Parliament by 15 seats. Singapore citizens would retain their citizenship but automatically become nationals of the larger Federation. The special position of Malays who were Singapore citizens would be safeguarded in a new constitution. Financially, because Singapore would administer its own educational and labour policies, it would retain 'a very large proportion of the present State revenue' to discharge those and other State responsibilities. The memorandum of agreement concluded, 'No terms and conditions can be liberal and generous to both sides; nor can they satisfy all parties on both sides of the Causeway. There are diverse local interests to be looked after. Singapore wishes to safeguard her local legitimate interests in many spheres; the Federation wants to secure her paramount interests in security and in the stability of the new Federation.'

This agreement paved the way for high-level consultations between the British and Malayan Governments. On 22nd November Mr. Macmillan and Tunku Abdul Rahman, after meeting in London, jointly declared that the formation of 'Malaysia' was 'a desirable aim'. They noted 'with satisfaction' the heads of agreement negotiated between Malaya and Singapore and added that before coming to any final decision it would be necessary to 'ascertain the views of the peoples of North Borneo and Sarawak' (whose future was the responsibility of the British Government) through an Anglo-Malayan Commission. At the same time the views of the Sultan of Brunei would be sought.

This conference also went into the general question of the future Malaysia's role in the defence of South-East Asia, a matter of considerable Commonwealth—and American—concern, and in particular the future of Britain's army, navy and air force bases in Singapore. The assurances that Britain obviously sought on these points were inherent in the final paragraph of the joint statement which said that in the event of the formation of Malaysia 'the existing Defence Agreement between Britain and Malaya should be extended to embrace the other territories concerned. It was agreed however that the Government of the Federation of Malaya will afford to the Government of the United Kingdom the right to continue to maintain bases at Singapore for the purpose of assisting in the defence of Malaysia and for Commonwealth defence and for the preservation of peace in South-East Asia.'

Events moved rapidly after this, particularly in North Borneo and Sarawak. A large number of political parties blossomed as the race for political power stirred these rural havens. In February 1962 an Anglo-Malayan Commission began its necessary inquiries into whether the peoples of North Borneo and Sarawak wished to merge with Malaya. It was headed by Lord Cobbold, a former Governor of the Bank of England. The British Government's nominees on the Commission were Sir Anthony Abell, a former Governor of Sarawak, and Sir David Watherston, a former Chief Secretary in Malaya, while the Malayan representatives were Dato Wong Pow Nee, Chief Minister of Penang, and Inche (Mr.) Muhammad Ghazali bin Shafie, Permanent Secretary to the Department of External Affairs. The Commission gave itself a formidable programme in order to ensure that it carried out its terms of reference thoroughly. Over 4,000 people in Sarawak and North Borneo accepted the invitation to give their views to the Commission which also studied more than 2,200 letters and memoranda from public bodies, political parties, religious leaders, local chiefs and individuals. It held 50 hearings in 35 centres, often going deep into the interior by light aircraft or outboard motor-boat to meet isolated tribes. It found 'Malaysia' a topic of everyday conversation in bazaars, clubs and coffee shops, and longhouses and huts in the interior. It completed its inquiries in two months and presented its report and recommendations in August.

The crux of the report lay in the Commission's unanimous assessment that one-third of the populations of the two States strongly favoured 'early realization of Malaysia without too much concern about terms and conditions'. Another third, of whom many were favourable to the plan, asked 'with varying degrees of emphasis, for conditions and safeguards varying in nature and extent'. The remaining third was divided between those who insisted on independence before union with Malaysia was considered and those 'who would strongly prefer to see British rule continue for some years to come'. The Commission added that there would remain 'a hard core, vocal and politically active' which would oppose Malaysia on any terms unless it was preceded by independence. This group was estimated at 'near 20 per cent of the population of Sarawak and somewhat less in North Borneo'. The opposition came largely from Chinese and mostly from those who supported the communist line. The Chinese, said the Commission, generally feared that Malaysia would mean discrimination against them and would affect their schools, their language and their culture, and that they would be reduced to 'second-class citizens'.

The Commission expressed unanimity on the point that Malaysia was 'in the best interests of the Borneo territories' in view of existing world conditions. It pointed out that the colonial administration could not continue indefinitely for pressures would inevitably mount both inside and outside the territories. Therefore the future of Sarawak and North Borneo would be much better assured if some more permanent arrangements could be made before those pressures mounted too far.

While the Commission achieved unanimity on a considerable number of subjects which had to be enshrined in a constitution, the British and Malayan members held opposing views on the phasing of the creation of Malaysia. The former were emphatic that 'the full realization of Malaya should be achieved in two distinct phases' with a transitional period of three to seven years during which the two territories could progress constitutionally to enable the people to understand 'the complicated machinery of Federation'; otherwise they feared a weakening in administration and stability leading to 'serious security risks'. The Malayans contended that the transfer of sovereignty should be immediate because a 'graduated constitutional and legal transfer of powers' would bring protracted delays, as State governments might be reluctant to transfer some of their power or the central government to assume the necessary responsibilities. This 'would leave the door open for destructive elements to impede the creation of a strong central authority by exploiting differences among various races and creating frictions between the central government and the State'. Lord Cobbold in summing up took the view that a transitional period was most desirable.

The Commission found that the most fundamental problem that emerged as the result of the Malaysia conception in both territories was race relations. It spoke of alarming signs of 'the conflict arising when a transfer of power is contemplated in some form and the indigenous people become aware of the prospect of having to share political power with the immigrant races at a time when they feel themselves still economically backward'. The bid for political power and the economic imbalances between the indigenous races and the Chinese had engendered strains among all the communities which once had lived on excellent terms with one another. This was apparent more in Sarawak than in North Borneo where racial harmony had been very much stronger because of assimilation by inter-marriage and social contacts generally. Nevertheless in both territories the alignment of political forces was clearly along racial lines.

In Sarawak the situation was aggravated by the intervention of a strong 'Clandestine Communist Organization' which since the proposal to form Malaysia had 'worked ceaselessly to exaggerate the fears which the Chinese community as a whole and members of other communities have of Malay domination and to make capital out of every possible issue, e.g., special position for the natives, citizenship, national language and religion'. North Borneo, while virtually free of communists, nevertheless possessed 'fertile material on which communist infiltration could work in the same way as it is already working in Sarawak'.

The Commission was undeniably perturbed by the possible future dangers from communists and from growing racial conflict. Lord Cobbold underlined the 'necessary condition that, from the outset, Malaysia should be regarded by all concerned as an association of partners, combining in the common interest to create a new nation but retaining their own individualities'. He added, 'If any idea were to take root that Malaysia would involve a "take-over" of the Borneo territories by the Federation of Malaya and the submersion of the individualities of North Borneo and Sarawak, Malaysia would not, in my judgment, be generally acceptable or successful.'

About this time a determined opposition to a Malaya-Singapore

merger as conceived in the agreements already reached, had mani-
fested itself among the small but very articulate left-wing parties in
Malaya and Singapore. In Singapore there had been a serious split in
the P.A.P. Three parliamentary political secretaries who had been
former detainees and 13 party members in the Legislative Assembly
had broken away and formed the *Barisan Socialis* (Socialist Front).
Lee Kuan Yew was left with a majority of only one in the Assembly.
This was the beginning of a bitter and critical battle for and against
Malaysia in Singapore. The *Barisan Socialis* pressed for the abolition
of the Internal Security Council and for full self-government for Singapore by 1963, after which Singapore could merge with Malaya and
have proportional representation in the Federal Parliament 'like the
other States'. The most crucial phase of this struggle for domination
was the Legislative Assembly's debate on a Government White Paper
which set out the terms negotiated with Malaya. It lasted 12 days and
ended in a Government victory. Then Lee Kuan Yew flung the
gauntlet down and declared his intention of holding a referendum to
ascertain the wishes of the people on the form of the merger with
Malaya. He said that, although the Government were legally and
constitutionally entitled to carry through the merger without a
referendum, they were prepared to hold one if only to rebut the
charge that Singapore was being 'sold out'. It may be added here that
the referendum on 1st September gave Lee Kuan Yew a decisive
decision. Of the 90 per cent of the registered citizens who voted, 71
per cent approved the terms of merger already agreed to between the
two governments, 1·1 per cent voted for merger on terms given to any
other State of the existing Federation of Malaya, and 1·4 per cent for
terms no less favourable than those to be offered to the Borneo territories. The remaining 25 per cent represented blank votes cast by the
opposition. Lee Kuan Yew's calculated risk had paid off clearly and
decisively. It ended the grim and relentless battle for Singapore's
membership in Malaysia.

In the middle of May 1962 Tunku Abdul Rahman, in a mood of
high optimism, arrived in London with a delegation for another
round of talks with the British Government. The report and recommendations of the Cobbold Commission formed the basis of the discussions. Some hard bargaining undoubtedly took place over the
timing of Malaysia and the question of safeguards for the two
Bornean territories; meetings often continued well into the night and

there were well-founded reports of 'hitches'. The talks lasted a fort-night but finally late at night on 31st July Mr. Macmillan and Tunku Abdul Rahman signed an agreement that Malaysia should be brought into being by 31st August 1963. A formal agreement to give effect to this decision would be signed within six months.

It would, among other things, provide for the transfer of sover-eignty in North Borneo, Sarawak and Singapore by 31st August 1963 and would include provisions governing the relationship between Singapore and Malaysia and detailed constitutional arrangements for North Borneo and Sarawak including safeguards for their special interests such as religious freedom, education, the position of the indigenous races, immigration, citizenship, representation in the Federal Parliament, and the State constitutions. To enable the new federal system to be effected as smoothly as possible, there would be, after the transfer of sovereignty, a transition period during which certain federal constitutional powers would be delegated temporarily to the State Governments (obviously a compromise formula on the main point of controversy among the members of the Cobbold Com-mission). An Inter-Governmental Committee would work out all these future constitutional arrangements for North Borneo and Sarawak. (It became clear later that the British Government had accepted almost all the unanimous recommendations of the Cobbold Commission.)

A week after the signing of this agreement, the British Government formally took up a side issue—a request from the Philippines Govern-ment for talks 'on the future of North Borneo'. The Philippines Government had claimed the return of parts of North Borneo on the ground that the transaction under which the Sultan of Sulu had dis-posed of his territory in 1878 to Baron von Overbeck and Alfred Dent had been illegal, and alternatively, if the Sultan had such a right, he had intended to lease and not cede the land. The British Government took the stand that the status of North Borneo was 'not open to dispute'. (The Philippinnes Government reopened the claim after North Borneo had become a part of Malaysia but up to the middle of 1964 had not presented formal details to the Malaysian Government.)

Then in December 1962 a rebellion broke out in Brunei—and its repercussions threatened the fulfilment of the creation of Malaysia.

CHAPTER 22

The Creation of Malaysia

The rebellion in Brunei broke early in the morning of 8th December 1962. Armed and uniformed groups calling themselves the 'T.N.K.U.'—*Tentera Nasional Kalimantan Utara*, Northern Borneo National Army ('Kalimantan' is the Indonesian name for their part of Borneo island)—seized control of the oil town of Seria and also attacked police stations in Brunei town and in the village of Limbang over the border in Sarawak. Within a few hours it became known that the revolt had been instigated by Sheikh Azahari, leader of the Party Rakyat, and that Brunei Malays were predominantly involved. Azahari had planned to capture Brunei, North Borneo and Sarawak and form them into a unitary State ruled by the Sultan of Brunei with himself as Prime Minister. The revolt was partly against the Brunei Government and partly an attempt to thwart the State's wish to become a member of Malaysia; Azahari had been an opponent of Malaysia in the form proposed by Tunku Abdul Rahman.

Earlier in the year, in July, the entirely nominated Brunei Legislative Council had approved the project of Malaysia in principle and the Sultan also expressed support for Brunei's membership in it provided the terms and conditions were satisfactory. Then, in September, Azahari's party won all but one seat in the first elections to the Brunei District Councils held under a constitution granted as far back as 1959. It thereby automatically gained all 16 indirectly elected seats in the new Legislative Council which was to have an official majority of one. The victory gave Azahari enhanced prestige in the circumscribed Brunei firmament. He began agitating for further constitutional reform (including, for instance, the conversion of the ruler from an autocratic to a constitutional monarch) and for further economic development of the State. The mood of the rural people

231

encouraged Azahari to believe that he would gain their overwhelming support for a federation of the three Borneo States as the first step towards independence. He then apparently decided to win support for his plans outside Borneo.

He made frequent trips to Djakarta where some of the top Indonesian leaders had known him for many years. In November 1962 he went to Manila to woo Filipino support for his opposition to the creation of Malaysia—and he was still in Manila when the rebellion was launched. It was from there that he proclaimed himself 'Prime Minister' of the 'new' State of 'Kalimantan Utara' (Northern Borneo) and declared, 'The Sultan is in our hands and supports the revolution.' Clearly his plans had included the kidnapping of the ruler and forcing him to sign a proclamation establishing the 'State of Kalimantan Utara'. Azahari did not know however that, on the first reports of the revolt, the Sultan had taken refuge in the Brunei town police station. There he denied knowledge of the plot and issued warrants of arrest for treason against Azahari and other leaders of the revolt. He also asked Britain for assistance in restoring law and order under the terms of its treaty with him, and troops were despatched immediately from Singapore by air and sea. They crushed the revolt in a few days. On 20th December, the Sultan suspended the constitution, dissolved the Legislative Council, and appointed an Emergency Council over which he presided. Azahari himself eventually left Manila for Djakarta where he temporarily faded from public view.

Although the Indonesian Government denied foreknowledge of the revolt, they had immediately announced their support of it. President Soekarno for the first time expressed strong opposition to the project of Malaysia—a surprising volte-face from the Indonesian attitude displayed in November 1961 when Dr. Subandrio, the Foreign Minister, said in the United Nations General Assembly, 'When Malaya told us of its intention to merge with Sarawak, Brunei and North Borneo as one federation, we told them that we had no objections and that we wished them success with this merger so that everyone might live in peace and freedom.' Soekarno described Azahari's revolt as an example of the power of 'new emerging forces'. Within a month of the failure of the revolt Indonesia began assembling its strident and provocative apparatus of 'confrontation' (which had been so successfully used against the Dutch in the demands for the return of Dutch New Guinea, now West Irian) against 'Malaysia' in general and Tunku Abdul Rahman and the British Government in particular. As 1963 opened, there were indeed doubts whether 'Malaysia' would 'get off the ground' at all in view of the strength of Indonesian opposition. And the fears that Indonesia would foment guerrilla warfare along its rugged frontier with Sarawak and North Borneo, using the 'T.N.K.U.' as a front, were realized. . . . With the help of volunteers from the Clandestine Chinese Communist organization in Sarawak, Indonesian guerrillas entered Sarawak territory, attacked villages and police stations, and killed and kidnapped people. British and Malayan forces were committed to immediate operations along the Sarawak border.

Azahari's revolt and Indonesia's war of words against Malaysia had the effect of strengthening pro-Malaysia sentiment in Sarawak and North Borneo. These two territories rapidly realized that once British sovereignty was withdrawn—as it would probably have to be sooner or later in the ordinary course of constitutional progress— there was no secure future for either of them if they stood on their own. They immediately became the most impassioned advocates of 'Malaysia'. The leaders of political parties, including the Sarawak United Peoples' Party which had opposed the concept of Malaysia, rejected Azahari and his 'Kalimantan Utara'. It was significant that North Borneo's first elections to District Councils (which were to form electoral colleges to a new Legislative Council) were fought on national rather than on purely local issues; North Borneo's membership in Malaysia was the main issue in everyone's mind. These elections resulted in an overwhelming victory for the candidates of a group of pro-Malaysia parties which had formed themselves into the 'Sabah Alliance'. They won 104 out of 119 seats, the remainder going to independents most of whom were pro-Malaysia.

In February 1963 the Malaysia Solidarity Consultative Committee issued a statement condemning outside interference in the affairs of the proposed Federation and expressed determination to create Malaysia by 31st August that year. In February too, representatives of the Malayan and Brunei Governments began to draw up draft heads of agreement for Brunei's membership of Malaysia. In Manila, President Macapagal declared, in a State-of-the-Nation address to a joint session of the Philippine Congress, that the proposed Federation 'was not in accordance with the principle of self-determination' and that its formation would make Malaya a new colonial power—a statement that promised poorly for the preservation of the Association of South-East Asia. And from Djakarta came threats of physical conflict in Sarawak. . . . The Malaysia plan came up for discussion too before a largely communist-dominated 'Afro-Asian Peoples' Conference' convened in Moshi in Tanganyika; a Singapore delegation was flown to Moshi to counteract the communist fulminations against Malaysia and, though it was barred from attending meetings, it succeeded in foiling attempts to marshal Afro-Asian opinion unanimously against the project. Nevertheless the dangers of hostile African opinion were recognized, and it might well be added here that in January 1964, Mr. Lee Kuan Yew set out, with a strong Malaysian retinue, to tour African States on a mission to win African friends and influence their leaders.

The reasons behind Indonesia's opposition became clear as the weeks passed, although they were never spelt out by Soekarno or his government who only alleged that Malaysia would be 'neo-colonialist'—meaning that it was designed simply to serve the interests of the British colonial power, that its dependence on British backing would perpetuate Britain's political, military and economic control of the territories concerned, and that it lacked popular support. Both these charges were quite unfounded but they served Soekarno's purposes. Basically however it was apparent that Malaysia—and the support it was receiving from peoples in the territories concerned—would frustrate Soekarno's personal dreams of ruling an Indonesian empire stretching from Sumatra to New Guinea and embracing Sarawak, North Borneo, Brunei and Malaya itself. There was probably a quiet fear too among the Indonesian leaders that if, as could be expected, Malaysia stood forth as a stable political and economic entity, it would inevitably raise dissatisfactions within Indonesia which was suffering from serious economic problems already, and would cast doubt on the validity of Soekarno's economic and political theories. Observers were also emphatic that another strong reason for the Indonesian antagonism towards Malaysia was Soekarno's personal antipathy towards Tunku Abdul Rahman whom he saw as a rival leader in regional and international affairs. Whatever the real basic reasons for Soekarno's 'confrontation', it had the backing not only of the well-organized Indonesian Communist Party (which with a membership of more than two million and a following perhaps four times as large was the third largest Communist Party in the world after Russia and China) but also of the powerful Indonesian Army.

The unexpected opposition of the Philippines was a little more difficult to understand because of its professed close friendship with Malaya and its membership of the Association of South-East Asia. The official Philippine reason for its attitude was the rejection of its claim to parts of North Borneo, but it also attempted to argue that the influx of Chinese into the Borneo States after the creation of Malaysia would present the Philippines with a 'Communist' menace less than 50 miles from its southernmost point. To observers this appeared a specious and weak argument which took no account of the determination of Tunku Abdul Rahman and his government to keep communism at bay.

On 27th February 1963 the Inter-Governmental Committee which had been set up out of a recommendation of the Cobbold Commission, published its report. It showed unanimity among the British, Malayan, Sarawak and North Borneo delegations that the constitution of Malaysia should be based on the existing constitution of Malaya. The Committee's principal task however had been to work out safeguards for the special interests of Sarawak and North Borneo on such vital subjects as religion (it recommended that while Islam should be the religion of Malaysia there should be no State religon in the Borneo States), immigration (the Borneo States should be given effective control over immigration), education (although this was a federal subject, the educational policy and system in the Borneo States would remain undisturbed until either government decided otherwise), the special position of the indigenous races (they would enjoy the same privileges that the Malayan constitution provided for Malays), citizenship (everyone born or naturalized in Sarawak or North Borneo would be a Malaysian citizen by operation of law and others would be able to acquire citizenship on the Malayan terms that applied to naturalization), and national language (Malay would be the national language of Malaysia but in the Borneo territories English would remain an official language until the State Government decided otherwise).

The Malaysian Parliament would comprise 159 members. Sarawak would have 24 seats and North Borneo 16, which indeed were special concessions when compared with the 15 agreed for Singapore and, as a further comparison, with the 20 granted under the Malayan constitution to Perak, the second largest State in Malaya with a population of nearly 1·4 million or more than that of the two Borneo States combined. The Committee recommended that the Borneo Members of Parliament should be elected by their State legislatures under the existing system of indirect elections until the first general election was held 'after the fifth anniversary' of the establishment of Malaysia. Sarawak and North Borneo would each have a Head of State who initially would be appointed by the Queen and the Yang di-Pertuan Agong for a period of two years, after which four-year appointments would be made by the Yang di-Pertuan Agong following consultation with the respective Chief Ministers. Sarawak's Head of State would be styled 'Governor' and North Borneo's the *Yang di-Pertua Negara*.

It was clear that Sarawak and North Borneo had been granted almost all the conditions they had set for entry into Malaysia. The Committee even indicated agreement that these States could retain a considerable measure of control over their own finances. As help and development had also been a Bornean condition, the Malayan Government promised to 'use its best endeavours' to enable Sarawak to spend $300 million and North Borneo $200 million on capital expenditure during the first five years after 'Malaysia Day'. The British Government also promised a grant of £1½ million a year for five years for development provided the Malayan Government would extend development aid for at least this period.

A few weeks afterwards, Sarawak and North Borneo took further steps in constitutional progress. In Sarawak general elections in mid-August formed the prelude to the introduction of a ministerial system of government under a Chief Minister (Mr. Stephen Ningkan, an Iban). In North Borneo, progress towards an elected ministerial system was begun in mid-March when six unofficial members of the Legislative Council were given departmental responsibility as 'Members', and in July indirect elections to the Legislative Council were held when Mr. Donald Stephens became Chief Minister. (By Malaysia Day, North Borneo had a Legislative Council with an elected majority and a ministerial system of government.)

On the international front, hope of a settlement of the Indonesian differences with Malaya suddenly sprang to life when Soekarno invited Tunku Abdul Rahman to meet him in Tokio. Their talks took place on 31st May and 1st June and built up hopes of better relations. Certainly before the world's press both joked and shook hands as they posed for photographers. Their communiqué said they had agreed to settle any differences between them 'in the spirit of the 1959 Treaty of Friendship', although as the *Straits Times* newspaper of Kuala Lumpur put it there had been 'times in the past 10 months when Malays might have been excused for believing that this Treaty had been denounced'. The communiqué foreshadowed a second meeting, this time in Manila with President Macapagal also present. The Foreign Ministers of the three countries met in Manila early in June as a prelude to the 'summit' meeting, and on 11th June announced agreement on the solution of problems arising out of the proposed formation of Malaysia. They did not go into details but conference sources suggested that Malaya agreed to an inquiry into the wishes of the peoples in the two Borneo territories under United National auspices or by a neutral commission. As a major side issue, the Foreign Ministers examined a proposal by President Macapagal that a confederation of nations of Malay origin—'Maphilindo' was the name adopted for this concept—should be established; they announced agreement on 'the acceptance of the idea as a means of bringing together their countries into the closest association'. It all promised a peaceful birth of Malaysia. . . .

In the meantime, talks between Malaya and Singapore on financial conditions for participation in Malaysia teetered on the edge of breakdown. The Singapore argument revolved around, first, a Malayan demand for $50 million as a contribution by Singapore towards development in Sarawak and North Borneo over the next five years, and secondly Singapore's insistence that the creation of a common market should be written into the constitution. There were also difficulties in the negotiations between Malaya and Brunei; these largely concerned the use of the State revenue from oil and of future oil royalties while Brunei, it was reported, also refused to recognize the right of the Central Government of Malaysia to levy and collect taxes, including an export duty on oil. It maintained that its sole contribution to the Malaysian exchequer should be a lump sum paid out of the annual revenue of the State. The Malayan Government was prepared to allow the Brunei Government to collect and keep the royalty on oil for ten years but asserted the central government's right to levy duties and taxes in Brunei as it saw fit. The Sultan of Brunei's precedence among the Malay sultans for election as the Yang di-Pertuan Agong was also a major issue.

Eventually to Brunei and Singapore went letters from the Malayan Government giving 'final terms' in the negotiations; Tunku Abdul Rahman also declared his intention to establish Malaysia on 31st August without either Singapore or Brunei. The scene for the solution of all these problems moved to London at the end of June when Malaya, Singapore and Brunei sought the assistance of the British Government in bridging the outstanding issues. Malaya's Deputy Prime Minister, Tun Abdul Razak, Lee Kuan Yew and the Sultan of Brunei flew to London. There the talks over Singapore's conditions all but reached breaking-point. Finally after $12\frac{1}{2}$ hours of continuous and dramatic roundtable talks presided over by Mr. Duncan Sandys, the Secretary of State for Commonwealth Relations, a compromise was reached. The hard bargaining that had occurred may be gauged by the fact that the first round of negotiations began at 9.30 one night and closed at eight o'clock the next morning; they were resumed at 11 a.m. and ended at 1 p.m. Terms relating to the establishment of a common market were agreed to after concessions by both sides. On aid for the Borneo territories, Singapore, although adamantly against making a gift of $50 million (the terms first offered) agreed to lend $150 million on the understanding that 50 per cent of the labour and materials to be used on projects under the loan would come from Singapore.

Tunku Abdul Rahman flew to London immediately to sign, with Britain, the final formal Agreement to the setting up of the Federation of Malaysia. But at almost the last minute on the day of the ceremony, 8th July, Lee Kuan Yew injected new difficulties with a final haggle, this time with the British Government, over the title to land in Singapore used by the War Department. He also asked for $15 million as the price for other land the War Department planned to use. The signing ceremony in Marlborough House kept being postponed from hour to hour while Mr. Sandys contrived to settle the new issues as he had helped to settle the others. In the midst of all this came word from the Sultan of Brunei that he had found himself unable to sign the Agreement because of the inability of the Malayan Government 'to give effect to terms previously agreed or to assurances repeatedly given'. Brunei's refusal was a setback to hopes of full accord among the five territories. Tunku Abdul Rahman expressed suitable regrets over the fact that the negotiations with Brunei had broken down.

Just before nine o'clock that night, the issue with Singapore was settled by the intervention of Tunku Abdul Rahman who called Lee Kuan Yew to his hotel for a talk. There Lee agreed to reduce his figure of $15 million for the land to $10 million. So a gruelling week ended. The formal Agreement was signed just before midnight, and the ceremony was all the more dramatic because of the preceding hours of intensive negotiation over matters of money. It was with delicious understatement that Mr. Harold Macmillan said at the ceremony, 'The Agreement which we have reached among us is the product of much anxious thought, careful consultation and keen argument. These processes have continued up to the last possible moment but I do not regret that.' He concluded with an expression of 'confident hope . . . that this bold and imaginative development in the evolution of our Commonwealth will establish a new focus of peace, freedom and stability in South-East Asia'. Mr. Lee Kuan Yew and representatives from Sarawak and North Borneo also signed the Agreement.

Hardly a week had passed before the dark clouds of Indonesian 'confrontation' gathered again. Although he was due to meet President Macapagal and Tunku Abdul Rahman on 30th July for another talk, President Soekarno suddenly declared, 'We not only disagree with Malaysia but we shall oppose it to the end.' He alleged that Tunku Abdul Rahman by signing the Agreement in London had broken faith and had gone back on his word that Malaysia would not be formed before the will of the peoples of the Borneo States on merger with Malaya had been ascertained. Tunku Abdul Rahman retorted that, although he had agreed to a United Nations inquiry in North Borneo and Sarawak, he had made it clear to Soekarno in Tokio that Malaysia would come into being as scheduled. He indicated his intention of attending the tripartite meeting. The question was whether Soekarno would attend for he never abated his hostility. Indeed as the meeting date approached he declared Indonesia's intention 'to crush Malaysia' (this became a popular phrase in the months to come).

Soekarno did go to Manila. After a six-day conference there emerged the 'Manila Accord' under which Tunku Abdul Rahman agreed formally to a United Nations assessment of the wishes of the people of Sarawak and North Borneo concerning membership of Malaysia with special emphasis on whether Malaysia had been a major issue—if not the main issue—in all the elections and whether these had been properly conducted. Tunku Abdul Rahman undertook to ask the British Government to extend the necessary facilities to the United Nations in the two Bornean territories and to agree to observers being attached to the teams. A paragraph of significance—reportedly put into the statement at the behest of the Malayans—made it clear that Indonesia and the Philippines 'would welcome the formation of Malaysia' if the U.N. investigation confirmed the support of the peoples of the two territories to the project. The three nations also agreed to 'take initial steps towards the establishment of Maphilindo by holding frequent and regular consultations at all levels'.

There were two significant points about the Manila Accord: Indonesia did not give any undertaking to abandon its policy of confrontation, and the United Nations inquiry would clearly mean a postponement in the date of the establishment of Malaysia. Tunku Abdul Rahman told his Parliament, 'We have to accept this inevitability (of postponement) in the interest of goodwill, understanding and peace.' He personally lost no prestige in Malaya for the compromise he had reached in Manila, but his partners-to-be, Singapore, Sarawak and North Borneo, turned and declared they were not bound by the agreement in Manila.

The British Government agreed, albeit reluctantly, to permit the United Nations to operate in the two Borneo territories although this created a precedent which might be invoked elsewhere. The Secretary-General of the United Nations, U Thant, in accepting the assignment insisted that his findings should not be questioned or subject to verification by any of the parties, and made it clear that the observers were not part of the team to whom he was entrusting the work, and therefore they were not essential to its fulfilment. On 16th August, two United Nations teams arrived in Sarawak and North Borneo to begin their task which they expected would take at least a fortnight. Britain agreed to permit two observers each from Indonesia, the Philippines and Malaya to watch the teams at work, emphasizing that this was to be their sole function and that they could not conduct any parallel or independent inquiry. Indonesia, supported by the Philippines, objected to the limitation on the number of observers and said they refused to accept the findings of the U.N. teams until 'the problem of observers was solved'. The U.N. investigators waited for instructions from New York. Britain offered a compromise—the attachment of a junior assistant of clerical grade to each observer. U Thant regarded this as reasonable and instructed his teams to begin their work even if neither Indonesia nor the Philippines accepted the offer.

On 27th August therefore the U.N. men set to work with Malayan and British observers attached to them. It was obvious by then that Malaysia could not come into being on 31st August, so on 29th August the Yang di-Pertuan Agong proclaimed that 'Malaysia Day' would be 16th September. This proclamation was constitutionally necessary. With all the agreements that had been entered into in London, a definite date had to be set for the transfer of British sovereignty; 16th September was chosen because it became known that U Thant's report on the findings of his teams would be published before that date.

The political executives in Singapore, Sarawak and North Borneo had to accept the new date but they appeared to judge it necessary to emphasize again that they and their peoples were partners in Malaysia and could not be taken for granted by Tunku Abdul Rahman, much less by Soekarno. On 31st August they held 'Malaysia Day' celebrations as planned. Singapore also proclaimed its 'complete independence', 'taking over' until Malaysia Day the powers over defence and external affairs. Sarawak and North Borneo also announced the introduction of internal self-government pending Malaysia Day. Malaya took strong exception to these gestures—which in fact they were, since no formal constitutional changes had actually taken place.

The United Nations teams completed their painstaking inquiries on 5th September. Three days before, Indonesia and the Philippines had finally despatched observers to witness the closing stages of the work and were also given access to the tape-recordings of all hearings by the commission. On 13th September U Thant presented his findings to the governments of Malaya, Britain, Indonesia and the Philippines. These corroborated the report of the Cobbold Commission and the evidence of the local elections that the majority of the peoples of the two States, as U Thant put it, wished 'to bring their dependent status to an end and to realize their independence through freely chosen association with other peoples in their region with whom they feel ties of ethnic association, heritage, language, religion, culture, economic relationship and ideals and objectives. Not all these considerations', added U Thant, 'are present in equal weight in all minds but it is my conclusion that the majority of the peoples of the two territories having taken them into account, wish to engage, with the peoples of the Federation of Malaya and Singapore, in an enlarged Federation of Malaysia through which they can strive together to realize the fulfilment of their destiny.'

The way was now clear to bringing the general wish to fruition. On 16th September, Singapore, Sarawak and North Borneo (which renamed itself 'Sabah') held ceremonies in which they formally declared their independence and their membership of Malaysia. (Officially 'Malaysia' was not considered a 'new' nation but the outgrowth of the former Federation of Malaya whose constitution had foreseen such a contingency. Thus there was no need for Malaysia's ambassadors abroad or for the foreign ambassadors within the territory to present new credentials; neither was new recognition of Malaysia in the United Nations necessary.)

The next day, 17th September, the Heads of all the 14 States of the new Malaysia assembled in the Merdeka Stadium in Kuala Lumpur for the formal proclamation of the admission of the three new States to Malaysia. It was in that stadium that the Queen's representative, the Duke of Gloucester, had in 1957 formally presented Malaya with its constitutional documents of freedom. On a long dais in the centre of the stadium sat the Malay rulers and the Governors with the Yang di-Pertuan Agong, now 'Supreme Head' of Malaysia, in the centre. It was another brilliant and memorable scene and it was from exactly the same spot where six years before he had emotionally declared Malaya's independence that Tunku Abdul Rahman, now Prime Minister of Malaysia, proclaimed that 'as from the Sixteenth Day of September in the Year One Thousand Nine Hundred and Sixtythree, corresponding to the Twentyeighth Day of Rabi'ul Akhir in the Year of the Hijrah One Thousand Three Hundred and Eightythree, Malaysia . . . shall by the Grace of God, the Lord of the Universe, for ever be an independent and sovereign democratic State founded upon liberty and justice, ever seeking to defend and uphold peace and harmony among its peoples and to perpetuate peace among nations'. The new flag of Malaysia, with its 14-pointed star and crescent and 14 red and white stripes, was raised to the playing of the national anthem.

But neither Indonesia nor the Philippines was represented in the great concourse of nations watching this event. On the previous day, both had announced their intention to withhold recognition of the new State because of 'flaws in the way the U.N. survey had been conducted'. Their ambassadors left Kuala Lumpur immediately. Tunku Abdul Rahman confirmed the rupture of diplomatic relations by recalling Malaysia's ambassadors from the two countries. On 17th September thousands of Indonesian demonstrators stormed the British and Malaysian embassies in Djakarta and other large groups sacked the British and Malaysian consulates in Medan, north Sumatra. The next day in Kuala Lumpur, the police had a difficult job preventing Malays from attacking the Indonesian Embassy. The Malaysian Cabinet decided to put the country into 'a state of preparedness' in case Indonesia opened hostilities. Britain informed Tunku Abdul Rahman that she was ready to help defend Malaysia's independence and integrity under the terms of the Mutual Assistance Treaty. That same day in Djakarta, Indonesian mobs sacked and set fire to the British Embassy and wrecked and looted British homes.

Indonesian hostility persisted strongly for the rest of the year and well into 1964 in spite of efforts by various heads of States and governments to get Tunku Abdul Rahman, Soekarno and Macapagal to meet again and settle matters. For instance, in January 1964 the United States sent its Attorney-General, Mr. Robert Kennedy, to the three capitals to try to persuade the three leaders to move the 'conflict out of the warfare that is at present taking place' (Indonesian-inspired incidents along the Sarawak border had increased in number and intensity) to a conference table. He succeeded to the extent that Indonesia, early in February, agreed to a cease-fire in the jungles of Sarawak and Sabah—which was fine in Indonesian theory but frequently violated in practice. The Foreign Ministers of Indonesia and the Philippines met Tun Abdul Razak in Bangkok. It was the first official contact between the three countries since the split in their relations around Malaysia Day. The Malaysians insisted on the unconditional withdrawal of Indonesian guerrillas from Sarawak and Sabah as a prerequisite to political talks, on which the meeting collapsed because the Indonesians refused to agree; they wanted withdrawal linked with a political settlement. Soekarno maintained his aggressive attitude and in speeches called on Indonesian 'volunteers' to 'crush Malaysia'. There were fears of an Indonesian Army invasion across the Bornean frontier and of Indonesian air raids on selected targets in Malaya and Singapore. The Indonesian sabre rattled noisily, and then in May 1964 President Soekarno accepted Filipino overtures for a 'summit' meeting in Tokio. Perhaps surprisingly Soekarno also agreed to Malaysian conditions that, before these talks could start, regular and irregular Indonesian forces inside Sabah and Sarawak should begin withdrawals through four designated checkpoints along the routes to which a cease-fire would operate; the withdrawals would be observed by Thai representatives. Tunku Abdul Rahman, President Macapagal and President Soekarno gathered in Tokio. When Thai observers reported the passage through one checkpoint of 32 Indonesian guerrillas, Tunku Abdul Rahman agreed to the opening of the talks. These began on 20th June in an atmosphere described by observers as one of 'superficial goodwill'. Within 24 hours, however, the expected happened again: the talks broke down. Tunku Abdul Rahman had agreed in principle to the appointment of an Afro-Asian conciliation commission which would recommend solutions for the existing political problems, but made it conditional on the cessation of all acts of hostility against Malaysia by Indonesia, an undertaking which, however, President Soekarno refused to give. Within another 24 hours, the Indonesians gave notice that 'confrontation' would continue. In Sabah and Sarawak, Malaysian and British forces prepared for increased guerrilla warfare or for an extension of hostilities by Indonesia.

On 25th April 1964 Tunku Abdul Rahman's Alliance Party won its third general election in Malaya with a sweeping victory; it was returned at even greater strength than in 1959. It secured 89 out of the 104 seats in the Federal Parliament. (In 1959, it had won 74 out of 104 seats.) It also retained control with greater majorities over 10 of the 11 State legislatures (the Pan-Malayan Islamic Party succeeded in holding on in Kelantan but with a reduced majority). Tunku Abdul Rahman's position in the Malaysian Parliament became impregnable for he could also count on the support of 36 seats held by Alliance supporters in Sarawak and Sabah. Thus he controlled a total of 125 seats out of the 159 in the House of Representatives.

The election campaign had been fought almost wholly on the issue of the establishment of Malaysia and the Government's stand against Indonesia's confrontation. The impressive result was a rebuff to Soekarno and to his supporters in Malaysia for the candidates of anti-Malaysian parties had suffered catastrophic failures. The Socialist Front saw only 2 of its 63 candidates returned (it won 8 seats in 1959) and the Pan-Malayan Islamic Party, sympathetic to Indonesian aspirations, succeeded only in 9 of 54 seats they fought (they had 13 gains in 1959). Lee Kuan Yew's People's Action Party had put up 9 candidates really to oppose the Malayan Chinese Association and the Socialist Front, but saw only one of them returned. Lee Kuan Yew was undoubtedly disappointed over this result but sent a telegram to Tunku Abdul Rahman congratulating him on his 'stupendous victory' and adding, 'No one in the world can now doubt that you lead the people of Malaysia in their desire to build an independent and democratic nation separate and distinct from Indonesia.' The P.A.P. with 16 seats (the other 15, it will be recalled, were Singapore's allocation under the Malaysia Agreement) became the largest single party outside the Government in the House of Representatives; its role, said Lee, would be that of a 'loyal opposition'.

On 31st August 1964, National Day, Malaya sombrely celebrated the seventh anniversary of its independence and Malaysia the first anniversary of its establishment. This first year had placed serious strains on the nation principally because of Indonesia's aggression. The situation was put succinctly by the *Straits Times* which said: 'Resources of men, money and materials have had to be diverted from development purposes. Trade between Indonesia and Malaysia has ended, a misfortune for both countries. The Association of South-East Asia is moribund, and the Maphilindo concept, which could have been the outstanding triumph of the Manila negotiations, died in the Borneo jungle.' And Indonesia had already switched its offensive from the Borneo territories to the peninsula itself. . . . Early on the morning of 17th August, about 100 men had landed by sea along Pontian, on the south-west coast of Johore. Malaysian security forces, which had long been placed in position along the west coast of Johore in anticipation of Indonesian invasion, quickly rounded up or killed almost all of the group. Then on 2nd September another Indonesian force, believed to number about 100, was parachuted into the Labis region of Johore, also in the south-west. Again most of them were either killed or surrendered to Malaysian troops. Many of the prisoners and the killed in both sets of invaders were identified as members of the Indonesian regular army and navy; the others consisted of Chinese communists and Malays of Indonesian stock who had been trained in Indonesia for sabotage and subversion in Malaysia. (Tunku Abdul Rahman later declared that more than 2,000 youths from Sarawak and Sabah, 300 from Singapore, and about 200 from Malaya, mostly Chinese but including some Malays, had gone to Indonesia in the previous two years for training in guerrilla warfare in Malaysia.)

With the Labis invasion, the Malaysia Government decided that the time had finally come to bring the subject of Indonesia's aggression before the Security Council of the United Nations; ever since 'confrontation' had begun, it had deferred presenting to the Security Council its charges of aggression against Indonesia although it had kept it informed of every Indonesian-inspired incident which had occurred on its soil. Its spokesman at the meeting of the Security Council which took place in the middle of September called upon the Council to 'condemn such international brigandage' and to order Indonesia to cease its aggression. Indonesia's permanent representative at the United Nations made no attempt to refute the charges but claimed that the Indonesian attacks in Malaysia had on the contrary been justified—because of British and Malaysian provocation against Indonesia. . . . The expectation that a resolution which criticized Indonesia in any way would be vetoed by Russia was borne out in the event; a Norwegian-sponsored resolution which deplored the landings of Indonesian paratroops on 2nd September, and which called on all the parties concerned 'to respect the territorial integrity and political independence' of each other, was met by a Russian veto and therefore could not be adopted. But as nine members of the Council had supported the resolution Malaysia won a moral victory. Since Indonesia was not expected to be impressed by this point, Malaysia prepared itself for all eventualities.

As it turned out, Indonesia's 'confrontation' policy had perhaps been the best gift that the people of the 14 territories could have been given on Malaysia Day 1963. It had accelerated the process of welding the multi-racial population into a nation as nothing else could have done; indeed the majority of the peoples were prepared to go to war with Indonesia if necessary. History may say that Soekarno's tactics did more than anything else to help in the creation of a Malaysian nation. Admittedly racial dissatisfactions existed but they were perhaps not so deep that they could not be solved by tact and persuasion.

But confrontation in its first year certainly had its adverse effects on the economy of Malaysia. The entrepôt trade of Singapore suffered most severely. Singapore used to import Indonesia rubber, petroleum, copra, coffee and spices which were then remilled, processed or graded largely for re-export to other countries. At the same time, Singapore re-exported to Indonesia textiles, rice and a large variety of manufactured goods. The Finance Minister of Singapore, Dr. Goh Keng Swee, declared that the cessation of all this trade would cost Singapore about 8·7 per cent of its national income and set development work back two years. The trade disruption had also caused the unemployment of at least 100,000 workers in Singapore to say nothing of about 900 sailors whose small ships used to ply between Singapore and Indonesian ports. Penang's entrepôt trade with Indonesia was similarly affected though on a smaller scale; in Sarawak, the major adverse affect was the reduction of the overland imports of Indonesian rubber.

External pressures apart, it seemed, on Malaysia Day, to have the best chance of any multi-racial Federation of surviving and becoming influential in international affairs, a stable force in South-East Asia, and a prosperous entity in itself. The fact that it was not an imposed Federation, but one sought by its people who also fashioned its federal and State constitutions, sent it off to a very good start. It must also be remembered that the federal idea had been successfully practised among the 11 States of Malaya since 1948, an experience that would be of enormous value and benefit to the new entity. And the fact that a spirit of compromise and understanding had been established during the negotiations that led to the Malaysia Agreement was a good augury in case of future controversy over points of principle.

Economically, Malaysia at birth stood more firmly and solidly based than any previous federation in the Commonwealth thanks to the revenue from the staple industries of rubber and tin and the judicious economic policies of the Malayan Government. In 1961 the territories comprising Malaysia exported rubber to the total value of $1,566 million (Malaya's own exports represented 55 per cent of its export earnings). But Malaysia is wary of depending too much upon rubber because of its vulnerability to the year-to-year fluctuations of the world markets and the impact of technological developments in America's synthetic rubber.

Malaysia however faces no competition as the largest single world producer of tin (one-third of the total world tin output), a commodity which remains at a fairly steady price level. In 1961, exports of tin from the peninsula were worth $307 million. In addition to tin, a new and considerable iron-ore field in Pahang holds great promise, while mineral deposits are expected to be developed in the Borneo territories in the near future.

A few other facts may serve to emphasize the promising economic future of Malaysia. Taken as a whole the exports of domestic goods and services in 1961 amounted to about $4,000 million or over 45 per cent of the combined national products. The total foreign exchange reserves of all the territories rose to about $3,800 million in 1962 or the equivalent of nearly one year's imports of goods and services; at the same time the public external debt was relatively small, totalling about $700 million altogether. Although the levels of income show significant contrasts in each territory, they are still, each of them, higher than in any other country in South-East Asia. Singapore has the highest with about $1,300 *per caput*, the peninsula next with about $800, Sabah third with about $700, and Sarawak fourth with $550. The average of $860 for Malaysia as a whole is computed in official Malaysian circles to be probably about twice the *per caput* income level of Thailand or the Philippines.

Industrial development which has been a considerable feature in Malaya and Singapore in recent years is likely to spread to the Bornean States. Economic development plans are being integrated to cover the whole of Malaysia. Malaya itself is moving towards the close of its ambitious Second Five-Year Plan (1961–5) and this will be succeeded by the first 'Malaysia' development plan. The ending of the Emergency had given a new momentum to development of the country, and the programme that was drawn up under the Second Plan had been set against some very pertinent economic problems which could not be tackled earlier because of the need to divert money towards crushing the communist terrorists. These were: an expected population increase of more than one million in the next five years which in its turn would put 340,000 young people in the market for employment; land hunger experienced by people in the rural areas who could turn to nothing but jungle for cultivation; poor living conditions prevailing over much of the countryside; and the over-specialization and excessive dependency of the economy on rubber (which accounted for over 25 per cent of the national income, nearly 30 per cent of employment, and about 60 per cent of exports).

The broad objectives of the Second Plan were therefore the improvement of life for the rural population, providing employment for all, widening the variety of Malayan production—for instance with oil palms—and extending the social services. The plan envisaged total development outlays of $5,050 million divided into $2,150 million of public investment and $2,090 million of private investment.

The highest priority was given to rural economic and social development—improving life for five million people in the hinterland. This was going to be a war against poverty, disease and ignorance in the Malay *kampong* and Chinese villages, and the Government tackled it as if it were a military operation. It adopted the technique so successfully used in the war against the terrorists—that is, 'war by committees'. A Ministry of National and Rural Development was established with a nerve centre in Kuala Lumpur which became known as the 'Operations Room'; it has its counterparts in every State and in every administrative district in the peninsula—and quite a number of villages have their own 'operations room'. The responsibility for planning development needs and carrying them out rests with Committees at State and district levels.

The Federal 'Ops room' holds complete reports on the progress of every development programme in every State and district. Wall maps, charts, diagrams, films, and even tape-recordings supplement written reports. Thus the Minister of Rural Development can see at a glance the stage reached in any project, however small, in the country—and does not hesitate to demand an explanation if any is behind schedule.

Under the vigorous impetus of this programme, the face of Malaya is undergoing another change. Several hundred miles of new roads have already been driven into the more isolated regions, bridges have been thrown across wide streams and rivers, and water and electric supplies installed in *kampong* and villages; schools, clinics and dispensaries have been built, jungle cleared for land-hungry settlers who have been given their own acres on which to grow rubber, *padi* and fruit and who can market their products through new co-operatives and farmers' associations. Bus services rumble along new rural routes. Low-cost houses have been built in the larger centres of population. Fishermen have been provided with outboard motors for their boats and they bring their catches back to refrigerated store houses. Even the telephone system is reaching into the hinterland— and adult classes are spreading.

The rural development programme is being extended to the two Borneo territories. Indonesia's confrontation however has not helped the general programme of development and there have been other problems. As an interim report by the Government published in

249

December 1963 put it, there are difficulties to be overcome. Some 'are inherent in our geographical situation and in our complex racial, cultural and linguistic backgrounds. Some spring from the international economy and Malaya's traditional dependence on exports of rubber and tin. Other difficulties arise from international politics.' However, although the need to divert money for defence against Indonesia's aggression reduced the pace of the economic development programme, the encouraging volume of capital that has been flowing into Malaysia as loans and investments has provided a counter-balance.

Like every other federation, Malaysia was expected to have its 'teething' troubles (setting aside those external influences which could submerge it or retard it). But once it had triumphed over those initial difficulties—for instance, the strains that might be imposed by the anomalous form of the federation, Singapore's special position in it, and the need for Singapore as well as the Borneo States, to allow time in which to accept the idea of working to and with a central government—Malaysia had all the elements for progress in stability and prosperity.

Postscript

At 10 o'clock on the morning of Monday, 9th August 1965, the Central Government of Malaysia and the Singapore Government announced simultaneously that Singapore had, by agreement, separated that day from Malaysia. The news burst like a bomb; the immediate reaction was consternation—not perhaps that it should have happened but that it had happened without warning and so swiftly—and also of apprehension over the future of the remaining federation. As the *Straits Times* said in an editorial, there had been nothing in recent events to prepare the public for the 'tragic' news and 'separation was the last thing the public expected'. The break came less than two years after the establishment of Malaysia.

The agreement for the separation of Singapore had been signed on the previous Saturday and it had been a well-kept secret for nearly 48 hours. Britain, Australia and New Zealand, so deeply committed to assisting in the defence of Malaysia against Indonesia's aggression, had not been informed; their diplomatic representatives in Kuala Lumpur had learned of the decision only late on Sunday evening. By then it was too late to persuade Tunku Abdul Rahman, the Prime Minister of Malaysia, to postpone the announcement and to reconsider the decision in the light of the very serious implications a break-up of Malaysia would have for Commonwealth political and defence policies in the Far East.

The general reason for the separation of Singapore is best given in the words of Tunku Abdul Rahman when he addressed the Malaysian Parliament that Monday morning: 'Since the formation of Malaysia, and this year in particular, there have been so many differences with the Singapore Government and these differences take many

251

forms, so much so that it has now come to a breaking-point. I cannot find any way out except the course of action which I am forced to take.' Efforts to find an understanding with the leaders of Singapore had been to no avail: 'As soon as one issue was resolved, another cropped up. Where a patch was made here, a tear appeared elsewhere, and where one hole was plugged, other leaks appeared. So it does seem completely impossible to arrive at a solution whereby we can hope to pull along together and to work together in the interest and for the common good of Malaysia.'

Serious political and racial problems had developed in a few swift months between the central Malaysian and the Singapore Governments and between powerful Malay and Chinese political groups in Malaya and Singapore. Basically they stemmed from the unseemly and suspicious haste—to Malays—of Mr. Lee Kuan Yew, the Prime Minister of Singapore, and his colleagues in his Chinese-dominated People's Action Party, in seeking to fashion, at a pace faster than the Malays wished, a multi-racial Malaysia in which all races were equal. In his speeches, Lee indicated that he was not aiming at removing all special rights for Malays, but his objection was to Malays assuming rights over and above the special privileges mentioned in the Constitution. Singapore Chinese criticisms of political inequality— 'Malay domination'—in the administration of Malaysia also helped to precipitate the racial crisis that eventually caused the break.

This internal confrontation had started with an initial antagonism between the People's Action Party and the Malayan Chinese Association of Malaya, the important second branch of the governing Alliance Party. Lee Kuan Yew attempted, futilely, to persuade Tunku Abdul Rahman that the P.A.P. would form a more worthy partner than the M.C.A. The Tunku also refused to have P.A.P. representation in the Malaysian Cabinet. (Lee's socialism, compared with the Alliance's right wing politics, alone would have made such participation impracticable, but there was no Singapore representation in the Central Government simply because there was no member of the Singapore Alliance elected to the legislature there. Lee in pressing for posts in the Central Government, seemed to be disregarding the electoral results.) Lee then went on to call for the abolition of racial distinctions—to wit, those favouring the Malays in Malaya—so that a 'Malaysian Malaysia' could be evolved. The P.A.P. next organized the formation of a 'Malaysia Solidarity Convention' composed of itself and four other opposition political parties in Malaysia, to agitate for the creation of a 'truly Malaysian Malaysia' in which the nation and the State was 'not identified with the supremacy, well-being and interests of any one particular community or race'. To the Malays it seemed as if Lee was reneging on the Malaysian Constitution which specifically provided for special rights for them and which he had accepted when he had signed the Malaysia Agreement in 1963.

Into the arena beside the M.C.A. against Lee came an extreme right wing group in the United Malays' National Organization, the dominant arm of the Alliance. It was led by Dato Syed Ja'afar Albar, the Secretary-General of the U.M.N.O., and included ministers in the Central Government and other powerfully placed Malays in the country. An acrimonious war of words with strong racial overtones developed between them and Lee and members of his Cabinet.

By early 1965, the division between the two governments and the opposing groups had widened. In an effort to find some solution, Tunku Abdul Rahman, in mid-April, invited Lee to Kuala Lumpur for talks which Lee himself described as an attempt to find 'means of ensuring that all areas of friction are resolved'. But the meeting did not have the desired result. Two days later, Tunku Abdul Rahman, addressing a congress of the Malaysian Alliance, said that Singapore's membership of Malaysia had been an essential requirement for the well-being of the whole State. He had dreamt of Singapore becoming the New York of Malaysia 'but little did we realize', he disclosed, 'that what the leader of the P.A.P. had in mind was a share in the running of Malaysia. This was considered unacceptable since the Alliance is strong enough to run the country on its own. . . . Unfortunately, however, the indications are that Lee took our refusal to let him have a share in the running of the Central Government as a challenge. It was not meant to be so. It must be clear to all that we must abide by the constitution; whatever party is returned to power by the will of the people, that party is considered to be the one which enjoys the confidence of the people, and as such it must accept the duties and responsibilities of running the government. . . . We must not be pushed around by a State government if this federation is to have any meaning . . . Singapore must try to make Malaysia workable.'

Towards the end of April, Lee spoke on the subject of Malay rights and criticized those who 'still believe that a certain racial group can dominate the political scene and that all other com-

munities must be satisfied with their activities in business success.'
He was not opposed to Malay rights, he said, adding, 'Our approach
is different from those who keep on stressing Malay rights. While we
uphold special privileges for Malays in the constitution, we believe
that the crux of the problem is how to raise the living standards of
the rural people who are mainly Malays and whose standards of
living are not advanced by special rights for a small number of
special Malays. Special privileges will only help a small group of
Malay bourgeoisie.'

The controversy began to boil furiously after this and particularly
after Lee, in a speech in Mandarin to Chinese members of the P.A.P.
said that 'no one race in Malaysia is more native than another, as all
their ancestors came to Malaysia less than 1,000 years ago. It is,
therefore, not logical for any one racial group to think that they are
more entitled to be called Malaysians and that other racial groups
can become Malaysians only through their good offices.' The
U.M.N.O. paper *Merdeka* construed Lee's remarks as denying the
rights of Malays to the 'ownership' of the country; it urged the
Central Government to revise the position of Singapore in Malaysia.
U.M.N.O. branches protested against Lee's 'insult to the Malays'.
On 9th May Tun Abdul Razak, the Deputy Prime Minister, attacked Lee's statement as being 'mischievous and dangerous' and
declared that if the people of Singapore 'wish to maintain this relationship with us, they must find another leader who is sincere. Mr.
Lee thinks he is the only one who can handle the situation; he has
heightened racial tension and this is very bad. We are all Malaysians
and we must work together for the country.'

A few days later, an effigy of Lee was burned before a meeting in
Kuala Lumpur to celebrate the nineteenth anniversary of the formation of the U.M.N.O. Malay feelings were given full vent at the
U.M.N.O. convention which followed on the 15th and 16th May.
Tunku Abdul Rahman was greeted by Malays flourishing slogans
such as 'Suspend Singapore's Constitution', 'Detain Lee Kuan Yew',
'Make Singapore a Second Kerala'. Delegates demanded Lee's
arrest and, after two hours' debate, passed a resolution which demanded that the Central Government should 'take firm action to
prevent incidents which may cause bloodshed'.

Towards the end of May, following the Speech from the Throne by
the Yang di-Pertuan Agong at a new session of Parliament, Lee
moved a provocative amendment to the Address. It regretted that

the Speech had not reassured the nation 'that Malaysia will continue to progress in accord with its democratic constitution to a Malaysian Malaysia, but instead had added to the doubts over the intentions of the present Alliance Government and to the measures it will adopt when faced with a loss of majority popular support'. Lee firmly declared that the P.A.P. was against secession by Singapore. It had a vested interest in constitutionalism and in loyalty 'because we know —and we knew before we joined Malaysia—that if we are patient, if we are firm, this Constitution must mean that a Malaysian nation emerges'. Secession would be an act of betrayal which would 'leave people in Sabah, Sarawak and Malaya' to the 'tender mercies' of those who spoke in terms of race. Malay privileges were accepted but not political inequality. Lee's remarks precipitated bitter attacks from Malay speakers before the debate adjourned for the week-end.

That week-end however, Lee in a speech in Singapore, declared that Singapore had never agreed to Malay rule when it had joined Malaysia. He spoke of the need for 'alternative' constitutional 'arrangements' in Malaysia which, he added, could more easily be made 'now'; one such 'arrangement' he suggested was the 'coming together' of states which wanted a Malaysian Malaysia, states such as Singapore, Sarawak and Sabah and 'possibly' Penang and Malacca.

When the debate resumed in Parliament, Alliance speakers returned to their attack on Lee. The Federal Minister for Home Affairs, Dato Dr. Ismail, suggested that the differences with Singapore were not over a Malaysian Malaysia which was the concept behind the constitution anyway, but 'the refusal of Singapore to reconcile itself to its rôle as one of the constituent states'. The P.A.P. way to a Malaysian Malaysia was by the imposition of immediate non-communalism; the Alliance way was by the establishment of racial harmony first, with non-communalism as the ultimate stage. Ismail accused the P.A.P. of using subtle, unscrupulous, and ruthless means to destroy multi-racialism. Replying for the Government, Tun Abdul Razak said that Lee's request that the P.A.P. should replace the M.C.A. in the Malaysian Government had been rejected because it was 'a Chinese party in search of power'. The P.A.P. was now prepared to break Malaysia up into a 'Malay' Malaysia and a 'Straits Settlements' Malaysia. Turning to Lee, Tun Razak said, 'I must warn him that although we stand for racial harmony, for goodwill, and for peace and unity, if as a result of his adventure, trouble should break out in this country, we must hold him responsible. What we resent is this attempt, in this time of our national crisis when we are facing a threat to our independence and sovereignty from outside, to blacken the image of our country in the eyes of our friends abroad, to create doubts and suspicions among the minds of our people, and to undermine the goodwill and harmony among the various races. . . . The gulf that divides the P.A.P. and the Alliance is now wide and clear.' Lee's amendment was rejected by 108 votes to 14, which included 10 P.A.P. votes, three from the Sarawak United People's Party, and one from the United Democratic Party. It was significant that the other opposition party, the Pan-Malayan-Islamic Party, voted with the Government despite their normal opposition to it.

On 11th June, Tunku Abdul Rahman left Kuala Lumpur for London to attend the meeting of Commonwealth Prime Ministers. There he spoke at length about the state of Indonesian confrontation of Malaysia and once again succeeded in getting the Prime Ministers, who represented one-quarter of the world's population, to reaffirm their support for Malaysia in her conflict against Indonesia. While the Prime Ministers did not openly condemn Indonesia, they disapproved of its aggression. A few days after the conclusion of the meeting, Tunku Abdul Rahman, who had planned a short holiday in Britain, fell victim to a sharp attack of shingles. After his recovery he went to the South of France to convalesce, and returned to Kuala Lumpur on 5th August after an absence of two months. Asked by newspapermen at the airport whether he would meet Lee—the situation between the two governments had deteriorated considerably while he had been away—Tunku Abdul Rahman, with disarming candour, replied, 'As soon as I have settled down, I shall ask Mr. Lee to come and meet me to discuss some of the things he has been shouting about.'

There was no hint in Kuala Lumpur during the next few days that Tunku Abdul Rahman had made a dramatic and fateful decision about Singapore and that senior members of his Cabinet had approved it. From what he said later to Parliament and during a plethora of newspaper, radio and television interviews, Tunku Abdul Rahman, while lying in his sickbed in London and while convalescing afterwards, had given considerable thought to the aggravating subject of Singapore's relations with the Central Government. He knew that on his return to Kuala Lumpur he

256

would be under the most intense Malay pressure to take repressive measures against Lee and his government. He realized too that, if he he did so, it would mean sending troops into Singapore and that this would inevitably result in bloodshed and the spawning of a disastrous and long-lasting hatred between the Chinese and Malays. The Tunku decided, as he said to Parliament later, that repressive measures were 'odious' and 'repulsive to our concept of Parliamentary democracy', and that, instead, Singapore should be severed from the body politic. While there was nothing in the Malaysian Constitution that permitted secession by any member state, there was equally nothing to prevent it.

Lee, on holiday in the Cameron Highlands, a hill resort in Pahang, was informed that Tunku Abdul Rahman would see him on the Friday. Observers assumed—and indubitably Lee also—that the talks might attempt to iron out many of the differences; perhaps there could even be agreement on some adjustment in the relationship between the two governments, but nobody, least of all Lee himself, expected an enforced withdrawal by Singapore from the federation.

Tunku Abdul Rahman presented Lee with the two alternatives— the first, drastic action by the Central Government against him and his government, the second, the secession of Singapore. Lee never disclosed what his emotions were upon being confronted with the second alternative but, to say the least, he must have been staggered. It may be assumed that he tried—vainly—to sway the Tunku in favour of a looser form of federation instead of taking a measure which meant the break-up of Malaysia which both of them, and Lee particularly, had so strongly believed in and, with single-minded devotion, had worked for. As Lee said later, 'After what the Tunku told me, I realized that there was no other way. We would have to leave Malaysia.'

It was necessary for Lee to consult his Cabinet colleagues and gain their approval to the proposal. Reports indicated that many of them —particularly those who had been born in the Malayan mainland— were appalled at the unequivocal ultimatum enunciated by Tunku Abdul Rahman. Indeed, the Tunku had to write a personal letter to Dr. Toh Chin Chye, the Deputy Prime Minister of Singapore and chairman of the P.A.P., to try to persuade him that separation was the only solution. The Tunku wrote: 'I have given the matter of our break with Singapore my utmost consideration. I find that in the interests of our friendship and security and peace of Malaysia as a whole, there is absolutely no other way out. I think the amicable settlement of our differences in this way is the only possible way out. I request you most earnestly to agree.' Toh replied: 'My colleagues and I would prefer that Singapore remain in Malaysia, and we felt that there could be other solutions to the present impasse. However, as you have indicated that the situation does not lend itself to any other workable settlement, and as you have impressed upon me that Singapore remaining in Malaysia will lead to a situation you may not be able to control, we have no alternative but to be resigned to your wish that Singapore leaves the federation of Malaysia. . . . Although lasting unification of Singapore and Malaya has not been achieved this time, nevertheless it is my profound belief that future generations will succeed where we have failed.'

With remarkable rapidity, an agreement was drawn up and signed that Saturday, 7th August, by Tunku Abdul Rahman and four members of his Cabinet, and by Lee Kuan Yew and his entire Cabinet. It said that Singapore would cease to be a State of Malaysia on 9th August 1965 (referred to in the document as 'Singapore Day') and would become an independent and sovereign state recognized as such by the government of Malaysia. The two governments would enter into a treaty for external defence and mutual assistance. They would establish a joint defence council and the Malaysian Government would give the Singapore Government 'such assistance as may be considered reasonable and adequate for external defence'. Singapore would give the Malaysian Government the right to continue to maintain the bases and other facilities used by its military forces within Singapore and would allow the Malaysian Government to use these as they might consider necessary for the purpose of external defence. Each party undertook not to enter into any treaty or agreement with a foreign country 'which might be detrimental to the independence and defence of the territory of the other party'. Both Governments would co-operate in economic affairs for their mutual benefit and interest and might set up joint committees or councils by agreement from time to time. With regard to any agreement entered into between the Singapore Government and any other country or corporate body which had been guaranteed by the Malaysian Government, Singapore should undertake to negotiate to enter into a fresh agreement. The Singapore Government undertook to indemnify the government of Malaysia fully for any liabilities, obliga-

258

tions or damage which it might suffer as a result of the guarantee.

The signatories to the agreement were sworn to secrecy until 10 o'clock on the Monday morning when both Governments would make simultaneous announcements about the separation of Singapore. Lee read his from the steps of the former offices of the City Council, and Tunku Abdul Rahman announced it at the beginning of a meeting of the House of Representatives that morning. He described his announcement as 'the most painful and heartbreaking news I have had to break. . . . In all the 10 years of my leadership of this House, I have never had a duty so unpleasant as this to perform.' He spoke of the difficulties of finding solutions to issues between the two governments, and said it seemed completely impossible 'to arrive at a solution whereby we can hope to pull along together and to work together in the interest and for the common good of Malaysia. We have tried everything possible to avoid separation of Singapore from the rest of Malaysia.

'We find that there are only two courses of action open to us. Number one is to take repressive measures against the Singapore Government for the behaviour of some of their leaders, and number two, to sever all connections with the State Government that has ceased to give even a measure of loyalty to the Central Government.' The Tunku went on to say that the peace and happiness 'of the people in this country depend on goodwill and understanding of the various races for one another. Without it this nation will break up, with consequential disaster which we have seen and read about happening elsewhere. . . . We feel that repressive action against a few would not solve the problem because the seed of this contempt, fear and hatred has been sown in Singapore, and even if we try to prevent its growth, I feel that after a time it will sprout up with more virulent force. . . . We had pledged to form Malaysia with Singapore but having given it a trial we found that if we persist in going on with it, in the long run there will be more trouble to Malaysia than what Singapore is worth to us. . . . In diversity, I am convinced we can find unity.'

Both Houses of the Malaysian Parliament that morning passed the necessary Bill to amend the constitution to allow Singapore to leave Malaysia and become a sovereign and independent state. So the break between Malaysia and Singapore was made in a clean, orderly and peaceful manner.

In Singapore later that morning, Lee broke down at a Press con-

R*

ference when he talked about the break. He said, 'Every time we look back on this moment when we signed this agreement which severed Singapore from Malaysia, it will be a moment of anguish. . . . All my life I have believed in Malaysia, merger, and the unity of these two territories.' He stressed that the years ahead would 'require our two governments to work in closest co-operation, not just in defence and security but also in commerce and industry'. He announced that Singapore would seek membership of the United Nations and the Commonwealth under the sponsorship of Malaysia. In the ensuing days, Lee declared that Singapore wished to settle any differences with Indonesia provided this did not endanger Malaysia. He also announced that Singapore would become a republic but he set no date for this. His Foreign Minister, Mr. S. Rajaratnam, the former Minister of Culture, declared that Singapore would follow a policy of non-alignment but with safeguards for the interests of Malaysia. On 11th August there came news of the resignation of Dato Syed Ja'afar Albar as Secretary-General of the U.M.N.O.

The news of the separation of Singapore was taken calmly enough in the island itself, and in Malaya, Sabah and Sarawak. Elsewhere, except in Indonesia and in Communist countries, there was shock and regret over the failure of another federation with a multi-racial society. Indonesia, as might be expected, rejoiced and claimed that its confrontation had caused the split between Singapore and Malaysia. The separation of Singapore was a major political setback for Britain, Australia, and New Zealand, all of which were closely concerned in the defence of South East Asia, and also for the United States. They each made apparent the fact that they would have to review their respective foreign and defence policies in the Far East. For Britain, there was urgent need to negotiate a defence agreement with Singapore about the use of British bases in the state, even though the Malaysian Parliamentary Act legalizing the separation agreement declared that the Anglo-Malaysian Defence Agreement remained in force as between Britain and Singapore and allowed Britain continued use of the bases and their facilities.

Lee Kuan Yew himself must have been under extreme pressure from within his own party to take up his unwavering stands. Few people in Singapore realized, however, that the Malays possess an innate strength which rises to the surface when they feel they are being pushed too hard in a direction which is against their national interests. There had been two examples of this in modern

Malayan history. First there was Britain's imposition of a 'Malayan Union' which converted the Malay States into colonies and divested the Malay rulers of their sovereign rights; on this occasion, the Malay population came to the verge of physical resistance against the British. The second occasion was the discarding of a great Malay, Onn bin Ja'afar, as national leader when he attempted to force Malays to accept non-Malays as members of the U.M.N.O. at a time when they were not receptive to a policy of non-communalism in their country. But history—in these two specific instances and in others—has shown also that, by tact and persuasion, and given time, the Malays can be persuaded to change their minds.

What are the chances of survival of what remains of Malaysia? On the withdrawal of Singapore, there were fears that Sarawak and Sabah might also seek to break away because of their own dissatifactions over their relations with the Central Government. These strains however were not as severe as those which had existed between Singapore and Kuala Lumpur—but they were obvious. And although the respective Chief Ministers announced in due course that the territories would stay in Malaysia, uneasiness remained. The eastern Malaysian states had two choices—that of continuing under the economic and defensive umbrella of Malaysia, or of breaking away—as economically non-viable independent states—and facing the probability of absorption by Indonesia. The optimists—and there were many—veered to the belief that Sabah and Sarawak, despite internal pressures, would hold to Malaysia. Indeed, there was also a very strong feeling in Malaya and in Singapore—and among their Commonwealth friends beyond—that Singapore would return as a constituent unit of Malaysia in the not too distant future.

31st August 1965

Select Bibliography

Colonial Office Papers.
Federated Malay States Annual Reports.
Singapore Annual Reports.
Straits Settlements Annual Reports.
Unfederated Malay States Annual Reports.
Federation of Malaya Year Books, 1961–3.
Federation Museums Journal. FMJ.
Journal of the Royal Asiatic Society, Malayan Branch. JRASMB.
Journal of South-East Asian History.
Malayan Historical Journal.
Albuquerque, Braz de, *The Commentaries of the Great Afonso d'Albo-querque* (4 vols). Hakluyt Society, London, 1875–84.
Anson, Sir A. E., *About Others and Myself.* London, 1920.
Barbosa, Duarte, *The Book of Duarte Barbosa* (Vol. 2). Hakluyt Society, London, 1924.
Baring-Gould, S. and Bakfylde, C. A., *Sarawak Under Its Two White Rajahs.* London, 1909.
Bird, Isabella, *The Golden Chersonese and The Way Thither.* London, 1833.
Brimmell, J. H., *Communism in South-East Asia.* London, 1959.
Brown, C. C., 'Sejarah Melayu (Malay Annals)'. JRASMB, 1952.
Buckley, C. B., *An Anecdotal History of Old Times in Singapore, 1819–1837* (2 vols). Singapore, 1902.
Cardon, Rev. R., 'Portuguese Malacca'. JRASMB, 1934.
Cheeseman, H. R., *Bibliography of Malaya.* London, 1959.
Clodd, H. P., *Malaya's First British Pioneer:* The Life of Francis Light. London, 1948.
Comber, L., *Chinese Secret Societies in Malaya.* Singapore, 1957.

Cowan, C. D., 'Early Penang and the Rise of Singapore, 1805–1832'. JRASMB; 1950.

Nineteenth Century Malaya. London, 1961.

Dobby, E. H. G., *South-East Asia.* London, 1957.

Emerson, Rupert, *Malaysia, A Study in Direct and Indirect Rule.* New York, 1937.

Gullick, John, *Indigenous Political Systems of Western Malaya.* London, 1958.

Malaya. London, 1963.

Hall, D. G. E., *A History of South-East Asia.* London, 1955.

Jones, S. W., *Public Administration in Malaya.* London, 1953.

Kennedy, J., *A History of Malaya.* London, 1962.

Keppel, Capt. the Hon. Henry, R.N., *The Expedition of H.M.S. Dido for the Suppression of Piracy.* 1846.

Lamb, Alastair, 'Miscellaneous Papers on Early Hindu and Buddhist Settlement in Northern Malaya and Southern Thailand'. FMJ, 1961.

Linehan, W., 'A History of Pahang'. JRASMB, 1936.

Makepeace, Brooke and Braddell (Editors), *One Hundred Years of Singapore* (2 vols). Singapore, 1921.

Maxwell, W. G. and Gibson, W. S., *Treaties and Engagements Affecting the Malay States and Borneo.* London, 1924.

MacMichael, Sir Harold, 'Report of a Mission to Malaya'. Colonial Office, 1946.

McNair, F., *Perak and the Malays:* Sarong and Kris. London, 1878.

Middlebrook, S. M., 'Yap Ah Loy'. JRASMB, 1951.

Miller, Harry, *Menace in Malaya.* London, 1955.

Prince and Premier. London, 1959.

Mills, L. A. 'British Malaya, 1824–1867'. JRASMB, 1925.

Malaya—A Political and Economic Appraisal. London, 1958.

Parkinson, C. N., *British Intervention in Malaya.* Singapore, 1960.

Peet, G. L., *Political Questions in Malaya.* London, 1949.

Percival, Lieut.-General A., *The War in Malaya.* London, 1949.

Pires, Tomé, *Suma Oriental, 1512–1515* (2 vols). Hakluyt Society, London, 1944.

Purcell, Victor, *The Chinese in Malaya.* London, 1948.

The Chinese in South-East Asia. London, 1951.

Malaya, Communist or Free? London, 1954.

Rentse, Anker. 'History of Kelantan'. JRASMB, 1936.

Runciman, Steven. *The White Rajahs.* London, 1960.

Rutter, Owen, *British North Borneo*. London, 1922.

Sheppard, M. C. ff., 'A Short History of Trengganu'. JRASMB, 1949.

Smith, T. E., *Population Growth in Malaya*. London, 1952.

Song Ong Siang, *One Hundred Years of the Chinese in Singapore*. Singapore, 1923.

Swettenham, Sir Frank, *Footprints in Malaya*. London, 1942.
British Malaya. London, 1948 (revised edition).

Tarling, N., 'British Policy in the Malay Peninsula and Archipelago, 1824–1871'. JRASMB, 1957.

Tregonning, K. G., *Under Chartered Company Rule* (North Borneo). Singapore, 1958.
North Borneo. London, 1960.

Wilkinson, R. J., *A History of the Peninsular Malays, with Chapters on Perak and Selangor*. Singapore, 1923.
'The Malacca Sultanate'. JRASMB, 1935.

Winstedt, Sir Richard, 'A History of Johore'. JRASMB, 1932.
'Negri Sembilan, the History, Polity and Beliefs of the Nine States'. JRASMB, 1934.
'A History of Selangor'. JRASMB, 1934.
'Notes on the History of Kedah'. JRASMB, 1936.
'Kingship and Enthronement in Malaya'. JRASMB, 1947.
Malaya and Its History. London, 1951.
The Malays, a Cultural History. Singapore, 1947.

Winstedt and Wilkinson, 'A History of Perak'. JRASMB, 1934.

Wright, A. and Cartwright, H. A. (Editors), *Twentieth Century Impressions of British Malaya*. London, 1908.

Wurtzburg, C. E., *Raffles of the Eastern Isles*. London, 1954.

Index

DATE DUE

4/12			
APR 4 1968			
MAY - 3 1968			
MAY 16 1969			
1974			
GAYLORD			PRINTED IN U.S.A.